Graeme Davison has been Professor of History at Monash University since 1982. He has taught at the University of Melbourne, at Harvard, where he was Professor of Australian Studies, Edinburgh and the Australian National University. His publications include *The Rise and Fall of Marvellous Melbourne*, which was jointly awarded the Ernest Scott Prize, *The Unforgiving Minute* and, as an editor, *Australians 1888, A Heritage Handbook* and the *Oxford Companion to Australian History*. He is a former president of the Australian Historical Association, Chair of the Victorian Heritage Council, and adviser to several museums, libraries and archives.

The Use and Abuse of Australian History

Graeme Davison

ALLEN & UNWIN

First published in 2000
Allen & Unwin
9 Atchison Street, St Leonards NSW 1590 Australia
Phone: (61 2) 8425 0100
Fax: (61 2) 9906 2218
E-mail: frontdesk@allen-unwin.com.au
Web: http://www.allen-unwin.com.au

National Library of Australia
Cataloguing-in-Publication entry:

Davison, Graeme, 1940– .
The use and abuse of Australian history.

Includes index.
ISBN 1 86448 720 8.

1. Australia—History—Philosophy. I. Title.

994

Set in 11/14 pt Sabon by DOCUPRO, Sydney
Printed and bound by t/c

10 9 8 7 6 5 4 3 2 1

Preface

FOR ALMOST twenty years I have been fortunate to combine my teaching and writing as an academic historian with a range of historical activities outside the university in such fields as historic conservation, family history, museums, cultural tourism, urban planning and national celebrations. I began this work partly as a hobby, partly through a sense of professional obligation. It was fun to work with enthusiasts who loved history for its own sake and satisfying to see history influence public policy. Only gradually did I begin to recognise that it was through these everyday forms of history-making, as much as the work of my academic colleagues, that our discipline was being challenged and transformed.

The following chapters are the fruit of my reflections on the uses of Australian history in these largely non-academic settings. The subjects covered are diverse, even seemingly serendipitous, but they are chosen because they illuminate some abiding concerns. Throughout the book I have sought, not simply to describe what goes on in the history business, but what makes it tick. How is the past being used? What kinds of arguments and images are being deployed? What interests and audiences are being addressed? Who gains and who loses from the uses of the past? And amidst so many users and abusers of history, what is the role of the professional historian?

I had been writing on these themes for some time before I recognised that they were indeed components of a single project. Tom Griffiths and Bain Attwood first encouraged me to think of bringing my ideas together as a book and John Iremonger offered me the opportunity to do so. I am also grateful to them for their perceptive comments on earlier drafts. Although some of these chapters have had an earlier incarnation as articles, chapters and conference papers, almost all have been revised and reshaped for this publication, some very extensively, and I have also taken the opportunity to bring the references up to date. Chapters 1, 8, 9, 12, 13, and 14 appear here for the first time. I am grateful to the editors and boards of *Australian Historical Studies, Quadrant* and the *New Zealand Journal of History* and to the Council of the Royal Australian Historical Society for permission to draw on material that appeared originally in their publications. I also thank the History Department, University of Melbourne for permission to reproduce Chapter 5, which appeared in a shorter version in Donna Merwick (ed.), *Dangerous Liaisons: Essays in Honour of Greg Dening* (Melbourne 1994). Chapters 6 and 7 were published in an earlier version in *A Heritage Handbook*; I thank my co-editor Chris McConville. My former research assistant the late Sheryl Yelland helped to locate useful material, especially for Chapter 2.

I owe much to the example and friendship of colleagues who have been my fellow travellers in public history. I learned much from Geoffrey Blainey with whom, along with the late Lloyd Robson, I once travelled the Victorian countryside as a member of the Norman Harper Safari to high school history students. With Greg Dening, my former colleague at the University of Melbourne, I shared the excitement of introducing final year honours students to the skills of ethnography and caught some of Greg's own passionate interest in how the past was made present in ritual and ceremony. Ken Inglis taught me that monuments are as important as documents in reading the past. My introduction to the heritage business came in the late 1970s with an invitation to join the Victorian Historic Buildings Council: I would like to record my appreciation to Ian Lonie, Boyce Pizzey, Ray Tonkin and David Yencken and to the staff of what is now Heritage Victoria for the windows they have opened for me. In the late 1980s Monash University inaugurated a Master's Program in Public History designed to prepare historians for work in heritage, museums, local history and other non-academic forms of history. To my Monash colleagues in public history—Ann McGrath, Chris McConville, Tom Griffiths, Margaret Anderson, Jan Penney, David Dunstan, Brigid Hains, Tony Dingle and Meredith Fletcher—to our students, and to Rosemary Johnston, who has been the generous friend and enthusiastic supporter of us all, I owe special thanks. It is to them that I dedicate this book.

Contents

chapter one

Introduction: Australian history on the eve of the millennium

I
T IS BOTH exciting and unsettling to be a historian in the late 1990s. We live amidst the ruins of so much that we once thought enduring, yet with such yearnings for a sense of our bearings, that the study of the past can seem either sheer self-indulgence or the most urgent intellectual challenge of our times.

History is often in the headlines. Never before, perhaps, have historians occupied as prominent a place in Australian public life. Some, like Manning Clark, Geoffrey Blainey and Henry Reynolds, have assumed the role of prophets, peering deep into the national soul and sometimes warning of wrath to come. And like prophets through the ages, they have attracted the slings and arrows of the naysayers and sceptics. Their prominence in public life is not simply a reflection of their own talent as writers and controversialists, but of the renewed salience of history in Australian public affairs. Mabo and Wik, the High Court cases that assert a continuing right of Aborigines to a native title in land, also signalled a new readiness among jurists and politicians to consider the claims of history. But to a generation raised on the school textbooks of the 1940s and 50s Mabo and Wik represented a new and troubling kind of history. No longer, it seemed, was the past the handmaiden of patriotism, but a source of division, no longer the foundation of national destiny, but a bone of national contention.

The crisis of Australian history is one facet of the general crisis of meaning that now afflicts democratic societies. Liberal democracy largely defined itself in opposition to the absolutism of king, church and Kremlin; when those opponents were defeated, democracy did not lose its appeal but it lost its historical dynamic. Much of the energy of modern democratic leaders is occupied by the mechanics of government, trimming the sails of the ship of state in accordance with the navigational data provided by pollsters, ratings agencies, money markets, lobbyists, talkshow hosts and backbench rumblings. But leading the nation also calls for something more—an ability to project a set of unifying national values and beliefs, what President George Bush called 'the vision thing'. Postmodernists may believe that history has come to an end but, in the high moments of national life, statesmen continue to find history indispensable. For the 'big picture' is always a moving picture, and the goals of current policy must seem to be aligned with historic goals.

The politics of history

Few Australian politicians are profound students of history but at important moments they must look as though they are. Possibly no modern Australian prime minister has uttered the word 'history' as frequently as Paul Keating. At Kokoda, where he kissed the ground on which the Diggers died, at Redfern, where he sought a historic act of reconciliation with Aborigines, at Winton where he reflected on 'Waltzing Matilda' and the class struggle, at Canberra's National War Memorial, where he presided over the burial of the Unknown Australian Soldier, and at Corowa, site of the 1893 Federal conference, where he pledged himself to the cause of an Australian republic, Keating sought to place himself in the path of history.[1]

There was more than a little political calculation in Keating's use of history. The appeal to Australia's past was designed, in part, to soften that other facet of his political profile, the economic rationalist and hard man of the NSW Right. When Keating spoke impromptu and from the heart—as in his famous Placido Domingo address to the National Press Club—it was his 'big picture' of the future, not his vision of the past, which came through. Australia, he confided, had no one to compare with the great figures of American history—a Lincoln or a Jefferson; its founders, the convicts, were 'rip-off merchants' and its politicians—even Labor's hero John Curtin—were no better than 'triers'. Doing the hard things, pulling the economic levers, 'spinning the great tale of economic change' was what Keating passionately cared about. But his minders also knew that this was an uninspiring vision to many ordinary Australians, for whom the numbers were meaningless abstractions and his 'big picture' too remote to be real. History became the soft packaging for Keating's hard politics. It called for a subtle blend of both inspiration and criticism, connecting Australians to their national past and encouraging them to embrace their international future. 'Legends bind nations together,' he observed on Anzac Day 1992. 'They define us to ourselves. But they should not stifle us. They should not constrain our growth, or restrict us when we have to change.'[2]

The speeches written by the historian Don Watson for Keating are among the best-crafted in recent

Australian political history. His eulogy for the Unknown Australian Soldier ('He is one of us') stands in the tradition of great funeral orations, from Pericles to Lincoln. It builds on the democratic tradition established by Australia's first official war historian, Charles Bean, but gives it a more pluralist inflection than its founder might have anticipated, or approved:

> This unknown soldier is not interred here to glorify war over peace; or to assert a soldier's character above a civilian's, or one race or one nation or one religion above another; or men above women; or the war in which he fought and died above any other war, or one generation above any that has or will come later.

The kind of multicultural, prosperous Australia Keating sought could be created, however, only by confronting 'the problems which beset the first Australians—the people to whom the most injustice has been done'. In perhaps the most quoted, and most controversial, passage in Keating's Redfern speech, the Prime Minister had acknowledged, more fully than any of his predecessors or successors, the moral responsibility of non-Aboriginal Australians for past injustices:

> We took the traditional lands and smashed the traditional way of life.
> We brought the diseases. The alcohol.
> We committed the murders.
> We took the children from their mothers.
> We practised discrimination and exclusion.
> It was our ignorance and our prejudice.

Australians should not wallow in a sense of guilt ('guilt is not a very constructive emotion') but 'open our hearts a bit'. By acknowledging a kind of collective and vicarious sense of responsibility for the sins of the fathers, yet avoiding the troubling moral (and legal) implications of collective 'guilt', Keating had offered White Australia seemingly painless relief from the burden of the past.

John Howard, too, believes that history matters, even if it is only to correct the distorted versions of the past purveyed by his opponent. 'One of the more insidious developments in Australian political life over the past decade or so has been the attempt to rewrite Australian history in the service of a partisan political cause,' Howard complained in his Playford Memorial Lecture in June 1996. This was a 'systematic', 'deliberate' and 'insidious' process and 'an abuse of the true purpose of history'. 'It read history backwards, imposing on the past a pattern designed to serve contemporary political needs.' It sought to 'demean, pillory and tear down many great people of Australia's past who had no opportunity to answer back . . .' The Keating view of history was divisive and disruptive of the national consensus; but 'the fact [was] that history of our nation is the story *of* all our people and it is a story *for* all our people'.[3]

Howard speaks as a newly elected prime minister and in defence of traditional conservative values, yet he positions himself rhetorically as the underdog attacking an 'officially endorsed' but mistaken view of history. There was, he implies, at some unspecified time in the past, a commonsense, factual history of Australia which unnamed ideologues have since 'hijacked', 'politically filtered', 'rewritten' and 'distorted'. Who these villains were he does not say, although the late Manning Clark, who was recently accused of sedition by sections of the conservative press, was probably at the head of the list. Howard's is a rhetorical strategy designed to damage his opponent's vision of history more than to advance his own. Although Howard acknowledges that 'there is certainly a need for Australians to understand their history better', the effect of his rhetoric is not to inspire historical curiosity but to reinforce historical prejudice. He suggests that the 'real' history of Australia is to be found by dismissing ugly versions of the past as ideological and embracing more positive ones because they rest on 'the facts of history'. But these 'facts of history' are never specified—it is a history lesson for people who know no history, but who want to be assured that Australia's past was not as bad as it is said to be.

The idea that history is simply 'the facts' and that 'interpretation' is something added to them would strike most practising historians as odd. 'Facts,' they would say, are constituted in the very act of interpretation. 'Just give me the facts' is something that detectives say but which no historian can really do, for the 'facts' are a response to questions, and one person's questions are never quite the same as another's. Yet while John Howard's history seems simplistic, his opponents can easily be dismissed as dangerously pessimistic. At Redfern Keating had used the authority of a national leader to install a critical view of Australian history; Howard was obliged to adopt the language of dissent in the attempt to reinstate his traditionally patriotic view of the national past.

The most severe test of Howard's view of history came in May 1997 when he addressed the Aboriginal Reconciliation Convention in Melbourne. The Human Rights and Equal Opportunity Commission had recently presented its report to the government, *Bringing Them Home*, documenting in heartrending detail the sufferings of the 'stolen generations' of Aborigines who had been forcibly separated from their families by churches and governments over the past century. Now, many of his audience hoped, was the moment when the nation's leader might offer a formal apology to its victims for that misconceived and devastating policy. But the Prime Minister seemed reluctant to face such a reckoning with the past. To be sure, he did express a 'deep sorrow for those of my fellow Australians who suffered injustices under the practices of past generations towards indigenous people' and for the 'hurt and trauma many people here today may continue to feel as a consequence of those practices'. But his words were lawyer's words, carefully crafted to avoid any specific implication of intention or collective responsibility. 'Australians of this generation should not be required to accept guilt and blame for past actions and policies over which they had no control.' He could acknowledge 'the interrelated histories of the various elements of Australian societies', but not the moral dimension of the relationship between the past and the present.

How can you say sorry for something you didn't do? For John Howard such questions seem to fly in the face of commonsense. But not all his political forefathers would have found that question puzzling. Traditional conservatives had an almost mystical belief in the bonds of obligation between generations as well as between classes, and some modern conservatives recognise the need for the nation to acknowledge shame for what its ancestors, sometimes unwittingly, did.[4] John Howard urges Australians to be 'proud of what this country has achieved', even if those achievements were not actually their own personal achievements; yet he seems unwilling to acknowledge the wrongs those past achievers also committed, or our own sharing in their consequences.

The truth, of course, is that we play fast and loose in our reckonings with the past, giving our forefathers credit when it suits us but ruling off their debts if the liability seems large. Keating offered an apology but assured his constituents that this involved no troubling sense of guilt. Howard refused to apologise, arguing that our ancestors had nothing to be ashamed of, or that, if they did, the guilt stopped with them. He later modified his stance, supporting the insertion of an expression of 'regret' for past injustices in the proposed preamble to the Australian Constitution. But he still declined to say 'sorry'.

Some Aborigines accepted this half-apology, perhaps because it was likely to be the best they could get; but others remained unreconciled. It needed someone to say sorry for their pains to be assuaged. And if the Prime Minister, as our representative, wouldn't say it—who would?

This question, so poignantly posed by the stolen generations, echoes the often anguished debates among Germans, Japanese and Americans over the moral legacy of the Holocaust and the Second World War. Does present-day Germany bear any responsibility to the victims of the Holocaust? Or did 'the grace of being born late', as Chancellor Kohl called it, excuse his own generation? Should Japan apologise for the crimes of its soldiers on the Burma Railway? And Americans for dropping the atomic bomb on Hiroshima?[5] Charles Maier, in a perceptive review of the *Historikerstreit*, the debate over the Holocaust that erupted among German historians in the mid 1980s, convincingly argues that 'insofar as a collection of people wishes to claim existence as a society or nation, it must thereby acknowledge that acts committed by earlier agents still bind or burden the contemporary community'.[6] As long as such wrongs go unacknowledged, they will tend to grow; to the extent that they are acknowledged and, if possible, compensated, they may tend to diminish.

What troubles some nationalists, and some historians, is that the history business may itself have begun to show a negative balance. A century ago the study of history seemed a sound investment, returning much more in patriotic fervour, national *esprit de corps* and wise statesmanship than it did in heart-searching and unexpected liabilities. Now, it seems, it is all burdens and no bounty, all boos and no cheers. Why, they ask, should we continue to subsidise an industry that makes us feel anything but comfortable and relaxed? Have the historians let us down or is it history itself that is to blame?

The uses of history

Such questions are symptomatic of the pervasive utilitarianism of our age. When every academic program is ranked according to the salaries of its graduates it is not surprising that history too should be judged by its usefulness. The 'bottom line' and 'cash value' have become the ruling standards of public as well as private good. Historians are often caught in the dilemma of whether to contest such standards (and implicitly concede their 'uselessness') or to fight the utilitarians on their own ground.

This book is about the ways in which Australians use the past, not just in national politics but in local and informal settings as well. It is written in the conviction that history matters, and matters to all Australians. It is a by-product of almost two decades of personal engagement in what historians have recently come to call 'public history'—as a participant in the heritage business, an adviser to museums, a writer of commemorative history, and a teacher of graduate and undergraduate students of 'the uses of the past'. Some of the most influential forms of history are informal, 'commonsense', semi-private ones, such as family history or local history. The forms in which the past is made present to us are as diverse as the forms of our national life; in the following chapters I have sought to reveal the historical dimensions of some current political debates (gun laws, managerialism, citizenship) as well as the political dimension of some popular forms of history (museums, family history, national celebrations). The topics are diverse but they are unified by an underlying theme—the continuing power of the past and the need to confront its uses critically.

History does not cease to be powerful just because it is not studied critically; on the contrary, as Ireland and Kosovo teach us, it is often most virulently powerful precisely when it is *not* studied. History, someone once said, was too important to be left to the historians; but it is also too important to leave the historians out. The abuses of history are many, and only some of them are matters of factual inaccuracy or bad method. Detecting the abuses of history requires an analysis of the uses to which stories about the past are put. It is as much a study of bad faith as bad method.

One of the most powerful critiques of historical knowledge and its use, Friedrich Nietzsche's *The Use and Abuse of History* (1873–76), was written more than a century ago, in the wake of the Franco-Prussian War when Germany, according to Nietzsche, was succumbing to 'a malignant historical fever'. Cynical, even nihilistic, Nietzsche may seem an uncongenial, and even treacherous, guide to the state of history in late twentieth century Australia. But his disenchantment with the chauvinistic nationalism of Bismarck's Germany made him a clear-eyed critic of some of the ways in which many continue to use and abuse the past.

History, Nietzsche asserted, was 'necessary for the living man in three ways: in relation to his action and struggle, his conservatism and reverence, his suffering and desire for deliverance'. To each of these needs, he suggested, there corresponded a characteristic type of history: the monumental, the antiquarian and the critical. We should probably think of these as dimensions of historical thought rather than distinct types of historian, since most real-life history, even of a simple kind, incorporates elements of each. Conservatives might seem to have a natural affinity with antiquarian history, liberals with monumental history and radicals with critical history; but in practice, as we have already seen, conservatives can adopt the stance of critical history and radicals use the language of monumental history when circumstances warrant it. Nietzsche's typology provides us with a useful guide to the ways in which various forms of history are linked to their use.[7]

Monumental history, he argues, serves the needs of the man of action who looks to the past as a source of moral inspiration and example. This was the standard form of history in new nations: tales of heroes and narratives of great events were the building blocks from which the myth of national progress or destiny was constructed. It was, until recently, the dominant form of history in Australia, reproduced in school textbooks, national birthdays, political speeches and most other forms of official history. It rested on the belief, as old as the Bible, that history had a purposeful direction, or *telos*, which could be discerned by the careful student and upon which the wise statesman might found his policy. At high moments of crisis or celebration national leaders are still sometimes expected to express such a sense of history, to discern in the flow of events an underlying purpose or ultimate goal. This was what an earlier generation of Australians meant by 'Australia Unlimited' or what Ben Chifley meant by 'the light on the hill'.

But monumental history, I argue in Chapter 3, has had a stormy passage through the twentieth century. The attempts of recent leaders to project a sense of historical destiny often seem contrived and unconvincing. President Bill Clinton's Second Inaugural Address was almost unanimously pronounced a failure—a collection of empty rhetorical gestures without a unifying vision. This, perhaps, was not just a moral shortcoming of the President, or his speechwriter; it may also have reflected a scepticism on the part of both speaker and audience towards the sense of historical destiny that such speeches are traditionally expected to express. When contemporaries speak of the 'death' or the 'end of history', it is the demise of this prophetic, monumental sense of history that they mainly mourn.

Recently, some influential voices have been raised in support of a revival of the monumental sense of the past. Australia, and especially its young people, need heroes, they say, and historians, by their irreverence towards Australia's great and famous, may have done a disservice to the nation. An interesting sign of the times, discussed in Chapter 2, has been the attempt to find and exalt new heroes, such as Weary Dunlop, and to build new monuments.

But monumental history is not the only way in which modern societies use the past. One of the striking features of Australian culture since the 1970s has been the rapid growth of such popular forms of historical consciousness as genealogy, local history, heritage, living history museums, historical re-enactments, antique-collecting and period performances of baroque and classical music and theatre. 'He is careful to preserve what survives from ancient days,' Nietzsche wrote of the antiquarian. 'All that is small and limited, mouldy and obsolete, gains a worth and inviolability of its own from the conservative and reverent soul of the antiquary migrating into it and building a secret nest there. The history of his town becomes the history of himself.'[8] While monumental history seeks to understand the past in order to transcend it, these newly popular forms of history seek to revive, restore and even re-enter the past.

The rise of antiquarian history so closely parallels the decline of monumental history that we might suppose their fortunes to be connected. In his stimulating book *The Past is a Foreign Country*, David Lowenthal perceives a reciprocal relationship between the decline of monumental history and the modern passion for preservation:

> Unwilling or unable to incorporate the legacy of the past into our own creative acts, we concentrate instead on saving its remaining vestiges. The less integral the role of the past in our lives, the more imperative the urge to preserve its relics.[9]

But preservation, as Lowenthal shows, is only one of the new forms of antiquarianism: in historical pageants, historically inspired consumer goods and living history museums Australians are also re-enacting, reproducing and imaginatively re-entering the past. The differences between antique and reproduction, documentary and re-creation, museum and theme park have become increasingly blurred. Is fidelity to history a matter of ensuring that the props are authentic, or that the plot is true to period? In later chapters, I seek to probe the source of our deep attachment to a past that is both tangible and familiar. Heritage, I suggest in Chapter 8, is a denatured form of piety, and in the tenacious struggle of Australians to preserve old stuff they are seeking both to celebrate the past and ward off mortality.

But we do not visit the past only as a form of escape from the present. If the past is a foreign country, it may also stimulate, challenge and disturb, as well as console. Active and ethical citizenship depends, among other things, upon the imaginative capacity to look at the world through the eyes of others. The past is a theatre of human experience. In attempting to understand the people of the past—for attempting is the best we can do—our imaginations are stretched, our moral sensibility strengthened. History is a rehearsal for responsibility.

Critical history—the third of Nietzsche's trinity—is the viewpoint of those who suffer the burdens of history and who see a radical rejection of the past as a precondition for their deliverance. 'Man,' he writes, 'must have the strength to break up the past, to apply it, in order to live. He must bring the past to the bar of judgement, interrogate it remorselessly and finally condemn it . . . Every past is worthy of condemnation.' Critical history has been a powerful thread in Australian historical writing, especially since the 1970s. The Vietnam War, the most divisive event in half a century, radicalised the generation of historians that largely dominated university history departments for the following twenty years. The battle cry of the young Humphrey McQueen in 1970 marked a sharp break with the traditions of monumental history that had dominated left-wing, as well as conservative, Australian history-writing. 'The past belongs to the enemy. We must understand it in order to end it,' he wrote in his preface to *A New Britannia*.[10] That battle cry has been taken up, in turn, by labour historians, feminist historians and, especially in recent years, by Aborigines. The slogan of Aboriginal demonstrators on 26 January 1988, 'White Australia has a Black History', was its authentic voice.

The most striking victory of critical history came in 1992 when six of the seven judges on the High Court of Australia overturned the doctrine of *terra nullius*—the belief held since the earliest days of the colonies that, since Aborigines were a nomadic people who did not lead a settled existence, they enjoyed none of the rights customarily associated with land ownership. In doing so, the Court had relied heavily upon the arguments first developed by Henry Reynolds in his book, *The Law of the Land* (1987). By upholding the principle of native title, documented by Reynolds in the legal debates surrounding early colonisation, the judges had created the basis for the most fundamental re-examination of land rights since European colonisation.

Critical history—the history that interrogates and condemns—is a powerful but volatile force; it can inflict considerable damage on its opponents but without a sustaining vision of its own its power is quickly spent. 'The history that merely destroys without any impulse to construct will in the end make its instruments tired of life; for such men destroy illusions,' Nietzsche observed.[11] By the 1980s critical history had taken a new turn: under the influence of postmodernism and poststructuralism it had redirected its energies from an attack on the capitalist state to an attack on the structures of knowledge through which, it alleged, systems of repression such as patriarchy and racism were reproduced. Taking their cue from Nietzsche, deconstructionists applied their corrosive logic not only to the interpretation of history but to the organising structures—or 'meta-narratives'—on which history itself was founded.[12]

The insistently critical tone of much Australian historical writing over the past twenty years has now produced a delayed reaction. In 1985 Professor Geoffrey Blainey attacked 'an influential group of socialists' for instilling a sense of unjustified shame about Australia's past. 'They have a deep sense of grievance about much of Australia's history—the past treatment of the Chinese, of Aborigines, of women, of shearers, of seamstresses, of Italians, of Irish, of factory workers, of miners, of trade unionists, of orphans—and maybe even the personal treatment of themselves, prosperous and independent as they are,' he wrote.[13] In 1993 he returned to the attack. We needed to draw up a more accurate 'balance sheet of our history', he argued. 'My generation was reared on the Three Cheers view of history. There is now a rival view, which I call the Black Armband View.' His old friend and former teacher Manning Clark was one of the sources of this gloomy view. Once, as he pointed out, the Left, as well as the Right, had seen Australia's history as a success; '[they] were alike in their congratulations though they rarely congratulated the same events'. There is, as in all Blainey's polemical writing, a tone of moderation, an apparent readiness to concede that his opponents have something on their side; he presents himself as the man of reason moderating the extreme claims of his opponents. 'To some extent the Black Armband view of history might well represent the swing of the pendulum from a position that had been too favourable, too self-congratulatory, to an opposite extreme that is even more unreal and decidedly jaundiced.'[14] Blainey's homely metaphors—the pendulum, the balance sheet, the loaded dice—are as telling as his arguments: they place him in the middle ground when, in fact, there is hardly a historian of any substance to the right of him. That he can credibly do so is a measure, not only of his own rhetorical skill, but of the distance which has now opened up between the intellectual milieu of academic history and the lay audience of professional and business people that Blainey now addresses.

The role of the historian

Monumental history, antiquarian history and critical history are ideal types; in real histories—even the simplified ones deployed by politicians on the stump—they are blended in complex and interesting ways. Each of the 'uses' of history, Nietzsche argued, had its corresponding 'abuse'. Monumental history, being centrally concerned with the political lessons of the past, was 'always in danger of being a little altered and touched up and brought nearer to fiction'. It was prone to false analogies, selected its explanations in accordance with preconceived ideas, traced causal continuities where none existed. In celebrating the achievements of history's winners, it marginalised the losers and diffused the pressure for change. Antiquarian history, on the other hand, was flawed by the very lack of a viewpoint, a principle of selection.

> The antiquarian sense of a man, a city or nation has always a very limited field. Many things are not noticed at all; the others are seen in isolation, as through a microscope. There is no measure; equal

importance is given to everything, and therefore too much to anything.

Critical history, as we have seen, also has its dangers: in comprehensively condemning the past it might lead to a dangerous condition of cynicism or demoralisation.

Nietzsche carries us to the brink of a great dilemma: if all these uses of history are flawed, is history itself a doomed enterprise? Some of his latter-day followers, such as Michel Foucault, have indeed veered close to this conclusion. But Nietzsche also hints at a way out of that dilemma. For each form of history can be seen as a corrective to the defects of the others—critical history for the false analogies of monumental history, antiquarian history for the preconceived ideas that corrupt both monumental and critical history, monumental history for the cynicism and disillusionment that infects critical history. The great historians move between these moments, blending them in complex and distinctive ways.

Even if we wanted to, we cannot escape history: consciousness of the past is one of the fundamental aspects of being human. But the uses and abuses of history may have consequences that are much more than academic. One of the important functions of professional historians is not just to write histories of their own, or to conduct debates in learned journals, but to maintain a watching brief on the varieties of history— some powerful and even virulent—that circulate in the larger community. This book is a small contribution to that task. Historians are sometimes seen, even perhaps see themselves, as policing the past, tramping their beat on the lookout for factual inaccuracies and other offences against the truth. There are indeed issues of truth and error, accuracy and inaccuracy at stake in the debates between historians, and some versions of history can have deadly consequences; but the most serious abuses are usually not just technical breaches of good historical method. Knowing what a history is being *used for* may be as important as knowing how it has been *argued for*.

In this book I have sought not so much to convict the abusers of history as to throw light on the process of historical interpretation. I attempt to draw out the implications of rival accounts of the past rather than to arbitrate between them; to provide matter for reflection rather than ammunition to support preconceived points of view. I am not a neutral, of course, in any of these matters, and in Chapters 12 and 13 I do give closer examination to specific abuses of history. But there is also surely a place for a kind of user's guide to the Australian past, which seeks, as honestly as possible, to show how the history trade is conducted not only by academics but by many Australians who live in, by, through, or even in spite of, the past. To those who love it, the utility of history may be the least of its charms; but we live in a utilitarian age, and in demonstrating history's uses I have also sought, unashamedly, to show the importance of taking it seriously.

chapter two

The last hero? History and hero-worship

N 1993 AUSTRALIANS mourned the death of Sir Edward 'Weary' Dunlop. Sportsman, surgeon, prisoner of war, internationalist. Dunlop had become a hero, not only to his own generation of Second World War veterans, but to a wide cross-section of Australians of all political persuasions, religions and social classes. His death inspired several commentators to reflect on the nature of heroes and the heroic dimension of Australian public life. 'Weary' was a hero in an age when there was a dearth of heroes, Sir Ninian Stephen had said at his funeral. 'Of all Australians he shares a lone eminence of sustained heroism.' The Melbourne *Herald-Sun* agreed: 'In a country where football players are routinely labelled heroes, the description is always in danger of losing its real meaning. It needed someone like Sir Edward 'Weary' Dunlop to restore the word's credibility.' The *Age* expanded on the theme:

> Can Australia expect ever to have another hero like Edward 'Weary' Dunlop? His state funeral today marks the passing of the last of his kind and in some ways this is a good thing. To have war heroes one needs wars, and we do not want more wars. Yet the nation today is in desperate need of real heroes . . . Sir Edward's values have proved a source of inspiration to more than one generation, yet few

modern Australians could stand alongside him. The
man was a natural hero, raised on ideals and principles and committed to old fashioned concepts like
faith and duty . . . Today, the people looked upon
as heroes are almost invariably creations of sport
where success is measured virtually exclusively in
monetary terms . . . Today's 'heroes' hold a short
span of public attention and acclaim, and once their
playing days are gone, the glory soon fades and a
new generation takes over. It is to be hoped that in
death as in life, 'Weary' continues to inspire the
young to a set of values beyond self-satisfaction and
materialism.[1]

This collective lament for Weary Dunlop posed a
contrast between the 'real', 'true' or 'natural' hero,
whose fame was grounded in enduring 'ideals and
principles', and the hero of the moment whose fame
was a product only of money and promotion. Weary
was the last hero, not just because he stood for values
and experiences that are past, but because he represented a concept of heroism that is said to be fading if
not extinct. That was one of the meanings of the almost
unparalleled mourning that accompanied his passing.
What it represented, we may suspect, was not a presence but a void, not continuity but rupture. Weary
Dunlop's funeral was the tribute of a more comfortable,
sceptical, uncertain nation to those who lived by a
simpler, harder code of honour, duty and sacrifice. It
was not just the absence of war—the external stimulus
for heroism—that caused these soul-searchings; it was
a suspicion, especially among the old, that the pursuit
of individual rights and wants had made old-fashioned
notions of duty and sacrifice obsolete.

Weary Dunlop was both an individual hero and a

representative of the Anzac tradition. Like the burial of the Unknown Soldier (1993), the Australia Remembers festival (1994–95) and the recent transformation of Anzac Day into an inclusive national festival, the funeral of Weary Dunlop expressed the determination of the diminishing band of ex-servicemen, aided by public officials and the media, to transmit the Anzac spirit to the next generation.[2] But while young Australians may admire the heroes of Anzac and acknowledge a debt for their sacrifice, will they also seek to emulate their virtues? Is the age of hero-worship over?

Heroes were once the soul of history. 'Great men are the inspired Texts of that divine BOOK OF REVELATION . . . called History,' declared the Victorian sage Thomas Carlyle in his *On Heroes and Hero-Worship* (1841).[3] The Victorian age was an age of hero-worship when the qualities of the heroic individual set the standard of morality and patriotism. Heroes stood for something more than themselves and won admiration by triumphing over circumstances. Like Tennyson's Lancelot, their 'strength was as the strength of ten because their hearts were pure'. Carlyle had drawn inspiration from the heroes of the Bible, ancient Greece and Rome, and the medieval Age of Chivalry, but he believed that a new industrial age also needed its own heroes. Australians inherited his message: they honoured the heroes of the Old World but they recognised, almost from the beginning, the need for heroes of their own.

The idols of the early Victorians were the warrior-heroes of Trafalgar and Waterloo, Lord Nelson and the Duke of Wellington. Military virtues—courage, daring, fortitude, love of country, self-sacrifice—became the measure of Australian heroism too. From the 1820s to the 1920s British military men—Drake, Nelson, Clive of India, Gordon of Khartoum—defined a pattern which Australians adapted to their own circumstances as well as they could. Explorers became the conventional heroes of colonial Australia, surrogates for the warriors Australia did not have. The explorers, reared on tales of heroism, were themselves often avid seekers after glory, conscious heirs to a tradition of heroic journeying that stretched back to the *Iliad* and the *Odyssey*. 'Ithaca itself was scarcely more longed for by Ulysses than Botany Bay by the adventurers who had traversed so many thousands of miles to take possession of it,' wrote Watkin Tench, chronicler of the First Fleet.[4] James Cook, who had claimed the continent for Britain, was perhaps Australia's first real hero, and his fame rose further in the nineteenth century when his humble birth, scientific skill and humanitarianism won the admiration of a democratic age.

Since heroes were seen as moral exemplars, especially for the young, schoolteachers took a keen interest in the cultivation of Australian hero-worship. While urging Australian boys to model themselves on soldiers and explorers, they also sought to create role models for Australian girlhood. Grace Darling, the lighthouse-keeper's daughter who had gone with her father to the rescue of a ship wrecked off the Northumberland coast in 1838, was a new kind of heroine—young, humbly born, brave and physically strong. Her fame spread quickly to Australia (a Collingwood pub was named after her) where she became, in turn, the model for such Australian heroines as Grace Bussell, who saved lives from a ship wrecked off the WA coast, and Jane Duff, the Victorian schoolgirl who helped her younger brothers and sisters survive the ordeal of being lost in the bush.

Australia itself was often personified as a woman, sometimes in the form of a warrior-heroine, like

Britannia, Boadicea or Columbia; sometimes, as Federation approached, as a fresh young debutante 'coming
out' into the company of nations. But these idealised
allegorical figures contrast with the relatively marginal
position of real women in the pantheon of Australian
nationalism. 'It is difficult to decide whether Australia-
as-a-woman was an affirming category for real women,
or whether she was associated with the more general
process of keeping woman in her place,' conclude the
curators of a recent exhibition of such images.[5] Australia had long thought of itself as a frontier nation
and gave precedence to masculine virtues and male
heroes. Women such as Jane Duff and Grace Bussell
combined feminine virtues such as tenderness and
mercy with qualities of physical bravery and strength,
conventionally associated with men.

For over a century Australians worshipped military
heroism without being able to prove themselves in
battle. When that opportunity came, in the Great War
of 1914–18, it was in circumstances that all but
destroyed the assumptions of individual valour, endurance and self-sacrifice on which their ideals were
founded. 'THRILLING DEEDS OF HEROISM' was the headline
of Ellis Ashmead-Bartlett's famous first despatch from
Gallipoli. The Australian war historian and classical
scholar Charles Bean also portrayed the Anzacs as
heroes in the tradition of Marathon and Thermopylae.
'They were hero-worshippers to the backbone,' he
wrote of the men who first enlisted in the AIF.[6] But his
ideal of heroism was strikingly different from the
romantic adventurer of pre-war *Boys' Own* stories; it
was the heroic qualities of the AIF as a whole, rather
than the deeds of the commanders or individual soldiers, which he sought to commemorate.

After the Great War democrats became wary of

hero-worship, a caution reinforced by the readiness of their opponents on both the Left and Right to embrace exaggerated and malignant versions of it. In the depths of the Depression a few misguided patriots may have sought to make John Monash into a *Führer*, or Jack Lang into another Lenin, but most Australians retained a healthy scepticism towards great men, an attitude which the war against Hitler and the rise of Stalin did nothing to disturb. 'The Australian people made heroes of none, and raised no idols, except perhaps an outlaw, Ned Kelly, and Carbine, a horse,' concluded Brian Fitzpatrick in 1961.[7] A peaceful property-owning democracy had little use for heroes, except perhaps for sporting heroes. Manning Clark, an admirer of Carlyle, put heroes at the centre of his *A History of Australia* (1963–) but, in the manner of Greek tragedy, they were all beset by 'fatal flaws'. The age of heroes, it seemed, was all but over.

In the 1990s, however, this traditional Australian resistance to hero-worship seems to have weakened. The old egalitarianism that insisted that Jack is as good as his master is now regularly denounced as a manifestation of the 'tall poppy syndrome'—a desire to cut down high achievers that threatens national survival. An Australian psychologist who recently conducted a survey to gauge the prevalence of the 'tall poppy syndrome' concluded that young Australians were very willing to give honour to high achievers, provided they thought their success was deserved. Sports people like Pat Cash and Alan Border were more admired than entertainers, such as Kylie Minogue and Paul Hogan, or politicians, such as Bob Hawke and Andrew Peacock. (A similar poll in the United States put Lincoln, Martin Luther King, Colin Powell, Jefferson, FDR and JFK ahead of the highest-ranked sports star, Michael

Jordan, who nevertheless outranked Bill Clinton by a considerable margin.[8]) Egalitarians were more likely to rejoice in the fall of the high achiever, but those who wished to cut down the tall poppies were outnumbered by those who wished them to grow taller.[9]

In the months following Weary Dunlop's death journalists often returned to the subject of the hero. A search of the CD-Rom *Age* turned up more than 500 references to 'heroes' in 1994–95. Most newspaper 'heroes' are not born great. Nor—except in a qualified sense—do they achieve greatness. It is in the daily struggle of the working journalist to find an angle that greatness is thrust upon them. As slayers of public reputations, journalists, it might be argued, have an indirect interest in fattening up new victims for slaughter. We can see the hero-making process at work in a number of standard media devices, such as the human interest feature in which ordinary people, such as Sydney's bushfire fighters, are 'hailed' as 'unsung heroes', 'local heroes' or 'reluctant heroes'. Contemporary hero-worship is also closely connected with the literature of motivation and self-improvement. It was during this period that Sara Henderson's inspirational autobiographies *From Strength to Strength* (1992) and *The Strength in us All* (1994), which recount her rise from financial and marital disaster to Businesswoman of the Year, headed the bestseller lists.

'Hero' is an old-fashioned word, invested with ideals now seemingly beyond our reach. Today it competes for use with newer, less demanding words. The 'celebrity' or 'star' enjoys renown without moral authority. The 'role model' has a kind of authority, perhaps of a prudential rather than a strictly moral kind, but need not be famous. Role models may prevail over adversity but, unlike heroes, they represent no one but themselves. The 'national icon' may have fame and attract a kind of worship, but people who become icons are on the way to becoming images rather than real people. (Vegemite and the Akubra hat are also national icons.) Like other icons in an iconoclastic society, they are always in danger of being shattered. The Civics Expert Group, headed by the historian Stuart Macintyre, called for a revival of civic education in which the study of 'exemplary individuals' would play a part; but it was unclear whether such individuals were to be 'exemplary' in the sense of setting a *good* example, or merely as typical of their times.[10]

Heroism is an intriguing, troublesome subject for the cultural historian. We shrink from praise as much as the founders of our profession once enthusiastically embraced it. G. M. Trevelyan, the last of the great Whig historians, declared that 'the presentation of ideals and heroes from other ages is perhaps among the most important among the educative functions of history'.[11] By contrast, our natural bias is to contextualise, relativise, explain away—to reduce the hero to the unspoken wishes of the hero-worshippers. Peter Cochrane introduces his *Simpson and the Donkey,* a subtle recent dissection of 'the pre-eminent legend of Australian heroism and self-sacrifice', with the observation that 'while heroism is an individual act, heroes are a social creation'.[12] He shows how the life and death of John Simpson Kirkpatrick, a working-class English immigrant and a man of the Left, was fashioned by recruiting officials and conservative historians into the patriotic martyr, Simpson, 'the man with the donkey'. Cochrane counterposes the phoney hero of the Right, Simpson, with the unheroic but admirable man of the Left, Kirkpatrick, but he leaves us to draw our own conclusions about the place, or absence, of heroism and hero-worship in contemporary Australia.

But in our irreverent dealings with heroes, academic historians may be out of step with public expectations. Academic reviewers of Sue Ebury's bestselling biography *Weary* quickly turned from admiration of the great man to puzzled reflections on his popular appeal. John Rickard, for example, deftly illustrated how Weary's life illustrated the themes of the 'Anzac Legend'.[13] Beverley Kingston pondered the balance between character and circumstance in the making of the hero ('Without the war, what kind of man would Weary Dunlop have become—an ageing ex-hearty, a crusty conservative driven to ever more heroic surgery?') and the ways in which his career reflected 'the complicated nature of leadership or masculinity in Australian society'.[14] Michael Cathcart noted that 'the Weary myth' had critics as well as devotees and posed the 'bewildering' contrast between the reckless and sometimes violent man and the 'Christ-like image which is now being promoted of him'.[15]

Readers of these reviews sometimes objected to all this criticising and explaining, as though, in accounting for the hero's popular appeal, the historians were somehow demeaning him. 'Cathcart talks of the "Weary Myth" and seems distressed to discover that Dunlop was not even remotely a Sensitive New Age Person,' one reader observed. There was no such thing as a 'Weary Myth,' objected another, although there was certainly a 'Weary legend soundly based on documented fact'. Mr Cathcart was engaging in 'the favourite sport of modern historians—deconstruction and reductionism. I prefer rugby', she concluded.[16]

These modern defenders of hero-worship echoed the impatience of their great nineteenth century predecessor, Thomas Carlyle, with the 'knockers' of his own time:

> I am well aware that in these days Hero-worship, the thing I call Hero-worship, professes to have gone out, and finally ceased. This, for reasons which it will be worth while some time to inquire into, is an age that as it were denies the existence of great men; denies the desirableness of great men. Show our critics a great man, a Luther for example, and they begin to what they call 'account' for him; not to worship him, but take the dimensions of him,— and bring him out to be a little kind of man! He was a 'creature of the Time', they say; the Time called him forth, the Time did everything, he nothing—but what we, the little critic, would have done too! This seems to me but melancholy work. The time call forth? Alas, we have known Times *call* loudly enough for their great man; but not find him when they called! He was not there; Providence had not sent him; and the time *calling* its loudest, had to go down to confusion and wreck because he would not come when called.[17]

Manning Clark, a latter-day follower of Carlyle, also deplored the tendency of his younger colleagues to reduce history to impersonal social processes. 'The people, not the mighty men of renown, have become the heroes of the new generation of historians. So far the people have not appeared in their articles and books as recognisable human beings,' he ruefully remarked.[18] Carlyle had seen the hero as called by destiny; the modern historian is more likely to see the hero as constructed by society. One saw his task as celebration, the other sees it as critique.

The making of a hero

Weary Dunlop is, at first sight, an unlikely hero for a multicultural Australia, especially considering his relatively recent emergence as a national figure. Revered from the first by his ex-POW comrades, it was only in his last years, and especially since the publication in 1986 of his *War Diaries*, that he became a truly national hero. Born into the old Protestant, imperialist, masculine Australia and bearing many of its traits to the last, Dunlop exhibited, if tentatively, some traits of the new Australia—an openness to Asian influences, including religious ones, and a readiness to forgive, if not forget, the bitterness of war. Michael Cathcart found these contradictions 'bewildering', but perhaps Dunlop's popular appeal lay precisely in his ability to represent, and thus symbolically to resolve, them. He was simultaneously tough yet tender, patriotic yet ecumenical, a believer and a sceptic, a boy from the bush and a man of the world, a sportsman and a scholar, man of action and a thinker. His example spoke most strongly to the older generation who shared his memories of war, but old Australia also saw in him a messenger to the young even if the young did not always get the message.

The outlines of Dunlop's character were formed early in life and seem to have altered remarkably little during its course. His magnanimity towards his Japanese captors, for example, was more a matter of old-fashioned chivalry than New Age internationalism.[19] His interest in cultivating closer relations with the countries of Southeast Asia long preceded Paul Keating's push to strengthen economic and cultural ties with Asia and refocus Australian nationalism around the Pacific rather than the European theatre of war, but these developments also gave Weary's story a new symbolic significance. It was because, in limited but crucial ways, the world brought itself more closely into line with his values, not because he changed his values to accord with it, that his heroic reputation grew. As the ranks of ex-POWs thinned and the story of their sufferings became better known, his reputation soared.

Like most of his generation Dunlop had been taught to worship, and in turn to emulate, heroes. Born in 1907, his earliest childhood memories were of what, in the 1980s, he still called 'the romantic chivalry of the Anzacs'.[20] As a state schoolboy he would also have read from the new School Readers in which heroes of the British Empire—Clive of India and Gordon of Khartoum—stood as moral exemplars beside Australian heroes—James Cook and Robert O'Hara Burke. He probably read Charles Kingsley's *Heroes,* the popular children's version of Homer which would later provide the theme for the ABC's long-running children's radio show, 'The Argonauts'.[21] The adventures of Ulysses—the warrior who journeys abroad, seeking fame and returning at last to the honour of his countrymen—touched a chord in his own life. If Weary was a hero, it was, in part, because he had heroes of his own, not just that heroism was thrust upon him.

What makes a good or brave or clever person into a hero is not the absence of weakness or wrong-doing. (Too good, too clever or too brave and the hero ceases to be someone we can identify with.) Nor is courage or moral force sufficient in itself to make a hero, at least not a popular or national one. What counts is the hero's capacity to present a personal resolution of values and interests we feel to be in contradiction. In admiration of the hero, moral and ideological opponents find, however temporarily, a common ground.

The very complexity of the hero's character and the diversity of his or her achievements afford multiple and divergent bases for loyalty and identification. Weary Dunlop, for example, was a figure capable of appealing to militarists and pacifists, nationalists and internationalists, capitalists and socialists, Christians and unbelievers, sportsmen and intellectuals. He was a born fighter—a big man, handy with his fists, a person who, as a young man, seldom flinched from physical violence. Witnessing the barbarities of his captors he experienced immense gusts of rage and the temptation to seek revenge; yet, when the opportunity for revenge presented itself, he chose the path of peace. He was a successful doctor who lived in a Toorak mansion; but the socialist and fellow POW Tom Uren remembered him as a leader who, in the hardships of the prison camp, had practised a kind of primitive communism: 'Under Weary Dunlop's leadership we were living by the principle of the fit looking after the sick—the young looking after the old—we collectivised our incomes,' he recalled.[22]

'Weary was no saint,' his biographer Sue Ebury remarks, pre-empting the words of some obituarists. His patients sometimes saw him as a 'god-like figure'; but those closer to him recognised a 'wild streak', a volatility of temperament which apparently even his wife never understood.[23] Yet others asserted the very reverse: 'WAR SAINT DUNLOP DIES' was how the *Herald-Sun* announced his passing. It went on to quote his personal physician's tribute to 'a most humble man who was able to strip away the superficial element of all humanity and see the godliness and goodness in everybody'.

These contradictory readings of Weary's character reflect an underlying unease among Australians about the emotional and moral underpinning of the national stereotype. Not being a saint is apparently a precondition for becoming a national hero. Roughness of voice, speech and manner was a key element in the public persona of Fred Hollows. According to this traditional reading, too much virtue, especially too much tenderness or piety, may be considered to unsex a man and to compromise his Australianness. Even Weary seemingly cannot be both a saint and hero at once. Obituarists tended to emphasise one image or the other; he was either 'The Christ of the Burma Road' or the 'Mad Elephant', the 'War Saint' or 'the surgeon with attitude'.

Within the traditional male Australian stereotype, loving kindness must be channelled through one narrow, officially sanctioned aperture—the code of 'mateship'. Yet Weary was emphatically not a 'mate'. He stood too tall to be considered an exemplar of an egalitarian virtue. (Admirers constantly invoked his height—'the tallest tree in the forest' said Tom Uren, 'a lighthouse of sanity' said Ninian Stephen—as a metaphor for his moral stature.) His heroism lay more in the capacity to inspire the practice of mateship among 'his' men than in his own identity as a mate. He expressed his admiration of the mateship demonstrated by others, but implicitly placed himself outside (or above?) the circle of mates. 'I shall always be uplifted by the memory of how men in the last extremity of illness so frequently took upon themselves the burdens of friends they felt to be in worse case.'[24]

The death of a hero demands acts of devotion and commemoration; and the diverse meanings that Australians attached to Weary's life were reflected in a baffling array of projects to commemorate him. The most traditional was a public statue, or rather two—one to stand in his own city, Melbourne, and one in the national capital. (These statues are discussed in Chapter 3.) A proposal to turn Weary's Toorak mansion into a shrine, which won favour among the members of the Dunlop family, failed to draw public support and the house was later sold. The Melbourne City Council received proposals to rename a city thoroughfare, perhaps the section of St Kilda Road traversed by the Anzac Day marchers ('Dunlop Drive') or the new walkway along the Yarra ('Weary's Walk') in his honour. Academics recalled Weary's role as a peacemaker in Asia to call for a scheme of international scholarships, similar to the Churchill awards, to foster cultural exchange. Doctors wanted fellowships for medical research. Television critics looked forward to a miniseries. The Mint made plans for a new 50 cent coin bearing his image and Australia Post issued a commemorative stamp.[25] Everyone, in short, sought to enlist the hero's memory in their own cause. At the moment of death, if not before, the hero relinquishes any further influence over his reputation.

Do we need heroes?

Everyone says we need heroes; but *do* we? If so, what do we need them *for*? And can the habit of hero-worship, once dead, be revived?

The cry for heroes is usually coupled with an anxiety about the moral direction of the nation's youth. Adolescents, according to the psychology textbooks, are natural hero-worshippers, and the call to promote 'real' heroes arises from the suspicion that the young are being offered only unworthy ones—models of self-indulgence rather than self-sacrifice, of hedonism rather than altruism. The worry is not an entirely new one— more than a century ago community elders were deploring the tendency of larrikins to adopt Ned Kelly as a hero. But it grows stronger in a postmodern, multicultural society as the elders themselves feel an ominous shaking of the foundations.

For two hundred years the pursuit of freedom was shaped by the claims of its enemies—the King, the Church, the Kremlin. Now, at once, it seems, those enemies are beaten and liberal democracy must ask: Is freedom enough? The question comes, these days, not only from traditional conservatives but former leftists.[26] It is, in muted form, the question that underlies the Civic Expert Groups' report: 'Rights,' the Experts affirm, 'entail responsibilities. There is a tendency to treat citizenship as if it were a magic pudding capable of providing benefits for whoever claims a slice; yet rights rely on reciprocal obligations. The emphasis on rights needs to be accompanied by an appreciation of duties.' But what duties—beyond voting—can the citizens of a multicultural society agree upon, and what sanctions or inducements are there to perform them? In the absence of a common morality, perhaps we take our lead from 'exemplary individuals'.[27]

G. M. Trevelyan had thought that 'individual great men' might become 'the model and inspiration of the smaller'. But, as he admitted, 'it is difficult to appropriate the essential qualities of these old men under new conditions'.[28] As the remaking of Weary illustrates, this process of appropriation is a complex one in which, under the influence of their enthusiastic worshippers, the historical individual may be transformed almost unrecognisably. The lead we take from their lives may be quite different from the lead they gave. What makes them heroes or saints is not the unambiguous message we may take from their lives, but the multiplicity of lessons we may read into them.

Thirty years ago democrats spurned hero-worship, fearing the reappearance of a Stalin or a Hitler. Now, it seems, that fear has receded. Heroism in the 1990s consists more in standing firm against the world than in conquering it. Weary Dunlop, at least as he is now portrayed, is a safe model for democratic youth— unselfish, courageous, benevolent and—importantly —dead. But being dead he is also remote and, try as we may to modernise him, there is no certainty that his example will survive the morality and faith in which he was reared. The life of the hero may be too removed from ours; he represents both virtues and goals beyond our reach. He belongs to a past no longer continuous with our present. The revival of hero-worship is both a lament for a lost world of moral certainty and a cry for its return.

chapter three

Monumental history: Do statues (still) speak?

NATIONALISM, IT HAS been argued, is a form of civil religion with its own creeds, rituals and shrines. The nineteenth century was the heroic age of nationalism, an era when many of the ceremonial forms of the modern state were invented or revived. In Britain, where the monarchy entered a new period of popularity under Queen Victoria, this civil religion assumed a traditional form, with the creation of ceremonies and orders of chivalry and the erection of buildings and public monuments designed to surround the monarch with the mystique of an ancient and glorious past.[1]

Australian colonists were proud to be part of this tradition, conscious how few, by comparison, were the reminders of a national past on their own soil. Australia seemed to be a land without monuments. Attuned to the classical traditions of Europe and blind to the more than 40 000 years of Aboriginal history beneath their feet, the colonists laboured without those tangible reminders of past triumphs and departed heroes which had everywhere surrounded them in the Old World. In his *First Fruits of Australian Poetry* (1819), Barron Field meditated on the dilemma of a poet in

A land without antiquities, with one,
And only one, poor spot of classic ground,
(That on which Cook first landed)—where, instead

Of heart communings with ancestral relicks,
Which purge the pride while they exalt the mind,
We've nothing left us but anticipation . . .[2]

Yet even as Barron Field wrote, the monumental
history of white Australia had begun. In 1822 members
of the Philosophical Society of Australasia had fixed a
brass tablet commemorating the landing of Captain
Cook and Joseph Banks—'The Columbus and Maece-
nas of their time'—to the rocky bluff of Cape Solander.[3]
It was the first modest step towards the creation of a
past that was at once tangible, public and permanent.

'As silent as a statue' we sometimes say; yet statues,
too, can speak, and the history of our public monuments is a vital clue, not only to what Australians have
chosen to remember but to the nature of public memory
itself. Tablets, columns and obelisks, such as those
bearing the signature of 'Lachlan Macquarie Esq.', were
the characteristically austere memorials erected by government bureaucrats in an age of predominantly
classical taste. It was not for another twenty years, as
the colony entered a more romantic and liberal age,
that the people of New South Wales erected their first
public statue in honour of their recently departed governor and champion of the people's liberties, Sir
Richard Bourke. At the dedication of the statue the new
Governor, Sir George Gipps, reflected on the social
utility of public monuments in a young colony. Of all
the arts, he remarked, sculpture was 'the most enduring
and therefore best fitted to transmit to remote posterity
the memorial of a people's gratitude'. By contemplating
the noble bearing of the subject and the lineaments of
his character, an onlooker might find inspiration to
follow in the hero's footsteps. Public sculpture also
served an ornamental purpose and Gipps perceived in

the commissioning of Bourke's statue 'a promise of the way in which the fine arts were henceforth to be cultivated in this young and rising land'.[4]

Homage to heroes, patriotic instruction for later generations, beautification of the city—these remained the main purposes of public statuary throughout the nineteenth century. With public parks, squares and museums they helped to create that sense of classical order which colonial conservatives sought to impose on the topsy-turveydom of the post-goldrush town.[5] Sometimes, when the hero had recently died, the motive of homage predominated and the monument itself was more elegiac than heroic in style. As the century advanced, however, and the education of the native-born became a more pressing public question, the didactic theme in public statuary became stronger. Governors and politicians usually directed their dedicatory speeches to parties of long-suffering children summoned from their new schoolrooms for an outdoor history lesson. Thus in 1879, when Sir Hercules Robinson dedicated Sydney's long-awaited statue of Captain Cook, he dwelt upon the great navigator's virtuous example to the young people of the colony:

> A monument of this kind cannot in any degree enhance the reputation of Captain Cook, whose name and fame will be remembered so long as the English language and history shall continue on the earth (Cheers). But such a statue is creditable to ourselves, as marking our admiration of the character and services of the man, and our gratitude for the benefits his discoveries have conferred, not only on Australia, but also on the world at large.
>
> It will serve also to bring home to all the lesson that great deeds and good reputation can be

achieved by those in the humblest station, and with the slenderest opportunity . . . I hope . . . that many a child in the future will learn at the foot of this statue how a faithful, patient cheerful attention to the details of daily duty, however monotonous and commonplace, will bring its own reward, and may perchance, as in the case of James Cook, leave behind a noble and imperishable memory.[6]

In a series of penetrating essays, and now in his masterly book *Sacred Places,* Ken Inglis has shown how much of the civic culture of colonial Australia may be reconstructed from a sensitive reading of its public monuments.[7] Erecting statues was an activity that focused the community's pride and gratitude for its successful heroes, such as Cook, and assuaged the sense of grief elicited by the deaths of its heroic failures like Burke and Wills and Gordon of Khartoum. They were large public projects supported by the monetary contributions of thousands of individual colonists including, in the case of the Gordon statue, businessmen and trade unionists, Freemasons and Catholics, schoolchildren and even the local Chinese community. Unveiling a statue was a great ceremonial occasion drawing tens of thousands of spectators, and the speeches that accompanied it were not only published in the public press but recirculated in pamphlets and school readers.[8]

Statues were sometimes designed to enhance this didactic function. The heroes themselves were often modelled on classical or biblical figures, thus elevating them to a status beyond the merely local and mortal. In Charles Summers' statue of Burke and Wills, for example, Burke is modelled on Michelangelo's Moses. Sometimes the plinth of the statue was embellished with panels depicting passages in the life of the hero. Hamo

Thornycroft's statue of General Gordon, for example, carries panels depicting his victories in China, his work among slum children at Gravesend, his governorship of the Sudan and his heroic death. They provided visual reinforcement of a narrative of patriotic courage and self-sacrifice already well grounded in popular memory through the stories in school readers and history text-books.

Sermons in stone

The heroic age of colonial statuary was the quarter-century preceding the Great War. In 1880 Melbourne, Sydney and Adelaide boasted only three great public statues between them: Sir Richard Bourke (1842) and Prince Albert (1866) in Sydney, and Burke and Wills (1865) in Melbourne. In the next thirty years private benefactors and public subscribers erected a further twenty-four statues as well as many smaller busts, tablets, cairns and other public memorials. Each capital demonstrated its fealty to the British throne with publicly endowed statues of Queen Victoria—Sydney in 1888 (replacing an earlier statue lost in the Garden Palace fire of 1882), Adelaide in 1894 and Melbourne in 1907—and of Edward VII—Melbourne and Adelaide in 1920, Sydney in 1922.[9]

Public statues were an honour reserved for men (seldom for women) of conspicuous fame or public service. Local worthies might deserve a plaque, obelisk or memorial drinking fountain, such as many Sydney aldermen are remembered by. More controversial were the claims of men distinguished for their wealth or power, but whose public services were less universally acknowledged. Judges, soldiers and explorers far outnumber politicians and businessmen among the subjects of Australian public statuary. In 1887 when Melburnians erected a statue of Sir Redmond Barry, founder of the University and the Public Library, their esteem for Barry's benevolence and high culture was contrasted with Sydney's respect for more mercenary qualities, as implied by their recently unveiled statue of the shipping magnate and woolbroker, Thomas Mort.[10] Melbourne, as it happened, would later erect statues of two of its richest men—Francis Ormond (1897) and Sir William Clarke (1902)—though ostensibly as philanthropists rather than tycoons.

Public statues were a reward for men of public spirit; sectional or partisan heroes might be honoured on their own symbolic turf, but not in a public street or park. When Governor Sir Charles Hotham, scourge of the Eureka rebels, died suddenly in 1855, the Victorian Legislative Council voted to erect a monument over his grave in the Melbourne General Cemetery. Even this circumspect gesture aroused opposition from his old opponents. Peter Lalor, by then member for Ballarat, declared that Hotham had sufficient memorial in the graves of the thirty-one men slain in the affray. Any monument should be paid for by public subscription, believed another. After an acrimonious debate the Council voted the necessary funds, more out of a sense of duty to Lady Hotham than admiration for her husband.[11]

Similar questions of public acceptability arose, in a more muted fashion, over monuments to homeland or religious heroes. While local Caledonians encountered no opposition to the erection of statues of Robert Burns in almost every capital and most provincial cities, the heroes of Irish Australia commanded less universal respect. Daniel O'Connell in Melbourne (1901) and Cardinal Moran in Sydney (1928) stand behind iron pickets within the precincts of Catholic cathedrals. Recently O'Connell has been moved from the west to the northern door of St Patrick's to make way for a striking new statue of another Irish-Australian hero, Archbishop Daniel Mannix. The most striking tribute to Irish nationalists, however, is a 1898 monument to the United Irishmen in Sydney's Waverley Cemetery.[12]

From the early 1900s progressive intellectuals had urged the erection of monuments to Australian heroes and heroines as an aid to the development of national pride among 'the coming race'. The men who led the movements to Australianise the teaching of history, to preserve Australian fauna and flora and to create national parks also spearheaded the movement to erect statues of Australian explorers and memorial cairns along the routes of their epic journeys. C. R. Long, textbook writer and editor of the Victorian *School Paper*, recognised that 'the history that reveals the development of the nation and the devotion of heroic souls down the ages is a powerful means the teacher possesses of inspiring the young with patriotic zeal'. In his *British Worthies and other Men of Might* (1933), Long placed the Australian explorers in a tradition stretching from Perseus and Marco Polo down to the latter-day heroes, Sir John Monash, Sir Ross Smith and Simpson (of donkey fame). With fellow members of the Victorian Historical Association's Historical Memorials Committee, Long travelled extensively throughout Victoria helping to erect more than one hundred memorial tablets and cairns along the routes of Hume and Hovell, McMillan, Strzelecki, Sturt, Mitchell and other notable explorers. With Sir James Barrett, Henry Gyles Turner and Sir Ernest Scott, he laboured for more than a decade to get Melbourne a statue of Matthew Flinders. 'The memorial to an explorer,' Long believed:

. . . may recall his long-tried patience and stubborn endurance, the battle he fought against great natural difficulties and obstacles, and the work that he accomplished for mankind by blazing a track into the unknown. They have, moreover, a national value, for, by the feeling of close relationship to the past and the recognition of race kinship which they engender, they aid in cementing together that race, and urging it forward through the sentiment of great possibilities. Let people but meditate on the worthy deeds of their predecessors, and it is not unlikely that they will strive to emulate them.[13]

Since 1911 Victorian schoolchildren had observed 'Discovery Day', the anniversary of Cook's sighting of Australia, as an occasion 'to reflect upon the heritage which was won for us by the toils, privation, persistence, warfare and even death of the sturdy pioneers and explorers'.[14] The history of exploration also claimed the attention of academic historians, its two foremost practitioners— Ernest Scott and George Arnold Wood—both writing or editing standard works designed, in part, for schools.[15]

The cairns and memorial tablets erected during the 1920s and 1930s represented a subtle shift in historical consciousness from the statue-building of the late nineteenth century. Their focus was on the deed rather than the man, on the process of exploration rather than the virtues of the explorer. Their builders aimed to remind the wayfarer, especially the growing number of motorists and hikers, of the invisible footprints of their hardier predecessors. Discussion among enthusiasts shifted from the moral qualities of the explorers to the reconstruction of their epic journeys. History was subordinated to geography as the new nation defined itself through the struggle to subdue the continent.

In 1923 a dispute erupted between rival factions of the Royal Society of Tasmania during a voyage to erect a monument at Abel Tasman's first landing place on the east coast. The question at issue was a seemingly trivial one. Should the memorial be erected on the spot where Tasman himself was reported to have stepped ashore or the place where his boat crew had landed a few days earlier? In other words, should they commemorate the belated landing of the great man or the act of discovery itself? Scholarly opinion was divided about the precise whereabouts of both sites. The dispute also had a sociopolitical dimension since it happened that the patriarchs of the Royal Society favoured the great explorer's landing place while the majority of the expedition to the east coast, who were less well connected, favoured the site of the earlier, more plebeian landing. The expedition began badly, with the leader accusing the minority of being 'bloody mutineers'. After they disembarked at Prince of Wales Bay the mutineers pitched camp at a distance and refused to assist in building the memorial, even though they continued to eat and drink with the rest. Controversy boiled up again after the expedition's return and was finally quelled only after the Society resolved to amend the wording of the proposed inscription from 'on this spot' to 'near this spot'.[16]

The decline of monumental history

Monumental history was so energetically promoted during the interwar years that it was not immediately apparent that its potency was waning. In 1921 a critic of Sydney's monuments expressed a revulsion for the 'theatrical' statues of politicians and explorers and noted a growing appreciation of memorials to 'artistic people'. He commended a simple obelisk erected by Governor Macquarie to mark the origin of road distances from Sydney. 'It is a monument that *does* something,' he remarked.[17] Increasingly, the public preferred monuments that did something to grand but useless statues of defunct statesmen.

The Great War had dealt a heavy blow to ideals of individual heroism. During the war itself public men had sometimes drawn parallels between the fortitude of the pioneers and explorers and the military prowess that would deliver Australia from its 'fiery hour of national trial'.[18] But as the sombre lessons of Gallipoli and the Western Front sank in, many Australians recoiled from the unthinking patriotism that had sent so many of their countrymen to their deaths. In his *History and Historical Problems* (1925), Ernest Scott insisted that 'the nourishing of patriotism is not the primary object of history, and that . . . the pressing of it into a patriotic mould has been one of the most fruitful causes of the manufacture of much pestilentially bad history'.[19]

In 1926, when Melbourne dedicated a monument to the martyred nurse Edith Cavell, it carried the eloquent inscription: 'Patriotism is not enough.' Monuments to the great warriors (Sir John Monash) were now balanced by tributes to humble angels of mercy (Simpson and his donkey) and both were outnumbered many times over by the simple white figures of Diggers standing to attention which sprang up in towns all over the continent.[20] The unknown Australian soldier became the prototype of a more democratic form of monumental history, for increasingly it was the representative type of soldier, working man, woman or athlete, rather than the heroic individual, who was honoured in Australian public statuary. The shift in terminology from 'monument'—with its associations of celebration and glorification—to 'memorial' or 'shrine' was indicative of the changing public mood.

The great war memorials, like Melbourne's Shrine of Remembrance and Sydney's Anzac Memorial, were more an expression of communal mourning than an incitement to national pride, though they contained elements of both.[21] Those who wished to pay homage to the heroism of the Anzacs had to overcome the objection that 'by building temples of memory they were perpetuating sentiments of enmity and strife'.[22] One response to this challenge was to ensure that the memorials served a useful as well as a patriotic purpose. Bruce Dellit, architect of Sydney's Anzac Memorial, had sought to portray 'neither the glory nor the glamour of war, but those nobler attributes of human nature which the great tragedy of nations so vividly brought forth— Courage, Endurance and Sacrifice'. His building was both 'aesthetic' and 'utilitarian', a memorial to the mighty dead and a welfare centre for returned soldiers 'broken in health and battered in their fight against the hardships of poverty'.[23] The onset of the Depression may have strengthened the hand of the utilitarians. A committee formed in 1936 to consider suggestions for a memorial to the late King George V received pleas for hospitals, playing fields, a conservatorium of music, a scientific institute and an opera house. 'It would be better to have a useful memorial than a bronze monument that would only make some poor people disgusted to think that people were starving while hundreds of pounds were being spent on a lifeless monument,' argued one correspondent.[24] It was not until 1954 that the present Queen dedicated a memorial garden in Sydney to her father and grandfather; Melbourne and

Adelaide, which had erected statues of George V, offered no similar tribute to his son.[25]

Between 1910 and 1940 about twenty statues of individual men and women were erected in Sydney, Melbourne and Adelaide, slightly fewer than in the preceding three decades but appreciably more than the fifteen that have been erected in the forty years since the end of the Second World War. Kings, governors and generals continued to be immortalised in bronze but they were now joined by the heroes of peace—the poets Henry Kendall, Henry Lawson and Adam Lindsay Gordon, explorers such as Matthew Flinders and Charles Sturt and their twentieth century successors, like the aviator Sir Ross Smith, whose statue was unveiled in his native Adelaide in 1927.[26]

A feature of the Victorian and South Australian centenaries of 1934 and 1936 was the creation of memorial gardens to the states' pioneer women. The garden—a haven of natural beauty and tranquillity amid the hubbub of everyday life—had long been recognised as a symbol of women's sphere. But by 1941, when Adelaide's garden was dedicated, sublime images of Manhood and Womanhood had become remote from the experience and taste of most Australians. On beholding Ola Cohn's madonna-like statue of pioneer womanhood in the centre of the garden, an onlooker was heard to object: 'That's not my idea of a pioneer woman. I see her bending over the cooking stove trying to make a fire light while water drops in through the roof of her wattle and daub hut, and with a couple of children hanging on her skirts.' One of the statue's sponsors tried to explain the symbolism of the statue—the signs of courage, resourcefulness and determination. But the sceptic remained unconvinced.

'Yes, I see what you mean,' he replied, 'even though I don't understand.'[27]

Seeing but not understanding, postwar Australians became more and more estranged from the traditions of monumental sculpture, and from the monumental sense of history on which it depended. The Second World War produced few heroic statues (Raymond Ewers' statue of Sir Thomas Blamey riding in a jeep was one of them) and the war memorials themselves were more likely to be useful, like the many memorial hospitals, crèches and swimming pools, or inconspicuous, like the forecourt of the Melbourne Shrine of Remembrance, than grandly monumental. Between the Second World War and the 1990s the only hero to be honoured with a statue in Melbourne was the American President John F. Kennedy, whose sudden death, in the days before political assassination became common, revived the sense of heroic tragedy that had inspired the monuments to General Gordon and Burke and Wills and drew Americans and Australians into a new fellowship of grief.

Since the 1920s public statues had come to be valued more for ornamental than for elegiac or patriotic reasons. New abstract memorials were designed to embellish the landscape; old ones were often moved around, like unwanted heirlooms, according to the dictates of traffic management and modern concepts of urban design. Thus Canberra's bulky memorial to George V was moved from its premier position in front of Parliament House to give a clearer view of Parliament House itself; in Melbourne the soldier General Gordon and the poet Adam Lindsay Gordon stand awkwardly at opposite ends of the recently created Gordon Reserve; while the unfortunate explorers Burke and Wills, after camping on several sites around the city, were relocated above the waterwall in City Square. When the waterwall was demolished, the thirsty heroes were moved to the edge of the new Swanston Walk. Now that the walk is to be opened to traffic again the explorers may have to break camp and resume their wanderings around the city.

The decline of monumental history was nowhere more apparent than in the changing landscape of the nation's capital. Walter Burley Griffin had sought to create a 'City Beautiful' in the style of Washington with long axial vistas and towering monumental buildings reflected in the waters of an ornamental lake. The 1928 National Memorials Committee had looked forward to the day when the city would be dominated by an Australian Acropolis or Capitol building.[28] Yet the city's rulers were inclined to draw back from the challenge and expense of monumental architecture, aiming instead at 'simple, pleasing but unpretentious buildings'. Was it something in the democratic ethos of the country or the horizontality of the Australian landscape that deterred them? Was it the aesthetic obsolescence of representational sculpture or the bureaucrat's resentment of politicians that ensured that only one notable politician is honoured with a public statue? Our first prime minister stands on the footpath outside the Barton government offices, gazing expectantly down King's Avenue as if waiting for a taxi. One or two other prime ministers are inconspicuously commemorated with bas-reliefs and busts outside the suburban high schools and shopping centres that bear their names. Canberra is not wanting in public statuary. The visitor is forever encountering concrete and stainless steel tributes to 'Growth', 'Knowledge', 'Relaxation', 'Togetherness' and other abstract democratic virtues. Such monuments may beautify the landscape and possibly evoke the admiration of visitors, but their purpose is very different from the public statues of the past.[29] It is in Canberra, rather than in Washington, that we witness the fulfilment of Alexis de Tocqueville's prophecy. 'In democratic ages,' he wrote, 'monuments of the arts have become more numerous and less important.'

To this rule, however, de Tocqueville allowed a significant exception for, while democracies might be slow to honour heroic individuals, their imaginations expanded infinitely when they thought of the State. Thus, he concluded, 'democracy not only leads men to a vast number of inconsiderable productions, it also leads them to raise some monuments on the largest scale; but between these two extremes there is a blank'.[30] He had particularly in mind the remarkable contrast between the raw appearance of the infant city of Washington and the astonishing grandeur of its public buildings, especially its pompously named Capitol. Australians may recognise a similar disparity between the 'vast number of inconsiderable productions' which embellish the environs of Canberra and the mammoth proportions of our Capitol, the new Parliament House. Few contemporary buildings demonstrate so vividly the political imperatives and aesthetic contradictions of monumental architecture in a modern society. 'The notion of a modern monument,' writes Lewis Mumford, 'is a contradiction in terms; if it is a monument it is not modern; and if it is modern it cannot be a monument.'[31]

The contradiction had been implicit throughout the long debate about the site for the new Parliament House. Should it be located on Capitol Hill, the site selected by the city's founders, or beside the lake? Should it dominate the landscape, a symbol of transcendent political values, or merge into it, symbolising the indissolubility of people and parliament? When the decision was made in favour of Capitol Hill these fundamental tensions were left unresolved. National pride required a building of a certain grandeur; yet democratic values and modernist aesthetics made the traditional forms of monumental architecture obsolete. Mitchell, Giurgola and Thorpe, the winning architects, have resolved this dilemma by the ingenious but costly expedient of constructing a building of monumental proportions and then burying it in the side of Capitol Hill. Is the result a monument or not? Any building of this scale, its architects concede, must exhibit 'a sense of grandiosity'. Their avowed aim was to express 'a simple sense of monumentality in concert with the honest, natural landscape' rather than 'a monumental structure imposed on the landscape'.[32] The result, as one critic noted, is a building 'distinctly unheroic in scale and style'.[33] Alongside its nineteenth century counterparts it appears almost devoid of the traditional symbols of authority. In line with the general tendency of postmodern architecture, it appropriates historical symbols in an essentially unhistorical way, playfully exaggerating and distorting them for architectural effect rather than drawing afresh upon their original sources. The gigantic flag and flagpole and the facade with its echoes of the 1927 provisional Parliament House are antiquarian gestures rather than the monuments of a new age. Within the building, dozens of distinguished artists have been commissioned to execute paintings, tapestries and sculptures telling the story of Australia. But their very number and variety—'a vast number of inconsiderable productions'—seemed to confirm the demise of monumental history.

In November 1993, with the entombment of the Unknown Soldier in the National War Memorial,

Australians completed the project of national remembering begun by Charles Bean more than eighty years before. The much admired dedicatory speech written for Prime Minister Keating by the historian Don Watson stands firmly in the line of democratic patriotism that runs from Pericles down through Lincoln to Charles Bean. 'He is all of them. And he is one of us,' Keating affirmed. 'Ordinary people' were 'the heroes of that war: not the generals and the politicians' and their heroism was of a democratic, fraternal kind. They taught us 'to endure hardship, to show courage, to be bold as well as resilient, to believe in ourselves, to stick together'.[34]

Yet in the very moment of its triumph this modern democratic concept of heroism was being politely challenged. No sooner had the Unknown Soldier been entombed than Australians were mourning and memorialising another very Well-known Soldier. As befits an old-fashioned hero, the monuments to Weary Dunlop were traditional ones. Rather than useful memorials—though there were some of these too—his followers insisted that Weary should be immortalised in bronze, and more than life-size. In Peter Corlett's Melbourne and Canberra statues, erected by public subscription, he appears as he did in later life—a tall, stooping gentleman in a business suit, a revered public figure. It is his reputation rather than his deeds that are commemorated here.

But in the public gardens of his old home town of Benalla a younger Weary, bare-chested and in army shorts, stoops to support the emaciated figure of a POW, while a second doctor tends his injuries. The ideal resolution between aggressive and nurturing qualities implicit in the public tributes to Dunlop (see Chapter 2) is also embodied in Louis Laumen's impressive statue, especially the strong masculinity of the figures themselves and the hints of femininity in the composition, which recalls that of a *pietà*. 'When despair and death reached out to us Weary Dunlop stood fast, a lighthouse of sanity in a universe of madness and suffering', reads the inscription, the tribute of one of his fellow POWs.

Alongside more traditional military monuments— generals on horseback, soldiers standing at the ready, Blamey in his jeep—the Dunlop statues impress by their resolute immobility. Weary becomes a hero, not by making war, but in 'standing fast' against 'madness and suffering'—not only that of the Burma Railway, we may feel, but of all those newer forms of 'madness and suffering' from which his hero-worshippers now crave deliverance.

Public statues and monuments were once an important means of civic education. By embodying large ideals and giving them a public presence, they helped to define the moral basis of social and political life. The statues of Queen Victoria, James Cook and Robert Burns which graced the colonial city usually bore no inscription beyond the hero's name and dates. Further details were unnecessary for their lives and characters were firmly inscribed in popular memory. The classical iconography of statuary was also probably more familiar to most people than it is today. But the educative role of the public statue has long since been assumed by other forms of mass media—the cinema, the TV miniseries, the popular press, the Internet. Soon the Shrine of Remembrance will have a visitors' centre with video displays where the story of Anzac can be retold to a generation for whom it no longer reverberates in memory.

So, are monuments just an obsolete survival of an

older form of nationalism? Not quite: for while a statue may seem mute compared with a movie or a website it is also more fixed and durable. By its very solidity and permanence it is a quiet protest against all those other powerful, omnipresent but ephemeral forms of remembering.

chapter four

The Great Voyage: National celebrations in three new lands

A S THE MILLENNIUM approaches Australians prepare once again to celebrate. In the year 2000 Sydney will host the Olympic Games and in 2001 we will commemorate the centenary of Australian Federation. Such 'major events' are now occasions of much more than local importance for, in the global competition for tourism and investment, cities prosper not only by how hard they work but by how spectacularly they play. National birthdays are not just for reinforcing national pride and identity; they are also an opportunity to put the nation on show to the rest of the world.

At the end of the twentieth century, nationalism—like almost everything else—is a global phenomenon and the ways we celebrate our national distinctiveness are not uniquely Australian. The Australia that is performed in the Opening Ceremony of the Sydney Olympics will owe as much to international precedents as it does to an indigenous folk culture. National history may provide the raw material for our celebrations but they are shaped in accordance with *our* view of what *others* expect.[1] Such emulation is not new: since the era of the American and French revolutions nations have modelled themselves on each other. National birthdays deploy a finite repertoire of narrative themes:

knowing which story to tell, and how to tell it, was what patriots debated as each birthday came round.

Historians played at most a supporting role in this process. More important have been the contributions of poets, politicians and, in our own day, of public relations consultants, advertising men and media moguls. National commemorations use the events of history but the stories they tell are determined more by the politics of the present than the ideals of the past.

Myths of nationhood

The histories of New World nations, like their classical prototypes, reproduce a limited repertoire of mythic themes—the heroic journey, the foundation myth, the treaty and the battle. The new land derives its legitimacy from the heroic acts of those who voyaged to the new land, who founded it, who conquered or made peace with the original possessors of the soil and who overcame the trials of fire, flood, pestilence, earthquake and revolution.

New lands such as America, Australia and New Zealand acquired historical significance, firstly, as the destination of the voyagers who founded them. The Pilgrim Fathers at Plymouth, James Cook at Botany Bay or Captain Arthur Phillip at Sydney Cove are endowed with something of the legendary aura of Moses and the Israelites or Jason and the Argonauts. They are themselves the forerunners of the thousands of other voyagers who have peopled the new land. The Great Voyage is a story of adventure, of risk, of pilgrimage, and by its capacity to include voyagers from many origins and generations it has—as we shall see—an enduring appeal as the warrant for a pluralist sense of nationhood.

It therefore stands in contrast to the more patriarchal sense of nationality based upon a foundation myth. In the minds of nineteenth century antiquarians and of some later historians, the primary event of a city's history was its foundation—the raising of the flag, the reading of a proclamation, the firing of a ceremonial volley of shots, the laying out of the first street plan. According to this tradition, the founding father (there were seldom founding mothers) was invested with special visionary qualities and seminal virtues that were often mysteriously transmitted to the city he fathered. Romulus and Remus, founders of Rome, were the classical paradigm; but their colonial counterparts, Governor Winthrop of Boston, Peter Stuyvesant of New York, John Batman of Melbourne, Colonel Light of Adelaide, Colonel Simcoe of Toronto, and both Captain William Hobson and John Logan Campbell of Auckland were often credited with similar heroic qualities. The foundation myth, like all such patriarchal histories, turns around ideas of legitimacy and pedigree. Though the character of the founder may subtly change as his story is retold, the essential purpose remains the same— to instil in the citizenry a reverence for the city's original, and fundamental, ideals.[2]

In possessing the new land the founders often went through the forms of conciliating the native inhabitants. To colonists themselves deeply imbued with the sanctity of property, the treaty was seen both as a legitimation of conquest and as a standard for regulating future relations between the races. Side by side with stories of exploration and foundation, therefore, they recounted stories of their clemency and justice towards the native peoples. William Penn, the Quaker founder of Philadel-

phia, had made his famous Great Treaty with the
Delaware Indians in 1682 and his example was
followed, more often in the breach than the observance, by other new nations. John Batman, 'founder of
Melbourne', signed such a supposed treaty with the
Doutta Galla Aborigines in 1835, and historian Henry
Reynolds has suggested that George Robinson, Protec-
tor of Aborigines, may have attempted some similar
agreement in Van Diemen's Land.[3] In no other national
history, however, does a treaty assume the pivotal
importance accorded to the Treaty of Waitangi in the
history of modern New Zealand.

The moral sustenance that citizens drew from their
history depended in part upon the legacy of stories,
ceremonies, monuments, and sacred sites handed down
by earlier generations; in part upon the felt needs and
anxieties that selected and reshaped those materials to
a present-day use. In times of rapid social change,
citizens clung to the stabilising virtues of the city's
founders. When ethnic loyalties threatened to divide
them, they recalled the shared experience of voyaging
and affirmed that, figuratively speaking, they were all
in the one boat. When the fate of the native peoples
they had dispossessed sat heavily on their consciences,
their thoughts returned to the principles of justice
enshrined in the founders' treaties.

But while citizens were free, within limits, to fashion
such usable pasts, their calendar of anniversaries and
centenaries was governed as much by arithmetic as by
social expediency. The events the calendar marked for
celebration were not necessarily the ones that citizens
felt most like celebrating. Boston, Sydney and Auckland
have enjoyed special places in the national consciousness of the United States, Australia and New Zealand.
Once the sites of historic events, they have now become

stages for the presentation of distinct, yet increasingly convergent civic rituals. How these rituals emerged, and later converged, is a valuable clue to the ways in which national history is played out on a world stage.

Boston 1775–1975

The American Revolution had no sooner ended than the process of patriotic myth-making began.[4] Boston, the self-styled 'Cradle of Liberty', was the home of some of the most famous revolutionaries—Benjamin Franklin, John Hancock and Samuel Adams—and it witnessed some of the Revolution's most momentous events—the Boston Tea Party, the 'Boston Massacre' and the battles of Concord, Lexington and Bunker Hill. The protests of Boston's artisans appropriated many of the symbols of British radicals—its bonfire and torch-light processions, its burnings in effigy, its feasts and orations, its Liberty songs and Liberty Tree.[5]

As memory faded into history, Bostonians developed a new reverence for the shrines and sacred sites of the Revolution. From the 1830s and 1840s, the city's liter-ary men, many of whom settled in suburban Concord, led the movement to immortalise the heroes of the Revolution in verse and monuments. In 1837 Ralph Waldo Emerson composed his 'Concord Hymn' to mark the dedication of a stone obelisk at the Old North Bridge where his grandfather had witnessed the slaying of the first British Redcoats.[6] In 1875, the centenary of the battle, Emerson, then in his 73rd year, returned to the bridge to witness the unveiling of a second monu-ment—a heroic bronze statue of a defiant Minuteman bearing an inscription from his famous poem. Many of the farms and homesteads around Concord and Lexington were still inhabited by descendants of the Minutemen. On Lexington Common, where the colonists had first faced British troops on the morning of 19 April 1775, visitors were assisted in their historical pilgrimage by local guides. 'Every spot having a history was duly labelled, like relics in an old museum.'[7]

Bostonians were eager to promote their city's historic significance, not least because of the commercial rewards of historical tourism. The 20 000 pilgrims who rode the railway out to Concord and Lexington in April 1875 were outnumbered ten times over by the visitors who converged on Boston—'the sacred Mecca of the American people'—for the anniversary of the Battle of Bunker Hill in June 1875.[8] Contemporaries recognised, in the more strongly urban focus of the 1875 celebrations, a sign of the forces that were reshaping the life of the nation as a whole. In their tributes at Concord and Lexington, centennial orators dwelt upon the characteristically rural virtues of the Minutemen: 'The men who fell on this green, under the shadow of the village church, willing martyrs, were men born and reared here, taught at the village school and from the village pulpit, freeholders of your own lands, voters in your town meetings, organised into the militia of your little community.' But they also recognised the irresistible, centripetal drift of the nation's life towards the great cities. 'In New England the characteristic village and local life of the last century perishes in the age of steam,' concluded George Curtis at Concord.[9]

Bostonians were eager to assert their solidarity with the cause of liberty. On the evening of 18 April a service was traditionally held in Boston's Old North Church to mark the anniversary of the moment when a lamp was raised into the belfry of the church warning the satellite communities of the approach of British troops.[10] The solidarity between revolutionary Boston and the Minutemen of Concord and Lexington was most vividly symbolised by the midnight ride of the Boston silversmith Paul Revere to warn the outlying towns of the British advance—an episode immortalised in the well-known poem 'Paul Revere's Ride' (1863) by the Harvard professor, Henry Longfellow, and since re-enacted on each anniversary.

Boston's own centennial celebrations culminated in the commemoration, on 18 June 1875, of the Battle of Bunker Hill, the confused and bloody encounter in which British troops dislodged the colonial militia from the heights overlooking the garrison at Charlestown, just a mile across the harbour from Boston. In the minds of most spectators, memories of the Revolution were overlaid by fresh, unhealed memories of that second, and even bloodier, national trial, the Civil War between North and South. A major feature of the anniversary was the presence of invited delegations of militia from the southern states and, in their speeches, Bostonians sought to further 'the benign work of reconciliation' by emphasising the solidarity between the sons of the South and the North who had 'stood shoulder to shoulder in that grand old time'.[11]

A hundred years later, when it was time for Bostonians to mark the bicentenary of the Revolution, the incongruities between the foundation myth and the nation's circumstances were even more striking. 'It would be hard to imagine a more painful approach to a time for national celebration,' remarked the journalist Anthony Lewis in 1976.[12] The Kennedy assassinations, the Vietnam War, Watergate, the energy crisis and continuing racial violence had tarnished the American dream of life, liberty and happiness. There was a tragic irony about celebrating the independence of a small colony from a great empire when America, now itself an empire, had so recently been humiliated by a small Asian nation fighting a so-called 'war of national liberation'. And it was hard, in the aftermath of Watergate, to celebrate the triumph of democratic rights over the excesses of monarchical government.

In 1970, when Nixon endorsed the plans of the Bicentennial Commission, he signalled a retreat from the grandiose mood of the earlier celebrations.[13] The Massachusetts senators, Edward Brooke and Edward Kennedy, had fought a successful campaign against the plans of Philadelphia, site of the original Declaration of Independence, to monopolise the Bicentennial celebrations with a colossal World's Fair similar to the 1876 Exposition. 'There can be no single Bicentennial city,' Nixon assured the jealous contenders. Of Thomas Jefferson's hallowed trinity of national ideals, Nixon played down the first two—life and liberty—but reinterpreted the third—'the pursuit of happiness'—in terms of that fashionable catchcry of the early 1970s, 'quality of life'.[14] The bicentennial organisers responded to the national mood with such environmentally conscious projects as tree plantings and building restorations.

In the months preceding the Bicentennial, as the scandal of Watergate unfolded, there sprang up a vigorous left-wing opposition to the official celebrations, under the auspices of the self-styled People's Bicentennial Commission. Led by the former Yippy, Jeremy Rifkin, the PBC sought to turn the revolutionary symbols of 1775 against the Republican administration and its big-business allies. In December 1973, when Boston re-enacted its Tea Party, protesters almost outnumbered the official celebrants. As one of the make-believe rebels cried out 'Down with King George', one of the modern-day rebels replied 'Down with King Richard'. At a meeting in Faneuil Hall, where Samuel Adams had once denounced British tyranny, one of his descendants, Thomas Boylston Adams, called for the impeachment of the President. 'It is the recurring tragedy of history,' Adams observed, 'that those to whom values inherited from a valiant past should mean the most are the last to perceive their destruction.'[15]

Eighteen months later, when the anniversaries of Concord and Lexington came round, the unloved President Nixon had departed but the protests continued. On the slopes overlooking the Old North Bridge at Concord, the long-haired, blue-jeaned supporters of the People's Bicentennial Commission held a Woodstock-style protest meeting. On the opposite bank, where the British troops had once assembled, President Ford addressed the official guests. He reminded them that it was here that the American colonists fired the famous 'shot heard round the world'. In a passage that would have surprised Emerson as much as it infuriated the protesters, he proceeded to develop the theme of America's expanding military might: 'From a newborn nation with a few ships, American seapower now ranges the most distant shores.' Boos and hisses erupted from the opposite shore, almost drowning out his words. Rejecting the spirit of passionate rebellion that had animated the Minutemen, Ford appealed to more conservative ideals of tolerance, reason and unity.[16]

The most memorable of Boston's bicentennial events came in July 1976 when the city hosted sixteen Tall Ships and welcomed the descendant of George III, Britain's Queen Elizabeth II. Hundreds of thousands of Bostonians and visitors lined the shore as the ships proceeded majestically down the harbour. Only a handful of IRA sympathisers protested against the Queen's arrival. As the Queen and the Duke of Edinburgh

toured the city's historic North End, spectators flushed
with the euphoria of the occasion were even heard to
call out the once-seditious words 'God Save the
Queen'.[17]

Boston, the 'Cradle of Liberty', enjoyed a rich
legacy of political rituals and symbols—the Liberty
Tree, the Tea Party, the raised lamp, the midnight ride,
the defiant stand of the farmers at Concord and Lexington. Yet in 1976 these powerful local symbols were
largely subordinated to the less authentic but more
consoling symbolism of the Great Voyage. The Tall
Ships did not stand for any specific historical voyage.
The *Mayflower*, whose 1957 re-enactment voyage was
still fresh in the minds of older Americans, was perhaps
their prototype, but they also called to mind a host of
other American odysseys—black slaves, Irish peasants,
Jewish refugees, Indo-Chinese boat people. The political
and social divisions of the 1970s had created an overwhelming need for a binding myth of nationhood. The
Tall Ships symbolised the common history of all new
nations—the migration experience. They evoked the
experience of voyaging, of movement from diverse origins towards a common, but still unknown, destination.
National identity, the myth said, was a process of
becoming rather than a moment of arrival.

Sydney 1788–1988

By 1976 Americans seemed almost embarrassed by their
revolutionary beginnings. Yet the American Revolution
and American styles of patriotic ceremonial had once
set the fashion for other nations to follow. 'I am by no
means sure that we should not act wisely by taking a
leaf out of the experience of our American cousins,'

declared Henry Parkes, Premier of New South Wales, in proposing a patriotic oration as the highlight of Australia's centennial celebrations in 1888.[18] Others, recalling the success of Philadelphia's Centennial Exposition, called for Australia to follow suit. A Sydney architect even suggested that Sydney Harbour should be adorned by 'a colossal statue consisting of an ideal figure of Australasia, such as that which has been erected at New York'.[19]

Anyone who pondered the histories of the United States and Australia could not easily overlook their fundamentally different origins. While 1776 marked a Declaration of Independence from British rule and the birth of a free society, 1788 had inaugurated the British conquest of a new land and the foundation of a prison camp. Americans looked back to their Revolution as a source of sustaining political values; Australians remembered Sydney Cove as a symbol of the bondage from which they had gradually won their freedom.[20] Many Australians therefore sought to avoid invidious comparisons with their 'American cousins'. 'I do not know if there is any exact analogy between our position and that of the United States on that occasion [the Centennial]; in fact there is no analogy at all,' insisted Sir Patrick Jennings.[21] Others conceded the validity of the comparison but drew a more radical conclusion. Rather than celebrating the anniversary of 26 January 1788, 'the day we were lagged', the republican *Bulletin* urged Australians to celebrate the anniversary of 3 December 1854, the date of the Eureka Stockade and the first engagement in the struggle for Australian independence.[22]

The American Revolution had created its own rich array of national symbols. But there was little in the ceremonial life of the Australian colonies, or in the environs of their cities, to inspire Australians with a similar sense of their country's history. 'Australia has no state religion; Australia has no shrine; Australia has no Capitol,' one patriot mournfully observed.[23] The solution, according to some politicians, was to create such shrines and symbols deliberately. Henry Parkes' grandiose proposal to erect a State House in the middle of the new Centennial Park on Sydney's eastern fringe was intended to supply such a national shrine. It would include Phillip Hall, named after the nation's founder, as a place for great national ceremonies; the Macquarie Institute, as a national library, gallery and museum; and a public mausoleum as a resting place for the nation's mighty dead. It was as though Australia's equivalent Capitol, Smithsonian Institution and Arlington Cemetery were to be rolled into one.[24]

Long before it was shelved for lack of funds, however, Parkes' scheme collapsed under the weight of public ridicule. 'It is not an edifice itself, but its associations, its surroundings, and the events belonging to it, that constitutes national building in the proper sense of the word,' declared the *Sydney Morning Herald*.[25] Regrettably, most of the associations and surroundings of Sydney's buildings were not inspirational in the desired way. Sydneysiders were left to mark their centenary with a lacklustre round of speeches, banquets, sporting contests, statue-unveilings and foundation-stone layings dressed up in the familiar rhetoric of British imperialism.

A hundred years later in 1988 Australian patriots were not much better off. Like the American Bicentennial, Australia's 200th birthday was approached amid a period of social and political turmoil. While memories of the Vietnam War were fading, the 1975 constitutional crisis, when Gough Whitlam's Labor government

had been dismissed from office by the Queen's representative, was still fresh in people's minds. Preparations
for the Bicentenary began under Whitlam's successor,
Malcolm Fraser, who appointed an Australian Bicentennial Authority (ABA) led by the Australian Democrat,
David Armstrong.[26]

Influenced by the style of the American Bicentennial
and by the vogue of multiculturalism, the ABA planned
a diverse, year-long program of celebrations under the
pluralistic slogan 'Living Together'. No sooner was
the slogan launched than it was torpedoed by the
objections of moral conservatives provoked by its implications of sexual naughtiness. The government
substituted the more chauvinistic 'The Australian
Achievement' but the program was little altered. With
the advent of the Hawke government in 1983 the old
slogan 'Living Together' made a comeback but it was
jettisoned again in 1985 when a reconstituted ABA, led
by the businessman James Kirk, substituted 'Celebration of a Nation'. This was an inaccurate, motto but
it had the kind of upbeat feel that appealed to the
advertising and marketing people who were to take a
dominant role in organising the celebrations.

Implied in the choice of a slogan was the question
of whether the Bicentenary was to be a celebration or
merely a commemoration. There were some Australians
who wanted a traditional patriotic birthday that re-
enacted the events of 1788, paid tribute to Captain
Phillip as the founder of the nation, and celebrated the
Anglo-Saxon civilisation he brought with him. They
feared that, under David Armstrong, the Bicentenary
would be hijacked by communists, feminists, Aboriginal
protesters and other 'unpatriotic' elements. One group
of enthusiasts led by Jonathan King, a descendant of
one of Governor Phillip's lieutenants, had begun prep-

arations to re-enact the voyage of the First Fleet from England to Australia. The ABA refused support for the venture. It was concerned—justifiably as it turned out—about its cost and, more seriously, about the moral and political implications of re-enacting the events of 1788.[27] It may have had in mind the unhappy precedent of the 1938 Sesquicentenary celebrations when, as part of a re-enactment of the arrival of the First Fleet at Sydney Cove, about thirty Aborigines from outback reserves were virtually kidnapped and brought to Sydney to perform a corroboree and shake their spears at the advancing Redcoats.[28]

The ABA also had its own more fitting symbol in mind. Since 1976, when he witnessed the progress of the Tall Ships up the Hudson River, David Armstrong had wanted to make a similar spectacle the centrepiece of Australia's birthday party.[29] What event could better express the multicultural ideal than the arrival of a fleet of Tall Ships crewed by the youth of many nations?[30]

The most appealing aspect of the Tall Ships was their affinity with that most spectacular of Australian outdoor theatres—Sydney Harbour. Its beauty and grandeur had captivated observers from the beginnings of the colony. 'I had the satisfaction of finding the finest harbour in the world in which a thousand sail of the line may ride in the most perfect security,' declared Arthur Phillip in his first despatch.[31] Two hundred years later an estimated two million Sydneysiders and visitors crowded the foreshore and hilltops to watch the Tall Ships and the First Fleet sail down the harbour with their immense escort of pleasure boats. It was an unforgettable sight.

In the months preceding the Bicentenary, the New South Wales government, seemingly possessed by the same 'edifice complex' as inspired Sir Henry Parkes'

State House, had been endowing Sydney with a new generation of public monuments. Along Darling Harbour the few remnants of Sydney's colonial waterfront were being erased to make way for the exhibition halls, museums, casinos, discovery villages and aquariums of a new leisure city.[32] Sydney, like Boston, was not without its historic sites. The stone footings of Phillip's own First Government House had only recently been found by archaeologists under a city building site. But among citizens captivated by images of modernity they did not seem as sacred as the Harbour Bridge or the Opera House.[33]

There was little in the ceremonies of 26 January 1988 to remind Sydneysiders of the historic event they were ostensibly commemorating. The only British naval officer to step ashore at Sydney Cove was that honorary Aussie, the Prince of Wales, accompanied by the popular Princess Di. On the concourse beside the Opera House Prince Charles inspected a detachment of Australian Army regulars dressed, for the occasion, in eighteenth century military garb, the so-called 'Heritage Guard'. In their speeches, neither the Prince nor Prime Minister Hawke once mentioned the names of Phillip or the First Fleet, although the Prince managed a cheeky allusion to his own youthful 'transportation' to Australia and developed the gratifying contrast between the prison of 1788 ('the worst place in the world') and the 'whole new free people' of present-day Australia ('the best place in the world').

Like President Ford at Concord, Bob Hawke steered his audience away from the painful facts of history towards the historically vague, but more reassuring, mythology of the Great Voyage. 'For the past 200 years and to this day,' he affirmed, 'we have been a nation of immigrants.' Australians not only enjoyed a 'common bond of institutions, language and culture' but 'our very diversity is an ever-growing source of vitality and strength'.[34] Instead of recounting or re-enacting the events of 1788, the Bicentenary organisers had settled for a vague and largely synthetic historicism. Like Mrs Hawke's jaunty Akubra and the slouch hat that the Prince later donned to protect the royal pate from the January sun, the symbols of nationalism had become articles of apparel to be worn for a day, doffed to the crowd and returned to the closet until the next anniversary.

The Great Voyage was an inclusive myth but it did not include everyone. The people who caused most anxiety to the organisers of the Bicentenary, and whose predicament perhaps made the speechmakers steer clear of specific references to 1788, were those whose fore-bears had been dispossessed by the first European settlers, the Australian Aborigines. In 1938 many Abo-rigines had marked the anniversary as a Day of Mourning. In 1976 Native Americans had also threat-ened to boycott the American Bicentenary. One of their spokesmen, using language similar to that later used by Australian Aborigines, declined to join the Bicentennial Wagon Train because 'we feel the invitation was like the Germans inviting the Jews to celebrate Hitler's rise to power'.[35]

The protests of 1988 in Australia were far more sustained and unanimous than those of 1975–76 in America. The Australian Bicentenary, after all, was not the anniversary of a revolution but of an act of European conquest. It highlighted the fact that the land had been taken without negotiation, without a treaty and without compensation. It came at the end of a decade that had seen the emergence of a self-confident political movement seeking the restoration of land rights to Aborigines and calling for a treaty between black and white Australians. And in the preceding months, the legacy of dispossession had been tragically dramatised by violent deaths among young Aboriginal men while in police custody. It was hard for white Australians to rejoice in their emancipation from the fetters of convictism while descendants of the country's original inhabitants were dying in prison cells.

As 26 January 1988 approached Aborigines throughout Australia began to mobilise. More than 500 people from the Northern Territory made their own symbolic journey in a convoy of cars and minibuses down through outback Queensland and New South Wales to Sydney. When the Tall Ships arrived in Melbourne a group of Aboriginal women carried out a mourning ritual on the wharf and cast wreaths of wattle into the water around the ships.[36] On the morning of 26 January about 15 000 Aborigines and their supporters marched through Sydney's streets, carrying their distinctive red, black and yellow flags, towards the tent embassy under Lady Macquarie's Chair, on the eastern shore of Sydney Cove, where their ancestors had once watched, amazed, as the white sails of the invaders came into view. Ironically, it was the Aboriginal protesters, not the official organisers of the Bicentenary, who staged the only re-enactment of the events of 1788 and it ended, not with the raising of the Union Jack, but with 'Captain Phillip' being thrown into 'the finest harbour in the world'.

Auckland and Wellington 1890–1990

New Zealanders—so like Australians in so many ways —rejoice in a prouder national pedigree. It was the more honourable pursuits of trade, agriculture and missionary enterprise that attracted the first free settlers to New Zealand, and their arrival in 1840, under the watchful eye of British humanitarians, was swiftly followed by the conclusion of a treaty with the native people, the Maori.

The Treaty of Waitangi, signed by Captain William Hobson, the Queen's representative, and more than 500 Maori chiefs, in its English text asserted the sovereignty of Queen Victoria over the land of New Zealand, guaranteed the Maori in the possession of their lands, forests and fisheries, and conferred on the chiefs the rights and privileges of British subjects. Not all the Maori chiefs agreed to sign the Treaty and not all the signatories, even on the British side, clearly understood its meaning, let alone that of the Maori text. No sooner had the Treaty been signed than some settlers began to break it and some chiefs to repent their compliance. In 1844, Hone Heke, the first Maori signatory to the Treaty, dramatised his opposition to British rule by chopping down the British flagpole at Kororareka, near Waitangi, and sacking the township. From the first, then, Waitangi has been a symbol of both trust and betrayal, of concord and protest. Yet it remains, as New Zealanders were reminded again in 1990, 'our founding document . . . the only symbol we have of our life together as a nation'.[37]

Fundamental as it is now to the sense of New Zealand nationality, the Treaty has not always figured prominently in national celebrations. In 1890, on the fiftieth anniversary of the British settlements at Auckland and Wellington, memories of the New Zealand wars were still fresh in people's minds. Many of the pioneers of 1840 were still alive, and the celebrations were designed more to honour their achievements than to recall New Zealanders to the principles of the Treaty.

The triumphant raising of the British flag, rather than the meeting of the two races on the level surface of the *marae*, provided the essential symbolism of the occasion. The first settlers were depicted as having come to 'a wild country tenanted by a wild people' but they had transformed it, in only fifty years, into a modern, urban society: 'The Maori with his fierce tribal wars, his mystic religious customs, and cannibalism, has vanished before the inevitable force of civilisation.'[38]

In the processions, pageants, speeches and sports marking the jubilee, Maori were generally assigned a separate and subordinate part. No attempt was made to draw upon the rich tradition of Maori ceremonial in devising an authentically national style of public ritual. In Wellington, where a symbolic tableau of New Zealand in 1840 and 1890 was played out, only a few Maori dressed in European costume joined the procession while the rest 'played the part of sightseers and holiday makers'.[39]

In 1940 New Zealanders marked the centenary of British settlement at a moment when Britain itself was about to face its sternest test. At Wellington, 5000 spectators gathered on the Petone foreshore to dedicate a monument incorporating a commemorative window showing a Maori chief extending a hand of welcome to the newcomers.[40] A few days later at Kororareka a smaller crowd witnessed a re-enactment of Captain Hobson's landing. Maori girls dashed into the sea chanting a song of welcome, while Maori men performed a *haka* on the shore.[41] Not all Maori were content with such a version of New Zealand history. In the interwar years, the Waitangi Treaty had become a powerful weapon in the hands of Maori leaders, like Sir Apirana Ngata, who sought Pakeha assistance to develop Maori lands. Tribal leaders of the Waikato and

Taranaki, locked in disputation with the government over confiscated land claims, boycotted the ceremonies at Waitangi and even those who took part, like Ngata, saw the Treaty as an agreement as much honoured in the breach as the observance. 'In retrospect, what does the Maori see?' he asked. 'Lands gone, the powers of chiefs humbled in the dust, Maori culture shattered and broken.'[42]

By 1990 New Zealand had become a more complex, urbanised and troubled society. One by one, the props of the old British-derived sense of nationality had collapsed. The *Rainbow Warrior* affair and the ban on nuclear ships had crystallised a proud, but lonely, sense of independence from the great powers. Economic decline and free market ideology had fractured the social compact that underlaid the country's tradition of state-provided social welfare. And the influx of settlers from the Pacific had transformed the bicultural framework of New Zealand society into a more complex multicultural one.

Coming in the wake of the American and Australian bicentenaries, the 1990 Waitangi celebrations could not but be influenced by them. The Opening Ceremony designed by Joseph Bleakley for the 1990 Wellington Commonwealth Games was a striking blend of traditional Maori ritual and the pizzazz of the Los Angeles Olympics. In the televised pageant which opened the Commonwealth Games, wave after wave of voyagers— Maori in their *waka*, British sailors and missionaries under billowing white sails, Pacific Islanders in their outrigger canoes—sailed across the blue plastic ocean of Mount Smart arena towards the welcoming shores of New Zealand.[43] At Waitangi, too, naval frigates and Maori *waka* were joined by tall ships, yachts from the visiting Whitbread round-the-world race, surfboats and outrigger canoes in an 'armada' of welcome to Queen Elizabeth. The Queen herself was to speak admiringly of New Zealand's 'diversity of cultures', while the Prime Minister, Geoffrey Palmer, underlined the 'common heritage' of a people whose 'ancestors navigated here by the same stars and . . . sailed out of the same sunrise'.[44]

The Great Voyage is a national myth that includes all New Zealanders while conferring a special dignity upon the first-comers, the Maori. At Mount Smart, the historical pageant was introduced by Maori ceremonies of welcome and by a symbolic re-enactment of the Maori creation myth of Rangi and Papa. Compared with the ceremonies of 1890 and 1940 there had been, as John Owens acutely observed, 'a reversal of roles for Maori and Pakeha'. The slackening of the British tie had undermined the foundations of traditional Pakeha nationalism, while the 'renaissance of Maori culture' had reinforced 'an increasing tendency for non-Maoris to turn to the Maori heritage for the quintessential New Zealand qualities'. In the approach to their Bicentenary, some Australians had looked forward to a similar convergence of Aboriginal and European cultures.[45]

The Treaty of Waitangi had become, as Erik Olssen noted, 'a symbol of Maori disaffection'.[46] 'We won't celebrate until you honour the Treaty' was the ultimatum of radical Maori. Like Bob Hawke in 1988, Geoffrey Palmer approached the national holiday with an attitude of indulgent neutrality towards the Maori protesters, admitting old wrongs, defending their right to protest, yet urging them 'not to dwell unnecessarily on the past'.[47] On 6 February, 50 000 spectators—more than the entire population of Auckland in 1890—assembled on the *marae* at Waitangi. Queen Elizabeth, descendant of the Queen in whose name the Treaty had been signed, made a circumspect speech regretting that the compact had been 'imperfectly observed' but rejoicing that 'progress had been made in putting things right'. A young Maori expressed her feelings more forcefully by hurling a black T-shirt at the Queen. But it was the Bishop of Aotearoa, Whakahuihui Vercoe, speaking more in sorrow than in anger, who best expressed the Maori sense of cultural loss. 'You have not honoured the Treaty,' he told his audience. 'We have not honoured each other in the promises we made on this sacred ground. Since 1840 the partner that has been marginalised is me—the language of this land is yours, the custom is yours, the media by which we tell the world who we are are yours.'[48]

Who could gainsay the Bishop's judgment? Whatever allowance is made for the ambiguities and defects of the Waitangi Treaty Maori are surely entitled to feel that they have been the losers, culturally as well as economically, in the making of modern New Zealand. Yet, in another sense, Bishop Vercoe's accusation may be mistaken— although the language, customs and media do not belong to the Maori, neither do they belong entirely to the Pakeha. In a world where English is spoken almost everywhere, where customs are increasingly standardised and where local media are but ganglia in a global network, it is to the marginalised indigenous minority that the culturally enervated majority often look to recover their sense of locality and historical tradition.

The convergence of New World cities like Boston, Sydney and Auckland towards the myth of the Great Voyage is one sign of their incorporation into a single transoceanic culture. The myth focuses our ideals on the experience of journeying—of national becoming— rather than upon our origins or destination. Yet, appropriate as such ideals may be in a world of migrants, many city dwellers continue to yearn for a 'civic religion' grounded in a deeper sense of place and tradition. The myth of the treaty, of which Waitangi is a powerful example, has also become a focus for contention, even though it remains an ideal towards which even those nations that have yet to make such a compact may continue to aspire.

Postscript: Towards Sydney 2000 and Melbourne 2001

It is, some would say, in the very nature of postmodern society to interrogate, criticise and ultimately to destroy all national myths. For better or for worse, they would argue, we live in an era when ties to kin, family, neighbourhood, city and nation are in radical dissolution. Yet the forces of globalisation, which dissolve national borders and national differences, also generate a deep, nostalgic and almost universal longing for local colour and ethnic tradition. When Sydney hosts the Olympic Games, it is the visitors as much as the locals who will demand demonstrations of Australia's authentic traditions, and it is above all to the first Australians that the rest will look to supply such local colour. A year later when the nation celebrates its centenary Australians too will look for ceremonies expressive of their national history.

No longer is there a clear consensus of what such occasions require. The pluralist myth of the Great Voyage, which became the dominant national narrative of the 1970s and 1980s, may now be viewed as a graceful leave-taking of the ethnic essentialism of the nineteenth century, as much as a sustaining new ideal. The ideals the Voyage celebrated—such as multiculturalism and Aboriginal and Maori reconciliation—

are less appealing to the conservative governments of the 1990s. There are signs—in the rhetoric of the Howard government, for example—of a longing to return to a more traditional patriotism; but few signs, as yet, that it can identify the symbols to make that patriotism plausible to a new generation of Australians.

The events of 1901, and of the federal movement that led to the creation of the Commonwealth of Australia, offer little material for inspiring public spectacles: Parkes and Deakin, for all their virtues, were not Washington or Jefferson, and the Australian Constitution cannot inspire like the Constitution of the United States or its Bill of Rights. The current debate over the insertion of a new preamble into the Australian Constitution is one attempt to endow that moment with a higher purpose. But the level of the debate, and the divisions it has already stirred, show how difficult it is to engage people's passions without fracturing national consensus. Constitutional democracy is an admirable cause, but it stirs less enthusiasm than the rituals of Anzac Day or even of Grand Final Day.

National birthdays, Greg Dening remarks, are 'metrical moments', celebrations ordained by the logic of the calendar rather than the mood of national life, much less the understandings of historians.

In 2001 Australians will celebrate their national birthday, whether they feel like celebrating or not, and whether history provides symbols to make those celebrations vivid and memorable. If historians cannot supply them, then, no doubt, advertising men and television producers will come to the rescue. Nature, and the mass market, abhor a vacuum. The symbolic void at the heart of liberal democracy is an ever-increasing one, and history is not the only force bidding to fill it.

chapter five

Ancestors: The broken lineage of family history

O NE OF THE most striking signs of our times has been the widespread revival of ancestor worship. Everywhere it seems—in libraries, archives, churches and graveyards—we encounter the ever-growing legions of genealogists and family historians. Since the mid 1970s genealogy and family history have been one of the most vigorous cultural industries in Australia and, unlike many of the other boom enterprises of the past few years, it shows no sign of collapsing. Australian genealogical societies have experienced almost a tenfold increase in membership over that period, far outstripping the growth of other historical societies. According to Nick Vine Hall, Australia, next to America, continues to have the highest per capita population of genealogists in the western world. It is, seemingly, in modern, recently founded, 'non-traditional' societies that the search for ancestors is most vigorously pursued.[1]

How should we account for the family history boom? One clue to its popularity may be found in the social background and motivation of the genealogists themselves. In 1988 Winnie van den Bossche asked almost 1500 Victorian genealogists to fill out a questionnaire about their personal background, their reasons for taking up family history and their thoughts about the family history boom.[2] (The questionnaire may be compared with a smaller survey among genealogists in New South Wales carried out by Noeline Kyle a year or two earlier.) The identikit genealogist who emerges from these surveys is a forty to fifty year old woman of middle- to upper middle-class background. She is more likely than her peers to have had a secondary or tertiary education. She was probably born in Australia of British or Irish parentage and is more likely to be a mainline Protestant than a Catholic by religion. Genealogy, one may speculate, is more likely to appeal to women, who are the customary nurturers and keepers of family tradition; to the middle-aged who are old enough to appreciate its attractions and to sense its fragility; to the well-to-do who have the education, leisure and means to pursue their hobby; and to the old Protestant Australia which, arguably, has been most threatened by the changes of the postwar era.

Part of family history's appeal is simply as an engrossing hobby. In 1932, in the first issue of the *Australian Genealogist*, one of the fathers of the movement made the point rather picturesquely. 'Collecting stamps, seals, badges and such like hobbies are not to be compared with collecting ancestors,' he remarked. 'Even that bizarre hobby of collecting cactus plants is not to be compared with it.'[3] Part of the charm of genealogy lies in the thrill of the chase, the challenge of finding the missing pieces of the puzzle, and the pride of being able to display the trophies of the hunt to an admiring group of fellow enthusiasts. Family historians often invite their readers to share the excitement of discovery, punctuating their narratives with triumphant exclamations. 'I had struck oil!' shouts one exultant researcher at the end of her quest. 'I was hooked on genealogy,' exclaims another addict.[4]

But family history is more than a hobby; it answers a widely felt need to reaffirm the importance of family relationships in a society where mobility, divorce and intergenerational conflict tend to dissolve them. In the United States there have been three major waves of interest in family history—one, in the 1870s, in the immediate aftermath of the Civil War; a second in the 1930s, the decade that also saw the birth of the Australian genealogical movement, and the third, paralleling our own family history boom, in the 1970s and 1980s.[5] These were times of social disruption when family links were threatened by war, depression or rising divorce rates. By lengthening the sense of generational memory, and by recalling family members to a stronger sense of their inheritance, the family historian seeks to shore up the links of kinship. 'The study of genealogy,' *The Genealogist* reminded its readers in 1978, 'tends to draw families together . . . In an age when national policies sometimes cause cruel disruption of families, genealogy is one of the counteracting forces that contribute to family reunion and family solidarity.'[6]

The sense of threat and cultural disorientation is a strong theme among the respondents to Winnie van den Bossche's questionnaire. 'I have heard the suggestion that there is a lack of stability in the modern world,' writes a retired insurance officer.

> One no longer trusts one's employer/club/municipality to show the same loyalty to one's self [sic] as say great-grandfather showed to and expected from his employer/regiment etc. Knowledge of one's forebears perhaps helps to fill this gap.

'In a rapidly changing world, individuals have difficulty in maintaining an identity; where they belong in a scheme of things,' confesses another family historian.

'As old truths crumble, the family is seen as a believable reservoir of stable values.' Because it is unalterable, the past is seen as consolingly secure. It is 'something solid in a shifting world', says one genealogist. 'The past is fixed,' declares another who questions 'the prevailing myth that truth and value are relative.'

The dissolving world from which family historians flee is reflected inversely in their family narratives. It is not a world without pain and conflict—since the 1970s family historians have shown a remarkable willingness to drag the old skeletons of illegitimacy, divorce and drunkenness from the family cupboard—but one that continues to provide a touchstone for the moral health of our own generation. It holds up the ancestors to admiration, if not for their virtue, at least for their fortitude. 'I have a deep respect for my ancestors,' declares one genealogist. 'Not only were the men tough, but more so the women. I'd like to see some of the feminists do the same chores under the same conditions as our great-grandmothers.' Some family historians see themselves as defenders of a (British) pioneer heritage against the diluting influence of multi-culturalism. 'The more "MULTICULTURAL" we become, the more risk of losing that pioneering identity,' remarks a male accountant. Feminism, multiculturalism, the new reproductive technologies, marital breakdown, inter-generational conflict—these are the perils against which the traditional family historian seeks to shore up the spiritual defences of family life.

Genealogy may be the last refuge of scientific his-tory. There is something reassuringly 'objective' about the task of compiling a family tree. Its lists of dates and names, of births, deaths and marriages arranged in chronological sequence convey an air of exactitude, completeness and inevitability. (Never mind that it suppresses as much as it recovers: a genealogy, after all, charts only one route, the male line, into the ancestral past.) The genealogists themselves are often formidable historical technicians, experts in the 'how' of history. Their domain, however, is essentially a private or tribal one that connects only tenuously with the concerns of national or international history. 'It is my firm opinion that a family tree, whether it boasts of kings or serfs, of bishops or highwaymen, is of little interest to any but the families who have sprung from it,' confesses one genealogist.[7] From the vantage point of the professional historian, the average family history may appear not only trivial but almost inscrutable. It seems plotless, disconnected, unselective. Only if we assume the subjective vantage point of the descendant rather than the universalistic viewpoint of the intellectual, only if we give as much weight to the idea of heredity as liberals customarily give to the influence of environment will we begin to understand its continuing appeal. It speaks, not to our sense of historical significance, but to our need for personal identity. 'I now have an identity, knowing exactly who I am and where I come from,' declares one triumphant genealogist at the end of her quest.

Often, it seems, the decision to begin a family history project is crystallised at those moments of birth, marriage and death when we become acutely conscious of the slender cords binding one generation to another. In the preface to his book, *A People called Pointon*, Bruce Pointon recalls that he decided to begin work on his family history 'just a few hours' after the death of his father, Horace. Heather Ronald concluded her book, *Wool Before the Wind*, with the merger of the family wool-broking firm into the Elders conglomerate. Peter Bottomley concludes his history of the Morgan clan, entitled *Just an Ordinary Family*, with the death of its matriarch and the sale of the old family home and effects at Castlemaine. Margaret Beasey first thought of writing the history of her family, the Fleays, after reading an old letter left in her father's safe when he died in 1933. 'Ancestral records are important to me,' she writes. 'I have no children—This Book is my contribution to the scheme of the Fleay family.'[8] It is often those who stand at the end of a family line, without children or spouses of their own, who most dutifully tend the memory of its past.

If awareness of the family's past is often stimulated by these moments of discontinuity, it is through the act of reunion that the family's enduring value is most strongly affirmed. 'People still need an extended family and [family history] is a legitimate way of reaching out to them,' writes one family historian. Doing the family tree is often the prelude or postlude to a family reunion; it is the device by which its often far-flung members are made known to each other and summoned back to the home turf. Family reunions are the present-day counterpart of the 'back-to' celebrations that were such a popular feature of rural life in the 1920s and 1930s. Then it was the old country town that the mobile city folk revisited. Now, as the ties of extended kin grow feebler, it is to the old family home that we reverently make pilgrimage.

A striking feature of modern family reunions is their traditional, and often explicitly religious, character. The family customarily gathers at the pioneer homestead or in the old home town, close to the original point of settlement. Often, it is the clergymen of the family who lead the proceedings which usually include a service of thanksgiving even when its members come from a variety of faiths, or none at all.[9] It is as though, by returning to the roots of the family, we seek to recover the certainties of a bygone, perhaps mythological, age of faith.

In recent years, however, family history has subtly changed its character. Thirty years ago, genealogy was still a rather select and selective pursuit, closely linked to the study of heraldry and to the search for a noble or gentle pedigree. In the early 1960s the main genealogical societies had only recently emerged from a period of 'dormancy'.[10] Many of their members were descendents of 'old pioneer' families, monarchists, pillars of the church, especially the Church of England, and of other ancient institutions. Their belief in the 'heredity principle' was at once mystical and scientific. In the person of the monarch they found a supreme example of the 'enduring principle of tribal and family stability'. The pages of their journals were filled with the pedigrees and armorial bearings of European nobility or self-styled Australian gentry.

At a time when eugenic ideas were still current, genealogy also had its scientific uses. Calculating the level of intermarriage in a country town might enable a physician to assess the risks of interbreeding.[11] Checking out a prospective partner's pedigree for possible hereditary disease might be a wise precaution before matrimony. 'The study of genealogy can be a useful preparation for a happy and successful marriage, and the planting of a healthy and fruitful Family Tree,' declared *The Genealogist* in 1977.[12]

In recent years, however, the movement has assumed a more popular and democratic character. In 1967 the editor of the *Victorian Genealogist,* the Pacific historian Neil Gunson, was still obliged to combat the suspicion that genealogists were 'snobs'. 'Nothing,' he replied, 'could be further from the truth. A pride in one's family, no matter how humble, an interest in people, in the human story of man and his way of life, his happiness and his sorrow, does not add up to snobbishness.'[13] By the mid 1970s the Australian Institute of Genealogical Studies opened its arms to all-comers. 'We are not like a trade union, where people are massed together for the purpose of improving their wages, working conditions or social status,' *The Genealogist* explained.

> Nor are we like a cricket or football club, where membership largely depends on specific skills or abilities, for anybody without any skills at all is welcome to join us. Nor are we an elite society where the high and mighty assemble to preen themselves on their importance and superiority, for even the lowliest of commoners has a genealogy and a family history of equal interest to all.[14]

By broadening its constituency, family history has also come to take a broader view of its subject. No longer is it sufficient simply to trace a genealogy—the skeleton of a family history—or to identify the notables in the family line. When even 'the lowliest of commoners' take their place in the story, the story itself broadens out to include those larger forces of social change that shaped their lives. Democratic family history is the story of those who suffered history, as well as of those who made it.

> Our forebears [writes one family historian] were not plaster saints; they were loving, feeling, caring human beings with as many vices and virtues as the rest of us; they lived life to the full and enjoyed their successes and suffered their failures.[15]

Modern family historian looks to their ancestors less as moral exemplars than as fellow sufferers. They give little weight to the influence of heredity in their own family fortunes. The bond they seek with their ancestors is an essentially sympathetic one, based more upon fellow feeling than the mystique of blood or ancestral piety. A gentle strain of feminism may be detected in these newer family histories. Instead of tracing the male line of her husband's family, the genealogist may sometimes choose to follow the distaff of her own. For a generation of women who often missed out on tertiary education, genealogy offers direct entry to an alternative world of scholarship, one insulated from the competitive pressures of academia with its examinations, ranking systems and relentless theorising; a democratic community in which everyone is an expert, if only upon her own family.

Patriarchal history

The private hobby of family history stands in contrast, not only to the public values of academic history, but to those elitist forms of genealogy that we may call patriarchal history. The attempt of William Charles Wentworth to create a hereditary Australian aristocracy may have been doomed to political failure, but the great pastoral families have remained the greatest reservoir of hereditary sentiment in Australian society. Land and lineage—the main axes of their identity—are the themes, not only of their own dynastic histories, but of broader accounts of national history into which they merge.[16] The transformation of this tradition in the late twentieth century offers another vantage point on the significance of family history.

The history of Australian family history begins a little later than its American counterpart, but follows a similar trajectory. During the last quarter of the nineteenth century many colonial landowners, and some merchants and politicians, sought to discover or, if necessary, to invent gentle pedigrees and to patent heraldic arms. 'An interest in genealogy,' writes Paul de Serville, 'was a declaration of love and loyalty for the home country' and its popularity—shared, so he says, 'by colonists of every class and background'—'was indicative of a desire to maintain one's links and roots, to preserve one's identity of background and inheritance, as much cultural as familial.'[17] The Victorian elite, whose origins were often far from illustrious and whose wealth was but newly gained, also led the rush to be ranked. *Burke's Colonial Gentry* (1891)—the most pretentious and the most controversial register of the best Australian families—was dominated by rich Victorians, including some heroes of the land boom whose fortunes had already dissipated before the book was published.

Ideas of blood and heredity—of 'the crimson thread of kinship'—were an integral component of nineteenth century British and Australian patriotism. Ideas of the British people as a great family, headed by the monarch; of the colonies as brothers and sisters; and of their political institutions as a priceless 'heritage' were but an enlargement of those transoceanic, yet intimate, ties which most colonists had recognised in their own family histories and which were regularly reinforced by the processes of migration.[18] Images of blood, kin and race were strong in the patriotic rhetoric of the early Commonwealth. 'These daughters of the Imperial mother will share in the greater conclave of the nation and make manifest in counsel the blood-tie and common racial instinct already proved on the South African battlefields,' declared the *Sydney Morning Herald* as it greeted the federation.[19] The imperial family, as these words imply, was both an inclusive and an exclusive concept; while strengthening brotherly and sisterly ties between fellow Britons, it placed 'lesser breeds', such as Chinese, Aborigines and even Irish, outside the family circle. A multicultural, pluralist Australia may be anxious to forget the extent to which earlier generations of Australians grounded their sense of national identity in notions of blood and breeding.

Pride of lineage is only one of the threads that links genealogy to national history for nationality is itself a genealogical concept, something that is thought to be handed down from generation to generation or, for the newcomer, conferred by a kind of adoption. National identity in a new country is constituted by descent from the first arrival. The 'three significant questions' to be asked by the Australian family historian were: 'WHEN did they come? WHENCE did they come? and WHY did they come?'[20] Descent, for practical genealogical purposes, meant descent through the male line. 'The simplest way is to begin with your father's pioneer forbear,' an experienced genealogist advised the novice. 'Give a brief account of his background overseas and go on to the *when* and *why* he came. Tell of his achievements, his marriage and his family then follow his line, generation by generation, to the present day.'

Genealogy was thus one of the main intellectual props for the pioneer legend, that account of national becoming that conferred the highest honour upon the first-comers. The Women's Pioneer Society of Australasia, for example, was founded in 1928 among female descendants of generally male pioneers. In the 1920s and 1930s members of the Society of Australian Genealogists joined members of the Royal Australian Historical Society in compiling a comprehensive list of the first European arrivals in New South Wales but it was not until 1969, the eve of the Cook Bicentenary, that the Fellowship of First Fleeters was founded.[21]

The Depression years of the 1930s, a period when domestic life and Australia's familial link with the 'Mother Country' were also experiencing new strains, witnessed a renewed interest in genealogy and family history. In the preface to his *Pioneer Families of Australia,* published to commemorate the sesquicentenary of New South Wales in 1938, P.C. Mowle emphasised the value of giving 'a permanent record' to the country's patriarchs and in demonstrating 'the close bonds of kinship which exist between the families in Australia and those of the Mother Country'.[22] In 1934 Victoria also marked its centenary with monuments, ceremonies and historical publications exalting the state's founders and pioneers, and celebrating the imperial connection.

The local genealogist, Alexander Henderson, whose *Pioneer Families of Victoria and the Riverina* was published to mark the centenary, viewed the state's history as the essence of innumerable genealogies. 'We have some measure of responsibility to make our own record worthy of all that is best in that which has been bequeathed to us,' he wrote. 'It is ungracious to forget how great is the amount standing to the credit account of the pioneers of this country in respect of human uplift and high example in treading new paths.'[23] Recording all that was best, totting up the credit account—these are phrases suggestive of a certain wilful blindness to the worst, or debit, side of the moral ledger of pioneering. In Henderson's pages the patriarchal mythology of the state's first families—with their romantic notions of blood, land and gentility—is held up to the admiration of a more democratic age. Like their British aristocratic models, Debrett and Burke, colonial genealogists emphasised the link between lineage and land. Instead of Norfolk of Arundel we have Murray of Borongarook and Wool Wool. Where the record permits, they rooted the history of the Australian pioneer family in a British or Irish prehistory, sometimes illustrating it with a photograph of the ancestral home and a sketchy summary of the British pedigree.

The legitimacy of the Australian pioneer family, however, resided less in the antiquity of its family tree than in the moral fibre and landed wealth of its founding generations. Early arrival in the colonies, preferably but not necessarily as a free settler, contributed to the prestige of the line. P.C. Mowle, for example, included only the most ancient white Australian families, those whose forebears had arrived before 1838. Henderson's pastoral pioneers, on the other hand, rest their claims primarily on the qualities of 'perseverance' and 'enterprise' which they displayed in possessing this 'land of promise'.[24] The imagery of the Old Testament, so familiar to this generation of Calvinistic Scots, provided the moral bedrock for a patriarchal interpretation of their family history.

What this history suppressed or skirted was the conflict between the claims of the pioneers and those of the original tenants of the soil, the Aborigines. Only the scholarship of the last decade has revealed how close to the surface of the land-takers' consciousness was the guilty knowledge of their trespass.[25] But in the family chronicles their descendants supplied to Henderson, the Aborigines—repeatedly characterised as 'troublesome' and 'treacherous'—become merely obstacles to be overcome by the intrepid pioneer.

It took another generation before the pastoral families produced genuine historians of their own, and then it was from the female line of dutiful, but not uncritical, daughters that they mainly came. Judith Wright's *The*

Generations of Men (1959), Mary Durack's *Kings in Grass Castles* (1959), Margaret Kiddle's *Men of Yesterday* (1961) and Elyne Mitchell's stories of the Snowy Country are among the first and finest of a remarkable postwar legacy of pastoral sagas written by the daughters of the great pastoral families. It is regrettable that recent feminist historians have so far given little critical attention to these grandmothers of Australian women's history for their careers offer subtle insights into the limits of intellectual independence among the daughters of the squattocracy.

Writing the family history was often a duty imposed by pastoral patriarchs upon their talented daughters, but the women's manner of discharging it did not always accord with parental expectations. 'My father had always wanted me some day to write of the family's pioneering efforts,' Mary Durack recalled in the preface to her story of her forebears, a pioneering family from the Kimberleys. 'He had a keen feeling for history,' she observed, and his journals, kept over sixty years, were an invaluable resource. Yet, she writes, 'only his death, that was so great a loss to me, left me free to write as I have done'.[26] Only as the pioneering age drew to its close, we may hypothesise, were its heirs freed to view their forebears with the pity and irony of the historian. By the time they wrote, the dutiful daughters had often left the land to their brothers or uncles and their writings breathe a wistfulness for a life near enough to remember, too distant ever to be regained.

Judith Wright was barely fourteen years old when her grandmother, Charlotte May Wright, matriarch of the pioneering family, died in 1929. She therefore stood in a less immediate relationship to the 'generations of men' chronicled in her book of that name, published in 1959. Hers is an affectionate, semi-fictionalised account of her grandparents' lives as pastoral pioneers in northern New South Wales and Queensland. It reproduces, yet subtly transforms, the standard themes of pioneer history—pride in land and lineage, the legitimating battle with the elements, the fertile heritage of sons, vines and flocks. But it is a story told largely from a woman's viewpoint, and shaped more by Wright's sense of the cyclical rhythms of the seasons and generations than the straight lines of material progress. Survival and continuity, rather than conquest and progress, are its leading themes. It begins at Dalwood, her family's property in the Hunter Valley, a place that already, at the beginning of her grandmother's life, had assumed 'the quality of legend'. 'There was about their story something of the atmosphere of the Book of Genesis,' Wright reflects. The life of her grandparents, Albert and May, and their search for new pastures in New England and Queensland assumes the shape of an Australian Exodus. And their story concludes, in the mood of Ecclesiastes, with May Wright's musings on the eternal cycles of life and death.

> By the end of the year [1929] she will have gone to her grave on the hill-slope near Wongwibinda— the grave she chose, as though even in death she must overlook what is being done on her beloved property. As for her world—perhaps by then it will have fallen and smashed with the prices on the world's stock exchanges, perhaps it is already vanishing from round her on the quickening tide of change. But at least she is secure; whatever changes, she and her century are unalterable now.[27]

Twenty years later Judith Wright returned to her family history, amplifying and revising it in ways that reveal, not only her changing commitments, but the

increasingly problematical character of patriarchal
family history. *The Generations of Men* was a hymn to
human continuity and growth; *The Cry for the Dead*,
published in 1981, is a lament for the victims, black
and white, of the European invasion. In the first ren-
dering of her family's story, Wright dealt briefly but
sympathetically with the fate of the Aborigines. 'The
whites knew that from the tribesman's point of view
they were trespassing on country where they had no
rights,' she observed. Into the mind of her grandfather,
Albert Wright, she inserted some of those awkward
'questions of conscience' that she had evidently begun
to ask herself.[28]

But it is only in the second account that these
questions are faced head-on. By the time she came to
write it, the author was a prominent advocate of both
Aboriginal land rights and environmental conservation.
The tone of *The Cry for the Dead* is less personal and
lyrical than its predecessor. It is as though Wright felt
a need to distance herself from her subject, to ground
her grim conclusions in verifiable fact. The union of
land and lineage that she celebrated in her own forebears' history is now relocated to the Aborigines they
dispossessed. Instead of the reassuring images of growth
and continuity that bathe the Epilogue of *The Generations of Men* in a kind of autumnal glow, Wright
concludes her second book on a tragic note. By 1980
the last speakers of the local Aboriginal tongue have
disappeared from the plains of central Queensland, the
native forests have been cleared, the grasslands stripped
raw by overgrazing and gouged by open-cut mining.
'None of the descendants of Albert and May Wright
now own land on the plain or beyond it; and perhaps
none of the descendants of the Wadja, if any remain,

have seen the country that once was theirs,' she mournfully concludes.[29]

It would be hard to imagine a more striking
evocation of the historical disjunction that Wright's
generation of pioneer families experienced in the 1970s
and 1980s. Her appreciation of the change—crystallised,
as it was, by her commitments to the causes of Aboriginal land rights and environmental conservation—may
have been more acute than some of her contemporaries.
(Mary Durack, always a more resolute upholder of
traditional values, continued to write within the broad
paradigm of patriarchal family history throughout the
1970s.[30]) It was no more than symptomatic, however,
of an entire complex of changes that were simultaneously reinforcing the longing for roots and loosening
the soil in which they were planted.

Not the least of these changes was a growing incli-
nation to question the patriarchal order that had first
cast the dutiful daughters of the homestead in the role
of family historians. In the eyes of their fathers and
brothers, we may imagine, family history was women's
work; although, as Wright and Durack were to prove,
it was not without its intellectual rewards. Only in the
next generation, however, did the limitations of the role
become fully apparent. Jill Ker Conway's *The Road
from Coorain* (1989) is at once an apotheosis and a
negation of patriarchal history. In its lyrical evocation
of the landscape of western New South Wales and the
affecting story of her father's heroic struggle against
war neurosis and the droughts of the early 1940s, it
stands—along with Wright's *Generations of Men* and
Patrick White's *Tree of Man*—in the mainstream of
pioneer history.

The crucial difference of *The Road from Coorain*
is in the denouement of the story and the stance of the

writer. Unlike the traditional story of pioneer life, in which shared trials build family solidarity, Conway's is a story of tragic family dissolution. Her father drowns mysteriously in a dam; her distraught mother returns to Sydney and seeks refuge in pills and alcohol; the children are dispersed to boarding schools. At university Conway eventually becomes a historian and begins a thesis on the colonial wool industry; but she chafes against the insularity and intellectual narrowness of her male colleagues. 'The place I was most at home was the bush,' she recalled. But she knew that 'as much as I loved it I would become a hermitlike female eccentric if I settled into that isolation alone'. In the end, she decides to abandon Australia and pursue higher studies in the United States. The only pang of parting, she implies, was saying goodbye to the family homestead, Coorain. As the plane waits on the tarmac, her mind flies back to the dusty cemetery where her father was buried:

> Where, I wondered, would my bones come to rest? It pained me to think of them not fertilizing Australian soil. Then I comforted myself with the notion that wherever on the earth was my final resting place, my body would return to the restless red dust of the western plains. I could see how it would blow about and get in people's eyes, and I was content with that.[31]

In this passage the link between land and lineage, which was the foundation of patriarchal history, has been stretched almost to breaking point. The cycle of generations has been arrested. The family no longer dwell on the land they fought so hard to keep. And the writer is about to leave her family and her native soil forever. All that remains, it seems, is the haunting after-image of nostalgia.

The reconstruction of family history

It would be easy, but too simple, to dismiss the family history boom as mere atavism, a clod thrown backwards by the chariots of time. Like fundamentalist religion, or voodoo economics, it looks like an essentially regressive symptom of postmodernity. It seeks a sense of continuity in a world of discontinuity, of concord in a world of conflict, of intimacy in a world of impersonality. But it is also something more, for family history has the potential to disturb as well as to console. Not all family histories, as we have seen, are consoling, at least in the sense that they are about happy families. Moreover, it is not necessary to love or respect one's ancestors in order to want to know their story. As the efforts of adoptees to find their natural parentage illustrate, people will endure a good deal of frustration and disillusionment to reclaim their past.

The radical possibilities of family history are well illustrated by the significant role it now performs in the political and spiritual life of those whose ancestral claims were most rudely denied by patriarchal history, the Aborigines. Among urbanised Aborigines, as well as those still living in traditional settings, lineage remains the bedrock of social life. The ancestral claims of the First Fleeters and white pioneers pale into insignificance beside those of the thousand or more generations of Aborigines who preceded them. Australians of European descent have increasingly come to acknowledge the spiritual affinity, if not the legal claim, of Aborigines to their ancestral lands and to look to

Aborigines as models of ecological consciousness. When Mary Durack claims that West Australians have 'long since developed an almost Aboriginal sense of identification with their environment', she both acknowledges, and seeks to qualify, the Aborigines' special claim to the soil.[32]

For many twentieth century Aborigines, the ancestral past has also been a hidden past. Separated from their mothers at birth and raised in foster homes or institutions, they know little at first hand of their ancestry, language or traditions. Robert Murray, raised on the Cowra Mission in southern New South Wales, compares his own faint memories of family and Aboriginal tradition with the more continuous oral traditions of Aborigines in the Northern Territory: The Territorians know their family stories 'because there they're retold over and over again to their children's children . . . Most of our knowledge [he says] comes from books, or from the screen, or from what people tell us. Not from our own people'.[33] Such people must now learn the same techniques of documentary research and oral history as other family historians to pick up the trail of their family past.[34] In her Foreword to *Lookin for Your Mob: A Guide to Tracing Aboriginal Family Trees*, Iris Clayton, a Wiradjuri family historian, reflects on the role of genealogy in the development of Aboriginal identity:

> As Aboriginal people become more aware of their lost lands, heritage and culture, they are increasingly feeling the need for their lost family genealogy. We want our identity returned. This is a need that is growing stronger every year. Our young people need their true identity returned to them with names and stories of their ancestors. This will in turn give them

back their self-esteem along with a purpose in life. Pride in their ancestors and culture will replace oppression, thus interest in Aboriginal culture will grow and hopefully our future generations will have a rich and living heritage to look back on.[35]

There is both irony and justice in the fact that, at a time when many Australians of European parentage look longingly to Aboriginal society as a source of spiritual inspiration, Aborigines should be borrowing the sources and techniques of European history to repair their own shattered sense of identity.

Sally Morgan's bestselling autobiography, *My Place*, describes the search of a young Aboriginal woman to recover her family history. Morgan had grown up unaware of her Aboriginal parentage and had to over-come the resistance of her relatives, long accustomed to the secrecy and shame of miscegenation, before she was able to trace her family tree. Her search led her back, not only to her Aboriginal grandmother, but to the scion of the well-known pastoral family, the Drake-Brockmans, whose child her grandmother had borne. In recovering her family history, Morgan thus illumi-nates a dark underside of pioneer history, but it is a revelation made without rancour. Far more important, in Morgan's own scale of values, is the release that her discoveries bring from the obscurity of her own origins. 'Can't you just leave the past buried, it won't hurt anyone then?' her mother pleads. 'Mum,' she replies, 'it's already hurt people. It's hurt you and me and Nan, all of us . . . I have a right to know my own history.'[36] It is this redemptive quality of family history, its capac-ity to release the guilt and pain of the past, which inspires other writers, too, to bring family history to the centre of their concerns.[37]

The last decade has also seen the emergence of a new kind of family history among European Australians. As the children of the rebellious 1960s and 1970s enter middle age, they often manifest an urgent need to rediscover the families they once sought to escape. Germaine Greer's *Daddy, We Hardly Knew You* (1989), Arnold Zable's *Jewels and Ashes* (1991) and Drusilla Modjeska's *Poppy* (1990) each describes a return to the home turf, the disinterring of a painful past and a quest to make peace with the ancestors. These searches are at once an extension and a radical rejection of the old family history. For the old family historians, establishing a lineage was a pursuit that reinforced a sense of certainty amidst doubt, of continuity amidst change. The new family history, on the other hand, is born of a sense of discontinuity, of broken lineages, fractured time and geographical distance. While the old family history records achievements, the new commemorates suffering. While the old celebrates family life, the new—often informed by feminism and Laingian psychoanalysis—radically deconstructs it. The search itself is therefore a more difficult and open-ended undertaking, one in which it is the journey rather than the arrival that matters.[38]

These new family histories are shaped differently from the old. The genealogist traditionally begins with the family founder, its colonial Abraham, and moves forward, generation by generation, tribe by tribe, to trace his large and fruitful issue. By its very shape, the story creates a sense of pattern or purpose that enables the descendants to identify their place in a larger patriarchal scheme. The new family histories, on the other hand, begin in the here and now, with the writer, and describe a journey backwards in time, and often through space, towards an uncertain destination.

Family history, to use Modjeska's metaphor, becomes the slow unravelling of a thread, a teasing out as well as a tracing back.

A preoccupation of the new family history, no less than of the old, is the idea of inheritance. 'There is no bucking the genes,' declares Greer, an enthusiastic, if selective, hereditarian. In tracing her father's past, she recognises mysterious affinities of physique and temperament between father and daughter—a strong jaw, a weak stomach, claustrophobia, even, she once fancies, a secret love of aliases.[39] Pondering her mother's breakdown, Drusilla Modjeska raises the resident ghost of genealogy—the fear of hereditary madness.

> When I was in my early thirties, I was afraid, for a long time that, like Lily, I'd have Poppy's breakdown, as if such things are part of our inheritance. The fear that we will follow the patterns laid down by our mothers seems deeply embedded in the female psyche.

But it is a fear she quickly dispels as 'irrational', as she subtly delineates the circumstances that brought her mother low. The inheritance that matters for Modjeska is not biological, but generational. For the feminists of the 1970s, the recognition of what is taken from, or owed to, their parentage is also a revaluation of the freedom they had sought to win. 'While my generation had been noisy in taking our freedoms, I wonder what it signifies in a world in which loneliness is endemic, sexual freedom too easy and too dangerous, and intellectual freedom institutionally hobbled, or fashion-bound,' she reflects.[40]

Like other family historians they follow the standard procedures of genealogical research—the devilling through birth and death registers, the pilgrimages to

graveyards and other sites of remembrance, the inter-
rogation of family elders. But there comes a point in
each of these narratives when the documents peter out,
the gravestones are mute and the elders fall silent. Then
the historian has nothing but imagination to sustain a
search that still cannot be abandoned. As his train
crosses the border into the Soviet Union, Arnold Zable
tears up his father's terse outline of the family past and
throws it out the window in a gesture symbolic of his
own transition from 'outsider' to 'insider'. 'Use your
imagination,' Drusilla Modjeska's mother replies, when
she cannot, or will not, fill the gaps in the factual
record. Even for Greer, the most indefatigable genealogist of the three, fact quickly gives way to conjecture,
and conjecture to fiction.

Always implicit, and sometimes quite explicit, in
their stance is a critique of the epistemological claims
of orthodox history. 'I used to think that truth was
single and error legion, but I know now that none of
us grasps more than a little splinter of the truth,' writes
Greer. For the feminist writers the truth of imagination
may be truer, as well as more healing, than the truth
of fact. Family history is part of that mysterious domain
of women's knowledge that feminists have now set out
to reclaim and assert in refutation of the false claims
of masculine knowledge. In a series of dialogues with
her mother, her lawyer-father and her ex-lover, Modjeska ponders the shifting boundaries between the
momentous and the ordinary, between 'evidence' and
'feelings', between what can be said and what cannot.[41]

In a similar dialogue with her brother, Greer insists
that her father's account of his own life, as a 'good
family man', was 'typical of the lie of *his*tory', whereas
her own more truthful account was 'a classic example
of *her*story, punctuating the ideology'.[42]

For each of the writers the return to the past is born of a sense of discontinuity more painful and profound than most family historians own up to. The gulf that divides them from their forebears is in part self-made—a legacy of the struggle for liberation that was the common thread of intellectual life in the 1960s and 1970s. More than thirty years later, Greer still rehearses the conflicts and bears the scars of her rebellion against the strictures of her parents' generation. As the limits of their liberation become evident, and as their own sense of mortality grows stronger, the claims of the parental past reassert themselves. 'We could imagine other ways of living,' Modjeska writes of her feminist contemporaries, 'but we didn't take account of our own histories . . .'[43]

Zable also hints at these strains. 'The arguments between us had been, at times, quite ferocious,' he remarks in passing of his relationship with his father, although the issues that were at stake are left unspoken.[44] Modjeska, on the other hand, deals with them head-on, trying imaginatively to reconstruct how their differences looked from her mother's angle as well as her own.

Their youthful desire to escape the family past, like their mature desire to rediscover it, is a frontal attack on that code of silence by which their parents' generation had kept their own painful family pasts at bay. War, racial persecution, sexual infidelity, childhood abandonment, mental breakdown—these were the ghosts that often haunted them, but in deflecting or denying their children's questions the parents of the complacent and conformist 1940s and 1950s had only postponed the day of reckoning.

That moment comes, for Drusilla Modjeska, with the death of her mother. 'My mother had died,' she writes, 'and it was true what I'd said, I did not know her . . . I knew that by not knowing her, I could not know myself.'[45] It was not that she was ignorant of the details of her mother's life for, as her book makes plain, she had been engaged for some time in an effort to reconstruct it. What she did not know, and what she urgently needed to understand, was the truth of those painful ruptures in a family history that had set out to be 'ordinary'—her parents' gradual estrangement, her father's infidelity, her mother's breakdown, her own banishment to boarding school, the anomalous liaison between her mother and a Catholic priest. She finds that the ruptures were, in a sense, implicit in the very pursuit of ordinariness, that her mother's breakdown, for example, came from an accumulation of small, silent injuries rather than the catastrophic onset of one big one.

It is death, too, that releases Germaine Greer from the compact of silence that had surrounded her father's past. 'Now that Daddy's need to have us not know is at an end, my need to know can be satisfied.' She had grown up knowing almost nothing about his parentage or early life. 'He never referred to any kin, neither father nor mother nor sisters nor brothers nor aunts nor uncles, not even in a chance anecdote. He was a man without a past.'[46] From her earliest years, his daughter had carried the hurtful memory of his departure as a RAAF officer during the war and his return as an emaciated and grey-faced invalid. Between father and daughter there had developed an emotional reserve that ripened in her teenage years into outright hostility. To make her peace, if possible, she must try to find that unknown father who preceded, and perhaps coexisted with, the father of painful memory.

Slowly, along faint trails and up dead-ends, Greer

unpicks the tangled skein of misadventures and decep-
tions that made Robert Hamilton King, son of a
Tasmanian servant girl, first into the adoptee and
Launceston draper's assistant Eric Greeney, and then
into the dapper Melbourne advertising salesman, Regi-
nald Greer. The child in her, she admits, had embarked
on her search in the hope of discovering a 'hero', a
'prince'. But the man she finds—a liar, a bounder,
perhaps a shirker as well—is product not just of his
own troubled upbringing and the stresses of wartime
service as an intelligence officer in besieged Malta, but,
as the author herself finally admits, of her own 'censo-
rious, scrutinising nature'. To understand all, for Greer,
is not finally to forgive all.[47]

In all three of these new family histories, the trau-
mas of war-torn Europe cast a long shadow over
modern Australia, in none more so than Arnold Zable's
Jewels and Ashes. Meir Zbludowski, father of Arnold
Zable, is the sole survivor of his family, one of only a
handful of the once great Polish–Jewish community of
Bialystok to escape the Holocaust. In faraway Melbourne, the old man hoards the few scraps of paper
that document the family past, but he always deflects
his son's questions '"There are not enough hours in the
day for what I want to do," he has told me many times.
"Why waste them in recalling things that have long
since gone?"' His obstinate refusal to raise the stones
of memory only reinforces the son's determination to
retrace the family's past. For the second generation, the
distance that separates their parents' experience from
their own is at once a barrier and an invitation.

> We were born in the wake of Annihilation. We were
> children of dreams and shadows, yet raised in the
> vast spaces of the New World. We roamed the

streets of our migrant neighbourhoods freely. We lived on coastlines and played under open horizons. Our world was far removed from the sinister events that had engulfed our elders. Yet there had always been undercurrents that could sweep us back to the echoes of childhood, to the sudden torrents of rage and sorrow that could, at any time, disturb the surface calm: 'You cannot imagine what it was like,' our elders insisted. 'You were not there.' Their messages were always ambiguous, tinged with menace, double-edged: 'You cannot understand, yet you must. You should not delve too deeply, yet you should. But even if you do, my child, you will never understand. You were not there.'[48]

In the effort imaginatively to 'be there', Zable returns to the ancestral town of Bialystok. Guided by a map drawn by his parents, he visits the neighbourhood where his grandfather Bishke, the newspaper seller, had rushed through the streets. He returns to the desolate village of Bielsk, once home to his mother's folk, the Liebermans, where he finds a tiny remnant of the Jewish community. He journeys to Pruzhany, a townlet on the edge of the Bialowieza forests, to which, in September 1941, the Gestapo ordered 12 000 of Bialystok's Jews, where his aunt Sheindl met her lover, the resistance leader Yanek Lerner. And he stands near the vacant lot, once known as Prager's Garden, where, on the evening of 5 February 1943, his grandparents, among 900 others, were shot in reprisal for an attack on a German officer.

Zable's journey can never enable him to understand the experiences of the Annihilation as those who were there do; but it is enough to make a bridge of understanding to those who survive. It is only when he returns to Australia and speaks to his father that the barrier of silence is broken down. Only if the past is first remembered can its victims begin to forget.

Conclusion

Our grandparents' generation had a rich vocabulary for describing the relations between past and present. They spoke of 'our heritage', of 'the legacy of the past', of ideas and values, as well as other 'proud possessions', being 'bequeathed' from generation to generation. Such ways of speaking came naturally to a society in which the obligations of children to parents, and notions of blood and heredity, were well and widely understood. When the servicemen of the Great War returned to meet the orphaned children of their dead comrades, it was natural, not only that they should think of assuming a responsibility for their welfare, but that the organisation they founded to do it should be called Legacy.

Such ways of speaking are no longer natural to us. Over the past twenty-five years, some of these words have acquired an antique ring and some, like 'heritage' for example, have abruptly changed their meaning. These changes are emblematic of a more pervasive shift in the ways we think of the relations between past and present, and of the mutual relations between the generations. The complex settling of accounts with the past, which is the theme of the new family histories, thus mirrors the preoccupations of national history. Feminism, environmentalism, Aboriginality—each in its way constructs a narrative of loss and guilt, and makes a claim for restitution. Pre-eminent among these claims is that of the Stolen Generations for apology and restitution. These claims raise matters that have to be remembered before they can be forgiven, though perhaps never quite forgotten. It's not that the past, to which we once considered ourselves debtors, can belatedly be handed a bill and somehow made to pay for its unacknowledged debts to the future. In that sense, at least, the past is dead and, if debts have to be paid, then it is only the present and the future that can pay them.[49] But that the past—at least the European past—has exhausted its credit, and that we no longer have to consider ourselves beholden to it, seems to be an unstated assumption of much contemporary culture.

The new family histories supply a telling commentary on that assumption and a partial corrective to it. They not only remind us that there are things we cannot change, but also that even the self that wishes to change them is a product of the past. Perhaps only a nation with a fading legacy of Judaeo-Christian belief, for example, would be susceptible to a claim for atonement and restitution. Just as our ancestors looked to genealogy as the model of nationhood so, perhaps, in these more complex renderings of family history, Australians may find a clue to a new sense of national becoming.

chapter six

Heritage: From patrimony to pastiche

F EW IDEAS ARE so expressive of our changing relationship with the past as the word 'heritage'.
'Heritage' is an old word, drawn from the vocabulary of traditional societies in which values were
derived from ancestral relationships. But in our times it
has become invested with a new cluster of meanings,
characteristic of a mobile, postmodern society. Tracing
its history is a valuable clue to the ways Australians
have used, and abused, their past.

In its original sense, heritage was the property ('heirlooms') which parents handed on to their children,
although the word could be used to refer to an intellectual or spiritual legacy as well. In the nineteenth and
early twentieth centuries, as new nation-states fought
for legitimacy, people began to speak of a 'national
heritage' as that body of folkways and political ideas
on which new regimes founded their identity. Australians, who modelled themselves on the new nations of
Europe and America, thus created their own national
myths based on the 'pioneer heritage' or 'the heritage
of Anzac'. School textbooks bearing the title *Australian
Heritage* showed how our love of democracy and fair
play was derived from the struggles of our pioneering
forebears. Charles Chauvel's film *Heritage* (1935)
dramatised that message in film.[1]

In recent times, however, and especially since the 1970s, heritage has become the special name we give to those valuable features of our environment that we seek to conserve from the ravages of development and decay. When the Hope Committee of Inquiry of 1974 defined the National Estate as 'the *things* we keep' and recommended the creation of a special body, the Heritage Commission, to guard it, the new usage became official. Thus we gained 'heritage studies' to investigate old buildings, 'heritage councils' to classify them and 'heritage advisers' to tell us how to maintain them.

But, surprisingly perhaps, things don't actually have to be old or historically significant to be described as 'heritage'. The word is now freely applied to almost any commodity that purports to reproduce past *styles* of architecture, furniture, household utensils or even food. In Britain a national chain of stores called 'Past Times' is devoted to the sale of Tudor brooches, medieval tapestries and other fake heirlooms. In Australia, the Tip-Top Bread Company invites jaded consumers to sample its wholesome, old-fashioned 'Heritage' loaf. Building companies offer 'Heritage' Federation houses. In the Bristol Paint Company's 'Australian Heritage' brochure the hallowed names of 'Phillip' and 'Macquarie', 'Ben Hall' and 'Ned Kelly' are used as labels for a range of 'authentic' Victorian and Edwardian paint colours. From the *values* of the past, to the *things* of the past, heritage has finally come to mean simply a *veneer* of pastness.

Heritage is something preserved for posterity so its framework of reference is the future—the generations yet unborn who will inherit—as much as the past. As early as the 1870s, as Tim Bonyhady has recently shown, the terms 'heritage' and 'national estate' were already part of the lexicon of those pleading for the conservation of Australian bushland and other places of natural beauty. In 1892 a plan to open a dairy farm on Tower Hill, a picturesque volcanic cone in Victoria's Western District that shortly before had been gazetted as a national park, met stern resistance from the *Warrnambool Standard*:

> The public park at Tower Hill is a priceless heritage that the generations of the future will highly prize, and it must be handed down to them with its privileges undiminished.

The nation's forests, its fauna, Sydney Harbour and Centennial Park were all described, at one time or another, as components of a 'heritage'—a gift of nature—that must be preserved for future generations.

Less commonly the word was applied to built objects.[2] The architect W. Hardy Wilson, for example, called for the preservation of early colonial buildings, not just for themselves but for the conservative aesthetic and social values they represented. Similarly, in 1948, America's National Trust for Historic Preservation referred to historic sites and structures as tangible remnants of the past and monuments to the national democratic heritage. In its *Criteria for Evaluating Historic Sites and Buildings*, it saw significance residing in those places 'in which the broad cultural, political, economic or social history of the nation, state or community is best exemplified, and from which a visitor may grasp in three dimensional form one of the larger patterns of the American heritage'.[3]

By the 1960s the two ideas—heritage as ideals and heritage as things—were becoming more closely intertwined. In 1960 the United Nations Educational, Scientific and Cultural Organisation (UNESCO) defined cultural property as 'the product and witness of the different traditions and of the spiritual achievements of the past and . . . thus an essential element in the personality of the peoples of the world'. It was the duty of governments 'to ensure the protection and preservation of the cultural heritage of mankind, as much as to promote social and economic development'. 'Cultural heritage' was a concept well adapted to the purpose of an international agency such as UNESCO. It enlarged the concept of heritage from a familial or national setting to an international one. By employing an anthropological understanding of 'culture' as embracing both values and the objects in which they were embodied, it strengthened the moral claims of the would-be custodians of cultural property while side-stepping difficult distinctions between its 'high' and 'low', popular and elite forms. One of the important uses of 'heritage' was simply as a convenient omnibus term for all those miscellaneous items—objects and sites as well as buildings—that were in danger of being lost. In 1963 the Victorian branch of the National Trust emphasised its concern, not only for buildings but for hitching posts, Aboriginal rock paintings, fountains, graves—anything, in short, 'whose destruction would be an important loss to Victoria's heritage'.

In the 1970s the new usage was officially recognised. A UNESCO Committee for the Protection of World Cultural and Natural Heritage adopted the term 'heritage' as a shorthand for both the 'built and natural remnants of the past'. The concept soon spread among Australian preservationists, especially those who participated in UNESCO conferences, although for a time it competed for popularity with the idea of 'the National Estate'—the term which Gough Whitlam, following the example of John F. Kennedy, had adopted to emphasise the responsibility of the national government to conserve the natural and built environment. In its report on the National Estate (1974) the committee of enquiry headed by Mr Justice Hope made sparing use of the term 'heritage', preferring more precise and neutral terms such as 'built environment', 'cultural resources' and 'historic buildings'. Labor ministers for the Environment, Tom Uren and Moss Cass, and David Yencken, later to head the Australian Heritage Commission, also preferred the idea of National Estate, perhaps because it provided a more solid foundation for a radical program of state intervention. But the statutory body belatedly formed under the Fraser government was called the Heritage Commission.[4]

In a period when 'quality of life' had become a leading public issue, 'heritage' was becoming a key word in the environmentalists' lexicon. When the Victorian government introduced its Historic Buildings Bill in 1973, the Leader of the Opposition, Clyde Holding, referred to the need to defend 'Melbourne's heritage in the form of historic buildings', but 'heritage' still competed in the rhetoric of debate with a host of other phrases—'historic landmarks', 'historic legacies', 'buildings redolent of a by-gone age'. By 1977 and 1978, however, when the New South Wales and South Australian governments introduced similar legislation, they naturally described their new councils as 'Heritage Councils' and the Acts themselves as 'Heritage Acts'. (In 1996 the Victorian government belatedly followed when its Historic Buildings Council became the Heritage Council of Victoria.)

In 1981 David Yencken, Director of the Australian Heritage Commission, introduced *The Heritage of Australia,* the illustrated register of the National Estate, with some remarks on the new terminology. 'Heritage,' he wrote, 'carries connotations of buildings and monuments; conservation suggests natural environments.' But even he was not consistent, referring elsewhere to the 'natural heritage'.[5]

Shades of meaning

The users of this newly popular word were often more confident of its acceptability than of its precise meaning. In his perceptive review of *The Heritage Industry* the British writer Robert Hewison quotes Lord Charteris, Chairman of Britain's National Heritage Memorial Fund, as saying that heritage means 'anything you want'.[6] Its value lay not in its analytical precision, but in its psychological resonance. It hinted at a treasury of deep-buried, but indefinite, values. It invoked a lofty sense of obligation to one's ancestors and descendants. And it secured the high ground of principle for the conservationists in their perennial battle against the improvers, developers and demolishers.

Heritage—what we value in the past—is defined largely in terms of what we value or repudiate in the present or fear in the future. In its preoccupation with the material remains of the past—'the *things* you keep'—it endorses our own materialism; yet in its reverence for what is durable, handmade or unique it also reinforces our underlying distaste for a culture of mass production and planned obsolescence. 'The impulse to preserve,' writes the geographer David Lowenthal, 'is partly a reaction to the increasing evanescence of things and the speed with which we pass them by. In the face of massive change we cling to the remaining familiar vestiges. And we compensate for what is gone with an interest in its history.'[7]

Ideas of psychic compensation are prominent in the

theories offered by sociologists and cultural critics for
the heritage boom. American sociologists, such as Fred
Davis in his *Yearning for Yesterday: The Sociology of
Nostalgia,* invoke generalised ideas of 'future shock'
and social dislocation.[8] In a fast-moving, atomistic society, heritage, he implies, offers a sense of spiritual
moorings. British neo-Marxists point to the sense of
national decline and to the complementarity between
a sentimentalised past and the political tenets of
Thatcherism.[9] Heritage offers the consolation of a glorious, if largely fictitious, past to a nation in the midst
of a painful present.

Each tradition of interpretation mirrors some of the
characteristic preoccupations of the society in which it
emerged. But it is hard to credit that a movement that
has assumed similar forms in Britain, the United States
and Australia is to be explained in purely local terms.
In Australia, at least, elements of all three interpretations—the senses of disorientation, of decline and of
national immaturity—may be detected in the ideology
and rhetoric of the heritage movement.

In the introduction to their Report of the National
Estate, the Hope Committee considered that

> It may well be that the rapidly accelerating rate of
> change in our society and surroundings is dis-
> orientating and bewildering to many people, and
> that a growing rootlessness and ugliness in their
> surroundings may be mirrored in aimlessness and
> violence.

They cited Patrick White's suggestion that Australian
society was heading for 'joyless warrens from which all
the peaceful and consoling aspects of village life have
been banished'. 'The shock of deprivation,' they went
on to argue, 'can be partly counteracted by identifying

and conserving buildings and whole areas of special quality as landmarks for our cultural past, present and future . . .'[10] The defence of neighbourhood integrity represented by the residents' associations of the 1970s often gave birth to an upsurge in local historical activity. The past was more than just a handy weapon against the bureaucrats and developers; the historical ambience and distinctiveness of the inner suburb was also a powerful source of community solidarity.

Australian society is not as overshadowed by an aura of national decline as British society. There, Robert Hewison has recently argued, the desire to save the past is largely inspired by a conviction that future choices are foreclosed.[11] Heritage is something that we must 'preserve' or 'save' rather than something to be 'created' or 'built'. It expresses the unspoken conviction that there is nothing that we have made, or can hope to make, that is as valuable as what we have inherited from the past. Often, it seems, items come to be recognised as 'heritage', not for their intrinsic qualities but by being 'saved' for posterity. In 1969 the Victorian National Trust stated that not everything that was old should be preserved and that only the best of the past should be cared for—this was how culture and heritage developed.

The appreciation of heritage often grew, therefore, in proportion to the sense of peril. In stagnant and declining regions in both Britain and Australia local history museums and historic precincts abound. To the locals they provide tangible evidence of the community's better days; to the visitors they offer a pleasant respite from the visual monotony of twentieth century architecture. As traditional industries decline, moreover, historical tourism often becomes the only economic alternative for some regions. At the Wigan Heritage

Centre in the derelict British industrial town made famous by George Orwell's depression-time study of the working class, *The Road to Wigan Pier,* visitors now enter an exhibit entitled 'The Way We Were' showing a nostalgic tableau of working-class life in the halcyon days before the Great War. In Australia, too, declining regions and towns, such as the towns of Victoria's central goldfields, the ghost towns of the New South Wales slopes and the mining fields of Moonta and Burra in South Australia, dominate the heritage business.

In *The Birth of the Museum,* Tony Bennett argues that the idea of 'heritage' assumes special significance in postcolonial societies.[12] When the sense of a real past is not deeply grounded, as in Australia, the 'vacuum' is filled by 'back-projecting' onto the land itself a sense of common nationality, which is now interpreted in terms of a common patrimony of natural and built, Aboriginal and European heritage. Australia, a new nation, thus acquires a history grounded in 'deep time' rather than just the last century since Federation. Bennett associates these tendencies with the 'new nationalism' of the Whitlam years and especially with the surge of heritage activity promoted by the Hope and Pigott enquiries into the National Estate and into Museums and National Collections.

Yet the process by which Australians came to identify old objects, buildings and landscapes with a sense of national heritage long preceded the specialised use of the word 'heritage' itself. The naturalists, painters and anthropologists of the nineteenth century, like the twentieth century promoters of national parks and pioneer monuments, were engaged in a systematic and more overtly nationalistic attempt to imbue the land with patriotic significance than the postwar heritage movement. What was new in the movement of the

1960s and 1970s was not its nationalistic focus, but its progressive redefinition from a spiritual to an essentially material concept. In this respect, as in others, Australians were following wider trends. The early 1970s was the heyday of the international environmental movement and the creation of the National Estate and the Museum of Australia might as readily be seen as an indirect creation of UNESCO as a symptom of Whitlam's new nationalism.

Heritage and history

Heritage and history are terms closely related, sometimes almost interchangeable, in the public mind. Is history the same as heritage? Are they fellow travellers towards a common goal, or are they, as some commentators suggest, rivals for that same valuable bit of turf, the past? In his stimulating book *The Heritage Crusade*, David Lowenthal has drawn a sharp contrast between the purposes and methods of history and heritage. History aspires to be objective, precise, accurate, universal, detached, to study the past in its own terms and for its own sake. Heritage, on the other hand, is concerned not with establishing the truth about the past for its own sake but for *our* sake or our children's. It is, he says, unabashedly 'partisan', 'shallow', 'chauvinist', 'mendacious'. It bends and reshapes the past to a present purpose. It sentimentalises, fabricates, distorts.

> Heritage . . . is not a testable, or even a reasonably plausible account of the past, but a declaration of faith in that past. Critics castigate heritage as a travesty of history. But heritage is not history, even when it mimics history. It uses historical traces and

tells historical tales, but these tales and traces are stitched into fables that are open neither to critical analysis nor to comparative scrutiny . . . Heritage and history rely on antithetical modes of persuasion. History seeks to convince by truth and succumbs to falsehood. Heritage exaggerates and omits, candidly invents and frankly forgets, and thrives on ignorance and error . . . Neither history nor heritage is free to depart altogether from the well-attested past. But historians ignore at professional peril the whole palimpsest of past percepts that heritage casually bypasses.[13]

As illuminating as it is, Lowenthal's contrast between history and heritage oversimplifies their complex relationship. Historians are by no means as unanimously dedicated to ideals of objective truth as our academic predecessors were. Even before the discipline was exposed to the influence of postmodernism and poststructuralism, historians had largely abandoned the pretence of objectivity. Any history, they would cheerfully admit, was written from a point of view and, while they might eschew deliberate fabrication and distortion, the pasts they portrayed reflected as much of themselves as their subjects.

Nor is heritage, at least in its institutionalised forms, as 'shallow', 'chauvinist' and 'mendacious' as Lowenthal makes it out to be. A leading goal of the international heritage movement, expressed in such bodies as UNESCO, ICOMOS and the Australian Heritage Commission, has been to objectify, professionalise and systematise the process of heritage assessment and evaluation. In the hands of professionals and bureaucrats much of the heat and subjectivity—and perhaps some of the enthusiasm too—has been taken out of heritage business. In this process historians have been willing, but not uncritical, accomplices. They have been prominent as activists, working with communities to preserve heritage places, as professionals evaluating their claims to historical significance, and as critical commentators on the heritage business itself. Heritage, I once wrote, is the cuckoo in history's nest. But the relationship is really more interestingly complex than that. History is also a free-rider on the heritage band-wagon.

The politics of the past

Heritage is essentially a political idea. It asserts a public or national interest in things traditionally regarded as private. 'Heritage belongs to the people, not to the owners,' remarked Evan Walker, Victorian Shadow Minister for Planning in 1980. He did not mean that because a building or place was part of 'the heritage' its owner ceased to have legal title to it. Rather he was insisting that the public retained a right to ensure its preservation that overrode the owner's right to alter or destroy it.

Opponents of heritage legislation sometimes argue that if, indeed, heritage belongs to the people, then the people should help the owners pay for its preservation or upkeep. The government, as the people's repre-sentatives, should either pay the costs of restoration or repair, or it should pay compensation for the develop-ment opportunities that the owners of the listed building have had to forego in order to preserve it.

Even in the prosperous 1970s, when 'quality of life' issues were to the forefront, Australian governments were loath to grasp the nettle of compensation. The grants paid in assistance to owners seldom equalled the costs of preservation. The provisions contained in some state legislation to allow the remission of municipal rates or land taxes to the owners of historic buildings have seldom been used. In 1987 the Australian Council of National Trusts and the state ministers for planning jointly petitioned the Commonwealth Treasurer to adopt, as a Bicentenary gesture, the American practice of allowing owners of certain listed buildings to claim the costs of restoration as an income tax deduction. If such pleas failed in the more expansive 1970s and 1980s they seem doomed in the mean 1990s. If politicians seek to 'compensate' owners of heritage buildings, it is more likely to be by relaxing controls on use and development than by foregoing public revenue.

Some leftist critics, on the other hand, welcome heritage legislation as a minor victory over the sacred rights of private property. They look back nostalgically to the days of the Green Bans, when conservationists and trade unionists made common cause against the onslaughts of the developers. Chris McConville maintains that buildings, once presented as heritage, are no longer simply pieces of capital to be exploited for the greatest possible profit.[14] The left wing of the conservation movement deplores the National Trust's timidity towards propertied interests and the readiness of governments—Labor and non-Labor—to compromise community values for economic development. The complaints have recently grown more vociferous as the Trust has become more preoccupied with securing the viability of its own portfolio of heritage properties.

Beyond the strict question of property rights, however, the idea of heritage also encouraged a sense of psychological or spiritual ownership over those buildings or objects brought within the National Estate.

When a squatter's homestead, a miner's hut, a Catholic church or a suburban town hall is identified as part of the heritage it ceases to be in exclusive possession of a family, church or local community and becomes 'ours'. 'Heritage conservation,' writes Jenny Walker in *South Australia's Heritage*, 'is not for governments alone; it is for us all to cherish and nurture the heritage so briefly entrusted to our care.'[15] It is a concept grounded in the first-person plural.

Whose heritage?

What does it mean to 'nurture' or 'cherish' our heritage? Recent critics of the British heritage movement detect in the idealisation of a 'peaceful' rural England and of its great country houses a process whereby an aristocratic or high bourgeois culture becomes identified with the national soul or spirit. National heritage, in the words of the British critic, Patrick Wright, is 'the historicized image of an instinctively conservative establishment'.[16] In Australia, too, the traditional concerns of the National Trust with squatters' homesteads and gentlemen's residences may be said to have reinforced a reverence for the conservative values of the class that inherited them. 'For the most part,' writes Chris McConville, 'the preserved building brought the ideal of the bourgeois Victorian family into the present. The balcony terrace in Gore Street and its imagined gentleman proprietor, the preserved town hall and its civic worthies, the suburban church and its lost congregation—these elements of Victorian society were represented through the preserved building.'[17]

Yet, as McConville concedes, the concept of heritage in Australia has gradually been widened to take in manifestations of many decidedly non-bourgeois ways of life.[18] Whereas Toorak matrons once fought to save Victorian mansions, the residents of small towns and unfashionable suburbs now seek to preserve workmen's cottages and disused factories. The National Trust, once the preserve of an Anglophile upper crust, now conducts walking tours of 'Little Italy' in Carlton, Melbourne. When Ballarat Council approved a scheme to buy and restore old miners' cottages, one of its supporters emphasised that 'an important element of the city's past is the working class life of its founders and their domicile'. The Victorian National Trust, in what may be a national or even international first, recently registered a public urinal.

An analysis of the Register of the National Estate or the National Trust, or state heritage registers, would still be likely to reveal a strong bias towards grand buildings designed for wealthy clients by well-established architects. Of approximately 100 buildings or sites listed in the National Register for the Newcastle area, almost 30 per cent dated from the period before 1850, about 60 per cent were from the period between 1850 and 1900 and only about 10 per cent were drawn from the period since 1900. The area is one of the most industrialised and proletarian in Australia but, in the Register, homesteads and mansions outnumber miners' cottages and industrial sites by almost ten to one. In their pioneering study of the cultural landscapes of New South Wales, *The Open Air Museum,* Dennis Jeans and Peter Spearritt document Newcastle's rich inheritance of twentieth century industrial buildings, but few of them have yet been included, officially, in 'the heritage'.[19]

Though most listings of the heritage invoke the language of democracy and aspire to some kind of

representativeness, the elitist values of the heritage consultants usually show through. 'We want to ensure that
examples . . . of structures and remnants of each
definable social group in each period, representing all
important historical trends are included in the Register,'
remarked David Yencken in 1981, though he conceded
that 'the search for what is representative is far from
complete.'[20] The author of *South Australia's Heritage*,
an illustrated listing of that state's Heritage Register,
claimed, with more justification, to include 'not only
architectural masterpieces of the past and present, but
the humble along with the great, the recent with the
remote'.[21]

One way of attempting to conserve a more democratic heritage is to collect items in accordance with the
main themes of Australian social history, or the social
history of a specific locality. Particular attention would
thus be given to the identification of sites or buildings
illustrative of important phases of Australia's development or of the way of life of representative groups of
people, including the humble as well as the great and
famous. In such a scheme, heritage items would be
selected in accordance with a general understanding of
social history rather than the social history being introduced to provide a background for items collected on
an *ad hoc* basis.

Thematic approaches to heritage identification have
had a mixed reception among historians. While promising
greater rigour and inclusiveness, they also lend themselves
to remote and bureaucratic application. They rest upon
a process of classification that comes more naturally to
botanists and zoologists than historians. The best way of
establishing the importance of a building or site, the
historian will tend to argue, is by telling a rich, evocative
and complex story about it; not by classifying it under a

preconceived theme, however important the theme itself may be. The higher one climbs on the heritage tree, from the local to the national, and from the national to the international level, however, the more such taxonomic methods tend to prevail. World Heritage assessments are the most rarified of all. The only way in which an Australian nomination for World Heritage can be advanced is by first establishing that it represents some theme of 'outstanding universal value'.[22] Historians, for whom context and narrative are the natural methods of interpretation, may welcome the inclusiveness of the thematic approach, but may resist the assumption, often made by bureaucrats, that once the historian has identified the important themes in the history of a region, the process of identification and assessment can be delegated to local planners or other heritage professionals.[23]

Creating a more representative 'heritage' is unlikely, in any case, to satisfy other critics of the heritage movement. Indeed, it is the very tendency of the idea of 'national heritage' to subsume and obliterate cultural differences that is at the basis of their objections. Tony Bennett, for example, draws attention to the ways in which the National Estate and the National Museum, by incorporating relics of both Aboriginal and white Australia, may unwittingly 'back-project the discourse of multiculturalism into the mists of time'.[24] How seriously one takes this objection may depend less on the rhetoric of those institutions than on their day-to-day practice and on how seriously one considers the alienation of those relics from their former custodians implied in the process of preservation itself.[25]

The democratically inclined social historian, therefore, will be concerned that heritage is not only representative of the people, and conserved for the people, but that it should also be identified and conserved *by* the people. Although the public is constantly exhorted by the experts to 'cherish' and 'nurture' their heritage, the job of identifying, classifying and ensuring it belongs largely to the coterie of heritage experts, architects, historians, archaeologists and planners. The heritage business is subject to a constant tension between the demands for bureaucratic consistency and impersonal expertise, on the one hand, and for popular participation and local autonomy on the other. Since the days of the Green Bans, the balance has swung heavily towards the rule of the expert. There is now a disconcerting gap between the arcane language and specialised concerns of the professional guardians of the heritage and its lay inheritors. Sometimes, it is true, the conservation consultant simply offers a scholarly rationale for aesthetic or historical judgments which the lay person makes more intuitively. But buildings often seem to be selected in accordance with antiquarian or scholarly criteria unrelated to the concerns of the public at large. When heritage consultants come to town they always inspect the buildings, but they do not always consult the locals. There is a danger, therefore, that the buildings they identify will not necessarily reflect the community's own sense of its past.

In historic Beechworth its historian Tom Griffiths argues that the city-based experts of the National Trust and the tourists who followed them to the town were often oblivious of the town's own sense of identity and community.

> Just as the countryside became defined earlier this century as a purely visual phenomenon—to be viewed but rarely understood—so, too, had the past, Beechworth's local past, become a thing to be visited and photographed, but seen as something

quite separate from the people living there. In serving the city so, the country becomes constrained to be the past. City-dwellers, who want to see 'progress' where they live, arrive in a country town and lament the careless destruction of quaint old things. Although they are ready to enter into debates about how the countryside looks, there is less concern about disappearing lifestyles or about existing relationships or feelings in that town.[26]

Griffiths may exaggerate the gulf between 'city' and 'country' attitudes and underestimate the degree to which the townsfolk, eager for tourist custom, collude with the outsiders in the transformation of their town into 'heritage'. The locals' sense of their past should surely not be regarded as sacrosanct from the more impersonal, but illuminating, interpretation of the outside heritage expert.

Sometimes, of course, the boot is on the other foot and the locals want to preserve a bit of local 'heritage' but the outside experts decree that it fails to meet the 'objective' criteria for registration. In his *Returning to Nothing*, Peter Read notes the powerful attachment, and consequent sense of loss, among residents of the old town of Yallourn, bulldozed to make way for an open-cut mine, and the residents of homes demolished in the path of a freeway in the Sydney suburb of Beecroft. These places may not 'make the grade' for heritage registration but as Read points out they are indeed someone's heritage; it is only the outsiders who fail to see it.

> Heritage and environmental impact assessors have not yet been able to appreciate the multitude of valuations among insiders who look out towards the threat. This should not be surprising, not

because such assessments are so difficult, but because assessors have not yet seen the need to appreciate the valuation of the individual, the family, the neighbourhood, the suburb and the town which co-exist within the 'community'.[27]

In recent years 'heritage professionals' (an oxymoron?) have responded to the disjunction between professional and community approaches to evaluation by debating the new criterion of 'social value'. In *What is Social Value? A Discussion Paper*, a Heritage Commission consultant Chris Johnson attempts to define the nature of communities' connections to the places they recognise and value. Social value, she argues, is not about the past or about social history, but about people's attachment to places *in the present*. Such places are important because they are 'recognised' by insiders rather than 'identified' by outsiders, and for the way they express and reinforce tradition rather than what they disclose about the past. Aboriginal meeting places, migrant hostels, main streets or pathways might have such social value. If you want to know whether a place has social value, she suggests, you can either just ask the locals, or 'threaten the place and wait to hear from the community if they care about it'. Since it was not practical (or presumably popular) to threaten every potentially valuable place, asking the community to identify valued places was the preferred methodology.[28]

Introducing the new criterion of social value might enable the community to have a bit more say in heritage assessment; or it might encourage the entry into the heritage business of yet another tribe of experts— anthropologists, sociologists, perhaps cultural critics —to join the architects, lawyers, historians and planners who have dominated the trade until now. It might ensure that heritage assessment was not dominated by the professionals; but by insisting on a distinction between 'historical' and 'social' value it might create a distinction between professional and community concerns that many historians would reject. The fiction of heritage as a scientific enterprise in which experts assess the relative importance of heritage 'items' has been useful to governments, as well as to the experts themselves; it created a set of rules and imposed implicit limits on the number of places that belonged to the national estate. But 'social value' introduces a new degree of uncertainty into the process of heritage assessment. It remains to be seen whether federal and state governments can accommodate such open-ended criteria into existing heritage legislation or whether—as seems more likely—the local community that recognises 'social value' will also have to bear the responsibility for protecting it.

What all these disputes underline is the impossibility of reducing heritage to a simple formula. It is, by its very nature, an unstable and contested idea, as must be any idea that attempts to capture the things we count most valuable in our collective life. As soon as the net of definition is lifted over it, it takes flight.

chapter seven

Antiques, shrines and documents: What makes a building historic?

I N 1873 THE globe-trotting English novelist Anthony Trollope made a visit to Australia's abandoned convict settlement of Port Arthur. For the people of Van Diemen's Land the ending of the convict era had not come a moment too soon, and they were as anxious to obliterate this place of pain and purgatory from their memories as they were to exchange the old unhappy name of Van Diemen's Land for the fresh, proud name of Tasmania. What would become of this sad collection of gaols, stores, chapels and barracks? 'They will fall into the dust, and men will make unfrequent excursions to the strange ruins,' he predicted.[1]

For almost fifty years, Trollope's expectations were fulfilled. The government sold off some of the buildings for removal, the land was subdivided and sold at auction, and what remained of the settlement was renamed 'Carnarvon'. Over the years bushfires razed several of the buildings and others became overgrown with bushes and weeds. Not until the 1920s did a few adventurous motorists and bushwalkers begin to rediscover the place. By then, the ruins had acquired a more romantic appearance. 'Like the ruinous tombstones of a neglected old graveyard,' one guidebook remarked, they created 'a longing desire in the minds of the curious to know something of its wonderful history'.[2]

In the wake of these first explorers came the inevitable souvenir hunters and grave-robbers, searching for old leg-irons, convict-made bricks and other relics of the colony's founding years. But it was not until 1949 that the Tasmanian government at last moved to reacquire the site and place it under the control of its Scenery Preservation Board. Later, at the cost of several millions of Commonwealth taxpayers' dollars, Port Arthur was carefully restored and the strange ruins became the site of increasingly frequent excursions by busloads of tourists from all over the world. Now, in a way that no one could have predicted, the 'Port Arthur Massacre' has added a new and macabre chapter to its history. A tradition of violence, muffled by the processes of decay and preservation, has been terrifyingly revived. But no one wants to preserve the physical remains of this history. The Broad Arrow Cafe has already been demolished. When history is so painfully close, mourning, rather than preservation, is the only way to remember.

Port Arthur is, by any standard, one of Australia's most important historical sites and the story of its death and resurrection illustrates not only the growth of preservationist sentiment in the twentieth century, but our changing views of what makes a building or place 'historic'. Like the word 'heritage', the concept of the 'historic' has gradually become a keyword in the vocabulary of conservation-minded Australians. What does it mean?

In the course of the past twenty years or so, architectural historians have developed clear and widely accepted criteria for determining the *architectural* importance of a building. Is it the work of an eminent architect? Does it

embody an innovative or skilful design solution? Is it an
outstanding or typical example of an important style?
Does it exhibit an important use of new materials or
building technology? The underlying assumptions of the
architectural historian's approach are similar to those of
an art historian or literary critic. The individual building
is placed, like a picture or a poem, within a classificatory
framework of authorship, style, period and so on, and
ranked according to its relative importance within a
canon. Connoisseurs will sometimes differ in their ranking
of individual buildings but everyone accepts the assumption that such a ranking is, or ought to be, possible. But
no such consensus has yet developed for the critical
assessment of historic significance.[3]

For most purposes, the words 'historic' and 'historical' are interchangeable. 'Of or relating to history;
historical as opposed to fiction or legend: relating to
historical events.' These are the standard dictionary
meanings of both words. But the word 'historic' also
has a narrower meaning when it is defined as related
to 'an important part or item of history; *noted or
celebrated* in history'. As the example of Port Arthur
reminds us, ideas of what are 'important', 'noted' or
'celebrated' may change with the times and vary between one observer and another. 'Historic', the word
enshrined in the Victorian Historic Buildings Act (1974)
and since regularly used in other heritage legislation,
has often been avoided in favour of the more neutral
and internationally recognised, but equally vague, idea
of 'cultural significance'.

When architects appraise buildings they implicitly
adopt the standpoint of a connoisseur, grading buildings according to a scale of relative excellence. But
when historians say a building is historically important
they are not giving it a rank amidst a range of other

possible candidates, but making a judgment of its significance in relation to a wider context of social,
political or intellectual history. The architect's method
of assessment is primarily intrinsic and comparative,
relating to the specific qualities of the building or
structure itself; the historian's is primarily contextual,
relating to the society of which the building is a physical relic. When architects wish to argue for the
significance of a building they are inclined to classify
it according to its style—Georgian, Victorian, Federation etc. When historians argue for its significance they
are inclined to tell its human story or locate it in its
past social and geographical context.

When people argue for the historical significance of
buildings or places, they often appeal, unconsciously of
course, to Nietzsche's trinity of 'monumental', 'antiquarian' and 'critical' history, discussed in Chapter 1.
The building is regarded as historic by virtue of its age,
of its association with great people or events, or
because of its contribution to a more critical understanding of the past. How these perspectives influence
the interpretation of the built heritage is the subject of
this chapter.

The building as an antique

In a lay person's language, however, historic often
means nothing more than 'old'. When local residents
band together to save an old building they usually
dignify it with the word 'historic'. During one week in
1986 the Yarram *News* highlighted the sale of the
'historic property' Woodlands, the *Dandenong Journal*
reported the local council's discussions with the Commonwealth government to try to save the 'historic

Berwick Post Office', the *Emerald Hill Times* voiced its concern about the deterioration of the 'historic' Kerferd Road pier and the *Essendon Gazette* featured a competition sponsored by the Urban Conservation Advisory Committee for the restoration of the district's 'historic homes'. A building, according to this ordinarily accepted usage, becomes historic if it is old enough, and in danger of demolition or decay. Just as serious illness reminds us of our mortality, so decreptitude and threatened demolition may heighten our sense of a building's historic significance.

People are attracted to old buildings for much the same combination of sentimental, aesthetic and solidly commercial reasons as they are attracted to old furniture, old books, old porcelain and other antiques. Old houses, real estate advertisements keep telling us, are full of 'old world charm' and 'the romance of yesteryear'. In a stark world of glass and concrete efficiency, they evoke an age somehow gentler and more harmonious than our own. Happily, buying them can also be good business for, as good examples become scarcer, their monetary value increases.

Reverence for age was one of the prime forces behind the development of the preservationist movement. The English architectural critic, John Ruskin, who strongly influenced the founders of the British National Trust, saw the buildings of the late Middle Ages as a source of inspiration to a generation living amidst the dark satanic mills of the industrial revolution. 'The greatest glory of a building,' Ruskin believed,

> . . . is in its Age, and in that deeper sense of Voicefulness, of stern watching, of mysterious sympathy, nay, even of approval or condemnation, which we feel in walls that have long since been

washed by the passing waves of humanity. It is in their lasting witness against men, in their quiet contrast with the transitional character of all things, in the strength which, through the lapse of seasons and times, and the decline and birth of dynasties, and the changing face of the earth, and of the limits of the sea, maintains its sculptural shapeliness for a time insuperable, connects forgotten and following ages with each other, and half constitutes the identity, as it concentrates the sympathy, of nations: it is in that golden stain of time, that we are to look for the real light, and colour, and preciousness of architecture . . .[4]

Ruskin's was a romantic approach to architecture. Modern-day historians may be inclined to dismiss his belief in the importance of age as more antiquarian than historical. Merely to be old, they would say, cannot make a building historically significant, even if it may exert a certain antique charm. Besides, in Australia at least, there simply are no truly ancient buildings.

Yet there are also dangers in drawing too sharp a line between antiquarianism and historial significance. In a country of recent European settlement like Australia, we need to keep a sufficient number of buildings and objects that remind us of our colonial origins. The antiquarian's love of old things can often lead to questions of a more truly historical kind. For many people heirlooms, old furniture and old buildings are a more accessible gateway to the past than books or documents. Some buildings and sites—Sydney's First Government House, La Trobe's Cottage, Fremantle's Arthur's Head—are important to us as a physical link with the earliest moments of European settlement.

The trouble with the antiquarian approach— reverence for old things simply because of their age—is that it may blind us to the historical importance of much younger things. The British National Trust was born of the movement to preserve ancient monuments such as medieval churches and castles. It was not until the First World War that it began to take an interest in Georgian architecture and not until after the Second World War that it turned its attention to the great industrial buildings of the nineteenth century. Early students of Sydney's architecture, such as Morton Hermon, concentrated almost exclusively on Georgian buildings. When Maie Casey and her colleagues made their first photographic survey of Melbourne's built heritage, *Early Melbourne Architecture* (1953), they concentrated on the few surviving examples of pre-1850 buildings and concluded their survey in 1888.

Only in very recent years have architectural and social historians begun to pay due respect to Australia's twentieth century buildings. The trouble with them, as Peter Spearritt reminds us, is that they are 'too common for their own good. If they were fewer in number', he believes, 'historians and architects would take them more seriously'.[5] Of the 600 or so buildings on the Victorian Historic Buildings Register in 1990 no more than 50 were constructed since 1900 and most of these were added because of their architectural rather than their historic importance. Over the last decade, however, the National Trust's Twentieth Century Buildings Committee has identified a much wider range of recent buildings, and the popular appreciation of period architecture has now widened to embrace not only Federation villas, but Californian bungalows and even cream brick veneers.

The building as a shrine

What makes a building historic, some people would argue, is not so much its age as its association with famous events or people. In his *Seven Lamps of Architecture,* Ruskin went so far as to claim that it was not until a building has been 'entrusted with the fame, and hallowed by the deeds of men, until its walls have been witnesses of suffering, and its pillars rise out of the shadows of death' that it gained an aura of the historic.[6]

It was some such idea that inspired the Melbourne businessman Russell Grimwade in the early 1930s to buy and transplant the alleged Captain Cook's Cottage from its original location in Great Ayrton in Yorkshire to Melbourne's Fitzroy Gardens. Grimwade believed that, by viewing this relic of the great navigator, Victorians might somehow be brought more closely in touch with the spirit of the man himself.

> We are certain [wrote Hermon Gill in a 1934 guide to the cottage] that something of Cook lives and lingers in the walls of the cottage today. Even if it were not his boyhood home, it is something more. It knew the great navigator as Australia knew him. Its doorstep rang to his heel as he entered. Its walls heard his voice, and the voice of his parent. Within them must be stored memories of the sacred bonds which tie loving father and devoted son . . .[7]

Modern Australian historians have generally been sceptical of the power of shrines and relics to establish communion with the mighty dead. Manning Clark, the last of the romantic historians, was unusual among Australian historians in diligently visiting the places where important events took place. In the footnotes of *A History of Australia* Clark often records his visits to famous sites such as the Burke and Wills Dig Tree or the windswept shores of the Bay of Islands where his forebear Samuel Marsden came ashore. But what he gleaned from such visits is seldom obvious from the text. He visited them, not for information, but for atmosphere; not as an investigator but as a pilgrim. His practice, in this respect, contrasts with that of Robert Hughes, whose brilliant description of landscapes such as Sydney Harbour and Macquarie Harbour are integral to the narrative.

Australians are not a people much given to hero-worship and, compared with Britons or Americans, we have very few shrines to our great men and women. In 1887, as Australia approached its centenary, the Premier of New South Wales, Sir Henry Parkes, proposed that the government should erect a great State House containing, amongst other things, a mausoleum for the nation's heroes. It is indicative of our democratic outlook, perhaps, that Parkes' scheme was laughed out of the legislature.[8] A recent proposal by the ACT government to create an Australian Arlington failed to stir the national imagination. Few of our prime ministers have memorials like the Lincoln Memorial, the Washington Monument or the Kennedy Memorial and their birthplaces and homes are not hallowed like those of Disraeli, Gladstone and Churchill. The only prime minister's home that has become a museum is Ben Chifley's—a simple wood railwayman's cottage on the wrong side of the tracks in his home town of Bathurst. The Jeparit birthplace of Sir Robert Menzies and Bob Hawke's childhood home in Bordertown are identified with plaques but many other prime-ministerial homes, including those of Stanley Melbourne Bruce, Jim Scullin and Harold Holt, are unmarked. Even Alfred Deakin's birthplace in Fitzroy failed to gain entry into the

Historic Buildings Register when it was nominated several years ago.

In the property pages of the metropolitan dailies associations, even very tenuous associations, with a great man or woman are sometimes invoked as a selling point. Under the heading 'Link with a famous artist', an otherwise nondescript Toorak house was advertised as the home of a 'family friend' of Sir Arthur Streeton, while a pleasant villa in Moonee Ponds was said to have been visited on one occasion by Sir Robert Menzies. But if the prospective purchaser feels a warm glow as he crosses the threshold in the steps of Sir Robert Menzies, it is unlikely that he seriously regards his new home as 'historic'.

Even when the association between the building and the great man is more enduring, it may still be quite uninteresting. As Sir John Summerson, the British architectural historian, once remarked, 'the objective fact that a certain man did live in a certain house is of purely subjective value'.[9] The connection becomes more than sentimental only if the historic personage and the building somehow help to interpret each other. Perhaps there is something about the character of the person— his or her taste, personal habits, lifestyle—that helps to explain the plan, architecture, decoration of the house. Perhaps something about the building offers a clue to the life of the person who designed, built or inhabited it. In this respect, Ben Chifley's humble house is a fitting memorial for the locomotive engine driver who became a prime minister.

An otherwise unprepossessing building sometimes acquires historic significance, not just for its association with a famous person or event, but as the historical basis of a famous fiction. The lakeside house at Chiltern once occupied by the young Henry Handel Richardson

takes on additional significance from the use the novelist subsequently made of it in *The Fortunes of Richard
Mahony.* Early in 1988 literary historians and local
conservationists formed a protest committee to oppose
projected extensions to Wyework, an unprepossessing
Californian bungalow at Thirroul on the New South
Wales south coast. For eight weeks in 1922 Wyework
was the home of the English novelist, D. H. Lawrence,
and his German-born wife Frieda. It was here that
Lawrence wrote all but the last chapter of his novel,
Kangaroo. Something, not only of events and daily life
in Thirroul, but of the physical and emotional climate
of the house itself is to be detected in the novel. The
proposed extensions to the house, one literary historian
argued, would not only change the character of the
house but rob it of 'the feeling of the emotional to and
fro between the Lawrences'.

The building as a document

What really makes the house of a great man or woman
historically important is what makes any building historically important—namely, that it throws light on a
significant aspect of the lives of people in the past. It
is not just as an *antique,* nor as a *shrine,* but as a
document, capable of contributing to a critical understanding of the past, that a building deserves to be
regarded as 'historic'. Some important consequences
flow from an understanding of buildings as documents.
Correctly interpreting a document requires that we
know and understand the language and idiom in which
it is expressed. Similarly, the attentive social historian
must take pains to understand the techniques, materials
and architectural vocabulary of those who constructed

the building as well as the codes of behaviour and way of life of those who occupied or used it. Only if they could place themselves in the position of those to whom a building was addressed, understanding every symbol and association called upon by its builder, could historians correctly interpret a building, argued Ruskin.

But buildings are capable of revealing our ancestors, not only through their conscious symbolism but through their unstated social assumptions. Ruskin believed that only the grandeur of past ages should be preserved. While castles and great houses were worthy of respect, mere villas and recreational buildings were not. 'We wish succeeding generations to admire our energy, but not ever to be aware of our lassitude; to know when we moved, but not when we rested, how we ruled, not how we condescended . . .'[10] But posterity has to decide for itself what it wishes to remember of past ages, and a more democratic and self-questioning society than Ruskin's may regard the nineteenth century villa, and even the factory and cottage, with more interest than he did. It may wish to be conducted through the stables and servants' quarters as well as the grand ballrooms and drawing rooms. As the past recedes from us, new generations may come to invest familiar places with a sense of the strange and exotic.

Since the 1970s Australian heritage bodies, in common with similar bodies around the world, have gradually broadened and refined their criteria of historical significance. A recent reviewer of heritage studies in the United States, for example, remarked on a broadening of criteria to include structures that are 'recent, vernacular and associated with ordinary lives and events'.[11] The Victorian Heritage Council suggested that a building may be suitable for inclusion on its Register if it was found to 'represent, or be an extraordinary example of, a way of life, custom, process or function'. In recent years it has registered a number of buildings of primarily social-historical significance such as the Victoria Brewery, the Bryant and May Match Factory, a Second World War air-raid shelter, a nineteenth century rural flour mill, complete with intact machinery and fittings, and a local newspaper office and printery. In 1995 the Victorian Branch of the National Trust placed an underground municipal lavatory on its register.

The necessarily broad criteria required to encompass items of social historical significance have sometimes been criticised by architectural purists as providing no firm basis for judgments of relative importance. Surely, they argue, any item that is not 'extraordinary' will be considered 'representative' and therefore any item at all—even the most mundane cream brick veneer—will become a potential candidate for registration. Claims based on 'representativeness' are implicitly comparative and therefore place an obligation on the historian to carry out a systematic search for comparable examples. They are not, however, claims for 'typicality'—a building may be 'extraordinary' in its capacity to illustrate some way of life or custom, while being quite atypical of the class of buildings to which it belongs. Judgments of social-historical significance may be subject, therefore, to similar kinds of comparative analysis to that usually undertaken by architectural historians. But since it is the 'ways of life' or 'customs' rather than the buildings themselves that are the primary object of the historian's attention, such comparative analysis is intrinsically more difficult than the stylistic categorisation of an architectural historian.

It is a standard principle of historical interpretation that a building acquires significance only in relation to its context. Similarly, establishing the historical significance of a building requires us to pay attention not only to its

intrinsic qualities but to its surroundings. In considering
architectural significance, lawyers and most heritage
bodies generally insist that each building is considered on
its own merits, that it cannot derive importance from the
architectural distinction of its neighbours, although
planning legislation often seeks to preserve at least the
external fabric of buildings that contribute to the general
ambience or stylistic unity of a street or neighbourhood.
In considering historical importance, however, a building's
relationship with its environs may be quite crucial. How,
for example, can we correctly assess the importance of
Melbourne's or Sydney's Customs Houses without reference to the busy wharves, chandleries, warehouses and
shipping offices that once surrounded them? How can a
country flour mill be understood except by reference to
the local patterns of grain production, transport and
consumption that once supported it? What significance
does a cable-tram engine house have apart from the lines
of cable that once powered the silently moving tramcars?
It may require a good deal of skilful research and historical imagination to discover the forgotten links between
some old buildings and their spatial context but it is the
only way in which the modern observer can truly enter
into the social world of which they were once a part.

Historical documents are not only the products of
their originators but of successive processes of editing,
revision, translation and interpretation. They are potential evidence about all those who participated in the
processes through which it was handed down to the
present. Viewing buildings as documents, therefore,
alerts us to their significance, not only as evidence of
the builder, architect and original owner, but also of
the processes of cultural and social change that have
subsequently altered, extended, truncated or refur-
bished them. We may liken some old buildings to

palimpsests—parchments that have been successively written upon, crossed out, erased and written over by different hands so as to leave several distinct 'layers' of writing. Reading such a manuscript calls for high skills in paleography (the study of obsolete scripts), contemporary idiom and knowledge of the various periods in which the document was composed. So, too, the social historian interpreting the fabric of an inner suburban terrace house that has been successively occupied by a late nineteenth century merchant, an early twentieth century boarding-house keeper, an Italian immigrant family and a trendy professional couple would need a good eye, not only for contemporary decorating styles but for the *mores* of the occupiers.

It was once the fashion among conservationists to seek to 'restore' such a building to its 'original' condition, treating the intervening layers of occupation as distortions of the historical significance of the building. Conservation architects sometimes recommended the destruction of the Victorian additions to a Georgian cottage in order to restore it to its 'original condition'. Yet such a conscientious attempt to recover the original feeling of the building can sometimes diminish its significance as a historical document. It is not just that the brightly restored paintwork obliterates the patina of age; the removal of those seemingly 'intrusive' or 'unsympathetic' additions deprives the viewer of a sense of the precarious passage through which the building has survived to the present day. To the critical historian the building testifies, not only to itself or its makers, but to all those—inhabitants, visitors, even vandals and demolishers—whose actions can be read in its fabric.

chapter eight

Sacred sites: The battle for historic churches

I F YOU WANT to know what places have 'social value', says a heritage adviser, try threatening them.[1] When the congregation of the Healesville Uniting Church decided to demolish their old and decrepit timber church hall to build a new brick one they could hardly have anticipated what a hornet's nest they would stir. After contracts for the new building were let, arrangements were made to clear the site for construction. Advertisements were placed in the local paper offering the old building to anyone who could find a suitable new use for it, but there were no takers. Eventually, with the contractors about to arrive, the church applied to the Shire Council for a demolition permit which was duly granted.

It was then that Mrs Pam Firth, proprietor of the Old Mechanics Institute Tea Room and Gallery and a veteran of earlier preservation battles in the town—the local paper dubbed her the 'Joan of Arc of Healesville's historic buildings'—appeared on the scene. Mrs Firth claimed that the threatened building had begun its life in 1860 as Healesville's first church, an unusual inter-denominational mission venture, and was probably the oldest building still standing in the town. She called upon the demolishers to halt operations until the church's historic significance could be investigated and appealed to the Shire Council to revoke its demolition permit while further information was obtained from the National Trust and the Historic Buildings Council. In their eagerness to preserve the building Mrs Firth and her supporters may have been inclined to exaggerate its antiquity—it was soon talked up from being merely 'the oldest timber church in the district' (which it very likely was) to possibly 'one of the earliest timber buildings in Victoria' (which it certainly was not).

The church people were anxious not to offend local feeling, but keen to get on with their new hall. The old one, their minister Rev. Darron Honey explained, was no longer safe to use and the demolisher was threatening to impose penalties for delay. An offer from Billanook College to transport the building to its campus in Mooroolbark for use as a school chapel appealed to the Parish Council who were pleased to think that their little church would continue to be used for a religious purpose. But Mrs Firth and the preservationists were more concerned with the local, than with the religious, history of the building. 'We are a small town,' wrote Richard Troon to the local press. 'To lose an important part of our town's history has far more impact than it would in a major city. The importance of this historic building, not necessarily as a church, but as a significant part of Healesville's history, is beyond replacement.' As news of the impending demolition spread through the district, the preservationists received heartening messages of support from people whose forebears had once been baptised or married in the ancient shrine. People who had never darkened its creaking doors were disturbed by the thought that a tangible link with their ancestors was about to be severed.

But although no one wanted the church to go,

neither did anyone know what was to be done with it if it stayed. Mrs Firth hoped to see it incorporated, together with some other historic buildings, in a tourist precinct near the soon-to-be-reopened Healesville Railway Station, but there were no concrete plans or funds. Public pressure nevertheless persuaded the regional planning authority to recommend the retention of the building and the Shire Council to revoke its planning permit. Having placated local opinion, most councillors were keen to wash their hands of further responsibility. It was now time, one remarked, for the preservationists 'to get off their backsides and do something positive to save it [the old church]'.

A public appeal for money and voluntary labour was launched through the local press but, six weeks after the controversy began, the only concrete plan that proved satisfactory to both the church and preservationists was to move the old building sideways on its present site to allow the new work to proceed. Volunteers, mostly local retirees, toiled in the blazing December sun to complete the job. The cooperation and goodwill that accomplished the relocation of the little church was a heartening reminder of the spirit of interdenominational cooperation that had first brought it into being, and some consolation to the harassed minister and parishioners for the frustrations of the previous weeks. But there was no disguising the fact that, after all the hue and cry, it was elderly church folk rather than the young people of the preservation movement who had shouldered the responsibility for preserving Healesville's heritage.[2]

Shortly after I became Chairman of the Victorian Historic Buildings Council in the late 1980s a small brown-paper package began to arrive each week in my mail. It came from a newspaper clippings service and it contained items culled from the suburban and country press on anything related to historic buildings. The clippings were sent to warn me of possible trouble ahead, but the habits of the historian die hard and I soon found myself looking forward to their arrival, not just as a source of political intelligence but as a weekly commentary on how local communities were interpreting and revaluing the material remains of their past.

One of the most common and poignant dilemmas to emerge from the pages of the local press concerned the fate of old or redundant churches. Everywhere, it seemed, as congregations shrank or merged with others, the churches that had once dominated the town or suburban skyline were emptying or falling into decay. The churchgoers themselves, who had borne the costs of maintaining the building and had long anticipated the painful moment of departure, often seemed less reluctant to give up their church than the rest of the community. For them, as they often said, the church was the people, not the building. But for the community, most of whom had probably never ventured inside the church, it was the building that mattered. And faced with the prospect of its loss, they were often prepared to fight with surprising tenacity to save it.

While the people of Healesville were agonising over the fate of their old mission church, other communities were undergoing similar trials. Down on the Mornington Peninsula the residents at Tyabb were up in arms about the decision to close their pretty little Anglican church. It was unfair, some of the locals thought, that the fate of the church should be decided by the Bishop and Vestry while families who had lived in the district for years were not given a vote. Out at St Andrews, on Melbourne's northern limits, controversy was raging about the decision to close down and remove the historic St Andrews Church that gave the place its name. One resident insisted that it should remain 'to preserve our children's heritage'. Down at Portland, a decision by the Uniting Church Parish to incorporate memorial windows from the now redundant Scots Presbyterian church into their main centre of worship at the former Methodist Church provoked an impressive display of local tribalism as descendants of former Presbyterians lodged 106 objections to the move with the Shire Council. To remove the windows, said one objector, would be 'sinful'.[3]

The local controversies reflect on a small scale some of the perennial dilemmas of historic conservation. What matters most—the survival of the building or the institution it houses? To whom do such places belong— just the present occupants? Or does the local community or the descendants of former members of the church also have a claim? In a secular age, why do people seek to save the churches they seldom attend? White man, as the saying goes, may have no dreaming and sacred sites, he may think, are for Aboriginal people. Yet in their determination to preserve the local church—the place where they or their forebears were baptised, married or mourned—European Australians were perhaps drawing on sentiments that went deeper than mere antiquarianism.

It is in losing loved places, as well as loved persons, that we come to recognise the nature and depth of our attachment to the past. Peter Read's *Returning to Nothing: The Meaning of Lost Places* (1996), the most moving exploration of this theme in recent Australian history, makes no mention of the sporadic, often unsuccessful, but impassioned attempts of small communities to save their churches. He tells how houses, gardens, lakes, suburbs and towns are lost to fires, hurricanes, highways, dams and open-cut mines and how those caught in the path of change mourn their loss. Attachment to place, he argues, comes hard to Europeans —harder at any rate than it does to Aborigines whose long, spiritual attachment to the land becomes the standard against which the attachments of all later-comers must be measured. Christianity with its partner, Capitalism, appears in Read's analysis only as a force radically opposed to such a spiritual sense of place. 'Christianity, a proselytising and formerly peripatetic religion, transports its sacred objects: a church can be erected anywhere, and the site may be deconsecrated as well as it can be sacralised.'[4] Many of those who spoke to him about their sense of attachment to lost places reached for a sense of transcendence, using words like 'sacred', 'mystical' and 'magical', but the framework in which they located it was more often pagan than Christian, New Age than Old World.[5]

Read overstates an important point. Protestant Christianity, it is true, is a religion rooted more firmly in a sense of time than of place. Yet official doctrine has often been in conflict with the outlook of ordinary parishioners who have upheld, sometimes tenaciously, their own forms of local piety. Christians continue, as most people did until very recently, to look to the past as a source of moral and spiritual values. The saints and heroes of the Bible and Christian history provide the narratives of courage, self-sacrifice and perseverance on which clergy, parents and teachers encouraged the young to model their lives. Buildings and monuments, by commemorating sacred history, may help to inculcate those ideals and in turn may become sacralised; but it is the persistence of the faith that matters most, not the preservation of the building or monument. When a young Uniting Church clergyman appeared before the Historic Buildings Council to argue for alterations to his church, a delightful little classical building in Portland, he underlined the differences between his Christian idea of history and the more antiquarian and materialist conception that he detected among conservationists. 'We do not see buildings as historical except as they are given meaning and value by the people who use them,' he remarked. 'It could be said that this view of history is a dynamic one, rather than a static one. It must be said that our view of history is people-centred and not object-centred.'[6]

When Protestant Christianity was in its missionary phase its leaders often resisted architectural pretension as a potential form of idolatry or Popery. They were more concerned with the state of people's souls than the surroundings in which they gathered. John Wesley, the founder of Methodism, directed only that preaching places should be built so as to ensure that the preachers would be heard by as many people as possible and that they should be 'built plain and decent, but not more expensive than is absolutely necessary'. Many of the earliest Methodist chapels were converted mills, barns, malt kilns and cottages. Even after Wesley's death, when his followers separated from the established church, their chapels continued to be built in a severely geometrical, often classical, form.[7] The more militant forms of Protestantism maintain this attitude: Salvationists, for example, happily sell, demolish or adapt their historic buildings as soon as they have ceased to fulfil their purpose. Attachment to buildings, in their view of things, is a form of idolatry and a symptom of decline. Some clergymen grow impatient with the seemingly irresponsible demands of the conservationists. They long for the church that travels lighter, responds more flexibly and presents a more modern face to the world.

But although, as these Christians insist, the church is people not buildings, this does not mean that buildings are of no account. A church building is not just shelter, any more than the body was simply clothing for the soul. In 1980 Rev. Graeme Griffin, a Uniting Church minister and grief counsellor, warned the church's property managers of the trauma already being suffered by many congregations, especially in rural areas, as they closed and sold off their buildings and merged with other congregations. 'When the buildings are threatened . . . what we face is not so much the loss of the specific bricks and mortar (or iron and timber) as the loss of a heritage, a part of something bigger than those particular buildings but symbolised in them,' he observed. Although the Kingdom of God was not made with hands, Christians could too easily 'underestimate the strength of the attachment we naturally feel for things'. The church had often fostered such feelings of attachment by putting building projects at the forefront of fundraising campaigns over the previous decades. The strength of people's sense of attachment could vary greatly and bore no necessary relationship to its duration: 'It is not necessarily the person who has been in the district for 75 years, and whose father laid the foundation stone of the church, who is most intimately tied to it.'

Griffin suggested ways in which the trauma might be eased, perhaps by incorporating windows or other memorials from the old church in the new. But when they lost their church building some people evidently concluded that they had lost their church as well. One clergyman estimated that as many as a quarter of the members of a closed or merged congregation left the church and did not rejoin a church elsewhere.

Piety and heritage

One of the signal features of our times is a nostalgic preoccupation with the material remains of the past. In his interesting book *The Past is a Foreign Country* David Lowenthal ponders the psychology of this nostalgia boom:

> Unwilling or unable to incorporate the legacy of the past into our own creative acts, we concentrate instead on saving its remaining vestiges. The less integral the role of the past in our lives, the more imperative the urge to preserve its relics. Because earlier modes of response to the past are now closed to us, because much of what survives is now foreign to us, preservation has become the principal, often the exclusive, way of deriving sustenance from the past.[8]

Why, we may wonder, is this so? Is it perhaps the gimcrack standardisation of mass production and planned obsolescence that makes us hanker for the handmade solidity of the old? Or is it possibly a more profound sense of the transience of human relationships, and of life itself, which causes us to cling to these remnants of an apparently more settled age? At all events, the passion to preserve is a strong one and, as the churchfolk of Healesville discovered, hedonistic, agnostic Australians will sometimes exert a lot of energy and political muscle to prevent the demolition of the church they don't attend.

What they seek to preserve, perhaps, is not a relic of the faith but a symbol of continuity and community. Churches are among the most distinctive and visible symbols of local community and it is no wonder, perhaps, that the locals feel their disappearance keenly.

Long after they have ceased to believe in the formal tenets of Christianity or to observe its rituals, they retain, it seems, a strong attachment to the church, sometimes merely for its architecture but also as a kind of local shrine. It is the place where the sense of family and local piety is given tangible form. The steel and concrete clock tower rising over the new suburban shopping mall is a poor substitute for the spire that once dominated the town.

Heritage—the impulse to save the material remains of the past—is perhaps a denatured form of piety.[9] 'Religious worlds,' writes Greg Dening, 'are full of contradictions . . . The problem for religious believers is how to sustain the contradictions, how to transform everyday experience into the "really-real". Clearly it only happens in sign and symbol, where action, gesture, artefacts are seen as pointing to something else.'[10] It is, we may argue, when the contradictions become overwhelming and the 'something else' recedes from view that artefacts cease to be symbols and become 'heritage'. Even in this apparently inert form, however, they do not entirely lose their power, even if it is only the power to reinforce a sense of the void left by their transformation.

In several recent novels the ruined, threatened or uprooted church becomes a powerful metaphor of the postmodern condition. It was the spectacle of a small timber church, much like the one at Healesville, being floated on a raft down the Bellinger River in northern New South Wales that provided novelist Peter Carey with the seed of his book, *Oscar and Lucinda*, and the fantastical project of its clergyman-hero to transport a glass church into the Outback. Towards the end of the story, the novelist meditates on the site beside the Bellinger River where Oscar's church had once stood.

After one hundred and twenty years this church, the one in which my mother sang 'Holy, Holy, Holy', the one of which my father was so jealous, the one my great-grandfather assembled, shining clear, like heaven itself, on the Bellinger River, this church has been carted away. It was not of any use.

Where it stood last Christmas there is now a bare patch of earth which is joined to the kikuyu grass by two great wheel ruts where the low loader was temporarily bogged. There are sixteen banks of old cinema chairs which had lately served as pews for the small congregation. But there is no sign of anything the church meant to us: Palm Sundays, resurrections, water into wine, loaves into fishes, all those cruel and lofty ideas that Oscar, gaunt, sunburnt, his eyes rimmed with white, brought up the river in 1865.

There are thistles everywhere. They are small and flat now, like prickly sunbathers, but by the end of summer they will be three feet tall, and they will be thickest beside the short fat stumps where the church has stood. No one will slash them because the ground belongs to the church and the church is not there.[11]

The church is a kind of absent presence: a site now unoccupied but irreplaceable and unable to be rebuilt.

In Penelope Lively's novel *Judgement Day*, the heroine, Clare Paling, a young middle-class wife and mother, finds herself drawn—rather like Healesville's Mrs Firth—into the campaign to save the parish church of Laddenham, a rapidly suburbanising village on the outskirts of London. Clare is an agnostic, but a keen student of architecture. 'Interest in ecclesiastical architecture,' she reminds the vicar, George Radwell, 'is not restricted to Christians. And infrequent amongst them, I've noticed.' She joins the committee of the Church Restoration Appeal, where she attempts to administer a strong dose of economic realism to the proceedings. 'We've got to think of what the church has got that people might feel they wanted to do something for,' she observes. 'And what the church has got is age. It's a very old building. And old buildings are well-regarded at the moment. They have a scarcity value.'

In the course of the novel, however, Clare's view of the historical significance of the church is challenged and changed. The turning point comes when a gang of bikies invade the church and desecrate it. In the aftermath of the outrage, the rather ineffectual vicar turns to her accusingly: 'You go into the church and all you see is carvings and different kinds of window, you might as well be in an art gallery. Or a museum. There's more to it than that.' 'I know,' she replies. On the nature of that something 'more' both Clare and the novelist are silent. What the experience has left is not a sense of illumination but an awareness of the lack of it. 'The trouble with people like me,' she admits. 'is not so much that we've got all the answers as that we are incapable of suspending disbelief.'[12]

Resurrection

Heritage is, among other things, the attempt of a post-Christian society to hold to the sense of transcendence and spiritual continuity represented in symbolically important buildings such as churches and war memorials. That is why the spectacle of a ruined church—its spire fallen, its stained-glass windows broken, its pulpit upturned—is so disquieting and why local communities often try so hard to stave it off.

Conservationists offer an appealing solution to this dilemma: disused churches may be 'resurrected' through 'sympathetic' adaptation to new uses. Even though the congregation has departed, the old church may live on as the home of another denomination, or as a house, an artist's studio, a concert hall or a museum. Driving around the suburbs or the countryside, one comes across many 'resurrected' church buildings. Sometimes an old Presbyterian or Methodist church has become the home of a thriving new congregation of Baptists, Pentecostalists or Greek Orthodox. But there are limits to this, perhaps the most sympathetic, form of adaptation simply because the number of new churches being founded is not large enough to absorb the number of old church buildings being closed. Almost eighty Anglican churches in the Diocese of Sydney have been closed over the past twenty years, but only a quarter were sold to other denominations, fewer than those that were demolished.[13]

Sometimes, a church can be used for other spiritual or cultural purposes. In Burwood, a Melbourne suburb, where two Uniting churches faced each other across Warrigal Road, the old Methodist building has become an undertaker's chapel. In Hawthorn, Box Hill and Richmond old churches have been converted to community theatres. In the countryside, some smaller churches have become artists' studios, restaurants, bookshops or weekend cottages.

How much adaptation is consistent with the aims of preservation? William Morris, the nineteenth century English designer and Socialist critic whose Society for the Protection of Ancient Buildings may be regarded as the fountainhead of the modern preservation move-

ment, took a hard line against the adaptation or restoration of medieval churches. 'The real, the essential
purpose . . . of our old buildings,' Morris declared, 'is
to be instructive relics of the past art and past manners
of life. If you can do so, *without altering* them or
making shams of them, use them for ecclesiastical, civic
or domestic purposes . . . That is the best way of
preserving them.'[14] What was not permissible, in Morris's view, was to alter the buildings in ways that
obliterated past 'manners of life' or defaced the crafts-
manship of their makers.

Modern conservation architects often take a more
flexible view. A British advocate of adaptive reuse cited
some convenient historical precedents. In medieval
times, when the church was usually the largest building
in the village, it was not unusual, he noted, for it to
be used for eating and drinking at weddings and funer-
als, dancing on church festivals and stalls on market
days.[15] An Australian architect, planning to convert a
partially demolished church into an office complex,
took a more radical theological approach: the fact that
the church could no longer be properly restored proved
that 'God no longer wants it as a church'.[16]

Yet, as William Morris implied, it is possible to
preserve a church, but in circumstances that undermine
the very purpose for which it was saved. Bairnsdale's
old Methodist church has now become a fish cafe while
Cranbourne's is 'The Heavenly Pizza'. Ballarat's lovely
Baptist church has become the 'Power House' disco, its
interior lit by strobe lights and its sunken baptismal
font a fish tank.[17] In Salem, Massachusetts, the former
Unitarian church has become a Witch Museum while
in Richmond, Maine, a Congregational church is hired
out to all-comers, from the Russian Orthodox church
and African drummers to midwives with a slide show

on underwater birth.[18] When the original religious and historical significance of the building is obliterated, preservation risks becoming a 'sham', and one is inclined to ask whether the building should not have been allowed to pass quietly away rather than 'resurrected' by such heroic, but culturally insensitive, measures.

In Montreal an atheist professor of architecture and a Christian minister joined forces to protest against the conversion of a former Presbyterian church into a condominium, *les jardins de l'église*. 'Sacrilege', 'prostitution' and 'perversion' were some of the words they used to describe the result. 'To use the facade of a church to lend unusual character to a building in use for purely secular purposes is not right,' the minister protested. 'If compromise can't be reached to perpetuate the original intention, at least in part . . . it were better taken down.'[19] Not everyone will agree with him: from a purely architectural point of view, it may seem more important to preserve a fragment of the original building than none at all. Postmodernists may go further, arguing that, in a culture characterised by fragmentation and parody, a cabaret in a church is no more objectionable than an apartment in a warehouse or a shot-tower in a shopping arcade.

In deciding the fate of their historic churches communities are testing the limits of the idea of heritage. Heritage, in Justice Hope's words, is 'the things we keep'. But in keeping them we aim to conserve something more than the things themselves. It is here perhaps that the aims of historic preservation come into conflict with those of history and even, in its original sense, with heritage. Because churches have traditionally represented the deepest and most enduring of human ties, their preservation seems imperative; yet it can also be self-defeating, if the ideals that once animated the building are erased. 'Unless the Lord build the house, they labour in vain that build it,' declared the psalmist. Something like the same principle applies to historic conservation: for once a church (or any other building) is removed from its original use, even if it is little altered physically, it becomes something else. Occasionally, it may become something more, as new chapters are added to its story; but sometimes, we must admit, preservation—the physical retention of the building—results in something less, a diminution or distortion of cultural significance. It is then, reluctantly but resolutely, that we must allow it the dignity of a quiet demise.

chapter nine

Living history: Touring the Australian past

F OR MANY AUSTRALIANS the past is not a straitjacket but a sanctuary. The antiquary, says Nietzsche, 'migrates into the past and makes his secret nest there'. There can surely never have been a moment in Australian history when the physical remnants of the past have been so prized. Collecting old stuff—old bottles, old postcards, old furniture, old clocks, old bricks—is a popular pastime and sustains a major growth industry. The more standardised, mass-produced commodities we ourselves produce and consume, the more we hanker after the handmade, durable wares of our forebears. If, as Marx alleged, industrialism induced 'the fetishism of commodities', postindustrialism has created the 'fetishism of antiquities'.

Collecting old stuff is a collective as well as an individual pastime. There are now more than 300 small museums in Victoria and comparable numbers in other states.[1] Every small struggling town sets aside an old shop, courthouse or mechanics' institute as a repository for its discarded household utensils, farm machinery and costumes. Like the local historical society, under whose aegis it is often founded, the small museum is usually dominated by an inner circle of community elders who jealously guard the collections and the tribal memories that go with them. Local museums are often symptoms of community decline. In Victoria the museum movement emerged first, and is still strongest, in the dying towns of the central goldfields where local councillors hoped to turn redundant buildings and discarded machinery into tourist dollars. This was always an idle hope and most attract no more than a trickle of visitors on the one or two afternoons they open. The real value of the museum is to the locals themselves for whom it offers tangible evidence of their community's better days.[2]

Five minutes off the Hume Highway and twenty from the NSW border is the old mining town of Chiltern. The young Henry Handel Richardson once lived here and the house, Lake View, is now a museum dedicated to her memory. Nostalgia has taken over the town's main street: there are shops selling old furniture, old jewellery, old books, even old radios and old electric jugs. The former Bank of Australasia dispenses bed-and-breakfast and old-fashioned afternoon teas while the former bank of New South Wales, now a craft shop, displays a colourful embroidered scene of the main street in its heyday. The Grape Vine Hotel, famous for its lovely courtyard and ancient grapevine, closed in the 1950s and is now a private museum run by the antique shop next door. Next door, the Chiltern Atheneum, a relic of the town's once vigorous culture of working class self-improvement, is a museum run by a little team of volunteers from the local historical society. They are getting older and fewer, explains the man on the door, a retired farmer, although they still have plans to buy the CFA store next door to accommodate their ever-expanding collection.

The Atheneum's transformation from a living institution to a museum has been a gradual one. New historical exhibits have slowly filled up the pleasant little auditorium, but without displacing the glass-fronted bookshelves of the old Atheneum; faded copies of Macaulay, Carlyle and Tolstoy, now securely locked away from thieves and borrowers alike, testify still to the old Chiltern's thirst for knowledge and the printed word. Where they have always been, facing visitors as they enter, are the portraits of Queen Victoria, the Union Jack and the honour board recording the names of Chiltern's sons who enlisted in the Great War. Crushed in between, in no apparent order, are cabinets of local curiosities—cups and trophies, old photographs, Aboriginal weapons, illuminated addresses, pots and pans, embroideries, old bottles, and cuttings from the local newspaper recording notable events, like the day in 1943 when a Wirraway fighter made a crash landing into Sister Carter's house. Chiltern's museum is an abomination to the modern museologist. It has no discernible themes, the handwritten captions are amateurish and little attention is paid to chronology, context or interpretation.

And that, perhaps, is its charm. Unlike the earnest former members of the Atheneum, the tourists who pull off the Hume for Devonshire tea and half an hour's browsing along Chiltern's main street are not in search of knowledge so much as romance. 'Very interesting,' is the standard but rather non-committal comment in the visitors' book. 'Well done', 'well laid out', 'well presented', 'thank you for keeping our heritage', say others, offering a kindly pat on the back to the volunteer curators. What the visitors find 'interesting', so far as one can tell, is the sense of being immersed in the past rather than being informed about it. 'Interesting and nostalgic', 'great nostalgia', 'took me back in time, I love it', 'a pleasure to journey back in time' are some of the more expansive remarks.

'Nostalgia,' David Lowenthal reminds us, is 'the universal catch-word for looking back.'[3] It once meant homesickness, but the place to which we long to return is no longer in the present but in the past. Old things, like the miscellaneous exhibits in Chiltern's Atheneum, trigger the memories that connect us to past times, or they may evoke a past that is imagined with the aid of television images rather than directly remembered.

Consider, for example, the picture of the Australian past purveyed in the many popular coffee-table books and glossy photo histories that weigh down the sales tables of suburban bookshops. Pop history, like video history, specialises in the careful recreation of a style, or veneer, of the past, leaving its human significance to be filled in by the reader. The message, once decoded, however, often turns out to be one of uncritical nostalgia. The pop historian views the past in soft focus through a sepia filter, looking back to a day when people were more virtuous and when society was simpler and more unified. An early specimen of the genre, John Larkin and Bruce Howard's *The Great Australian Book of Nostalgia* (1975), begins with a candid statement of their social message:

Nostalgia is the kingdom lying somewhere in the tranquil valley of our minds. A place where the girls were softer, the men more manly, the kisses sweeter, the sunshine warmer, and the river gums smelled sharper after the January showers. Nostalgia is the intimate refuge of every man and every woman in a world seemingly gone mad. George Orwell's *1984* is but a few seasons away and man has the capacity to blow his own habitat off its axis. We recognise this and are apprehensive. And we slip away to the realms of nostalgic fantasy.[4]

Larkin and Howard knew that their collection of old photos, advertisements and bric-a-brac was a 'fantasy', but in other books the boundary between fact and fantasy, history and nostalgia, is less candidly acknowledged. In Stephen Brooke's *Life was Simple Then* (1983), the sharp black-and-white images of a horse-and-buggy rural Australia conjure up a lost world in which moral and political choices were also sharper and clearer. 'In those days,' Brooke writes,

> most things of importance were judged in very black-and-white terms—issues were right or wrong, good or bad, and no-one was compelled to think in terms of grey areas. This led to an almost child-like acceptance of the principles of God, King (or Queen) and Empire, that all policemen were honest [the book is published in Sydney!] and that the father—the bread winner—was the undisputed head of the household.[5]

The captions of *Life was Simple Then* seldom indicate precise dates or places; they present only a generalised 'then' and 'now', the good old days and our own sordid present. The picture-historians recycle a limited repertoire of stock pioneer images—the 'stalwart settler' beside his bark hut, the bullocky and his strong team, the lone prospector and the poor, but united, pioneer family.

Pioneer villages and folk museums

These frozen black-and-white images are brought vividly to life in the 'pioneer villages' and 'folk museums' which now punctuate the tourist routes of inland Australia almost as regularly as the memorial cairns erected

by an earlier generation of historians. Like the historical
society museums, the folk museums usually began as a
repository for historical artefacts and buildings from
the surrounding locality. In their early days, the dating
and interpretation of these objects was often rudimen-
tary—like the pop historians, their creators worked
within a simplified historical framework of 'then' and
'now'—and the vision of pioneer Australia that they
presented to the visitors was purged of disturbing social
and political conflicts. The people of the pioneer village
worshipped at the one church, sent their children to
the only school-house and lived frugal but happy lives
in slab pioneer cottages.

Swan Hill's Pioneer Settlement, founded in the
1960s, was among the first of Australia's so-called folk
museums. Like the small local museum it was devoted
to the collection and display of objects of historical
interest from the surrounding locality, but instead of
putting them on shelves or locking them in glass cases
it displayed them in an authentically recreated rural
setting. The Pigott Committee, reviewing Australia's
museums in 1974–75, commended Swan Hill's founders
for their pioneering enterprise but was troubled by its
'unsystematic' approach to collection and display,
though randomness, it admitted, also had its rewards.[6]
Since the 1960s Swan Hill has been joined by dozens
of imitators: Korrumburra has its Coal Creek Historical
Village, Moe has Old Gippstown, Jeparit has its Mallee-
Wimmera Historical Museum. Far away in outback
Queensland, Winton has its 'Qantilda Centre', dedicated to the town's links with the pioneer Qantas
(Queensland and Northern Territory Aerial Service)
airline and to Banjo Paterson's famous song 'Waltzing
Matilda', first publicly performed in the North Gregory
Hotel just across the road.

Living history

The folk museums appealed strongly to the antiquarian's nostalgic identification with things of the past.
Historical theme parks and 'living history' museums
sought to enhance that experience by enabling their
visitors imaginatively to re-enter the past. 'A visit to
Sovereign Hill can be more than just a pleasant day's
outing,' its guidebook promises; 'it can become an
intriguing expedition into a living past where the excitement of heady gold rush days can still be felt in the
air.'[7] 'Experience', 'participate', 'interact', 'hands-on'—
these are the key words of the 'living history' approach.
Like its famous American counterparts in Colonial
Williamsburg and Plimoth Plantation, Sovereign Hill
aims to transport the visitor into a past made tangible
through authentically reconstructed buildings and
objects, and peopled by authentically costumed 'diggers'
and 'diggeresses' who play out the everyday dramas of
their society. It is a theatre without walls in which
patrons and museum staff conspire in an elaborate
game of historical make-believe.[8]

The Ballarat citizens who conceived Sovereign Hill
in the late 1960s were inspired by something very like
Nietzsche's monumental sense of history. Their 'primary
object' was 'to provide for present and future generations a worthy visual reminder of the lives and work
of the men and women who, in the many fields of
endeavour, pioneered and developed this great city'.[9]
Ballarat was not wanting in monuments but by the
1960s there was a feeling, perhaps, that bronze and
stone were not equal to the challenge of inducting a
new television generation into the pioneer tradition.
There was also a secondary, and increasingly important,
aim: to secure the town's economic future by the cre-

ation of 'one of the great tourist attractions' in the state.

Since its foundation, Sovereign Hill's manager and curators have skilfully balanced these educational and commercial objectives. They are justifiably proud of the historical skill and technical ingenuity behind their reconstructed buildings and landscapes. In the 1960s when the project got under way, Weston Bate was researching the first volume of his history of Ballarat, *Lucky City*, and Main Street, the nucleus of Sovereign Hill, drew on his detailed reconstruction of the town's main street which achieved literary form in the chapter 'Main Street Heyday'.[10] Over the succeeding years, the interpretative emphasis has gradually shifted, from 1850s Ballarat to the broader mining experience, from the techniques of mining to the workings of society, and from accurate reconstruction to a more vivid re-enactment.[11]

Sovereign Hill's historical staff are conscious of the need to avoid the nostalgic, consensual vision of the 'pioneer village'. The storylines given to the volunteer guides who help to 'activate' the setting may include reference to the hardships and hazards of life on the goldfields. Yet high staffing costs and the customers' notion of a happy family outing severely circumscribe the kind of 'living past' that the visitors enter. Australians are more reluctant than Americans to engage in the uninhibited dressing-up and play-acting that go with 'living history', although they unbend more readily than the Japanese and Chinese tourists who tend to steer clear of the dirt and mess of the diggings and head straight for the souvenir shops along Main Street. The truth, of course, is that the goldfields of the 1850s were a noisy, dirty and insanitary environment where large numbers of people—mainly young working-class men—toiled incessantly under conditions that no modern unionist or health inspector would tolerate for a moment. The reconstructed goldfields of Sovereign Hill are necessarily quieter, cleaner and more orderly. The handful of young men in spotless dungarees and red neckerchiefs who drive the gold escort are far outnumbered by the middle-class matrons in crinolines and bonnets who form the nucleus of the park's band of volunteer guides. Sovereign Hill is a pleasure resort rather than a real mining town. It has many shopkeepers but few miners, several entertainers but no prostitutes, a picturesque school-house but no undertaker.

Sovereign Hill embodies the belief that by experiencing an authentically reconstructed historical environment we are able to relive the past. Authenticity is something that most museum visitors prize. Four-fifths of the visitors to three South Australian social history museums agreed that 'museums should tell what life was really like in the past'. They should focus on 'the lives of ordinary people' rather than 'famous people or events'. A museum might reinforce a sense of national or local pride, many visitors thought, but they were more reserved about museums that were too escapist or too challenging.[12] Showing 'what life was really like in the past', however, did not necessarily require the museum to be 'full of old and interesting objects', since many of those who wanted it to achieve the first did not want the second. In a television age, the primary signifiers of historical authenticity may not be intrinsic—the antiquity of the objects on display—but experiential—the success of the museum in evoking for its patrons the look and feel of the past.

From the viewpoint of the visitor, 'realism' or 'authenticity' is something that can only be judged by its effects. Making things seem real may require a good

deal of contrivance behind the scenes. As Umberto Eco
has noted, the distinction between the real and what
he calls the 'hyper-real' becomes increasingly blurred in
contemporary culture. The tourist is constantly challenged to spot the difference between the 'Almost Real'
and the 'Absolute Fake'—and in the end may not care.[13]
Recreating the past calls for the very latest in high-tech
electronics. Yet in 'living history' more can sometimes
be less, for the more the past is simulated with
cinematic images or animatronics, the less scope there
is for the visitors to exercise their own imagination.
In its latest and most successful exhibition, 'Blood on
the Southern Cross', Sovereign Hill has taken a step
away from the cinematic approach by activating the
nocturnal vista of mines, tents, flagpoles and commis-
sioner's camp through a spectacular sound-and-light
dramatisation of the Eureka story. 'The magic of a
sound-and-light experience lies in the fact there are no
actors,' the program explains. 'It is your imagination,
with the help of clever sound effects and lighting techniques, that makes the story live.'[14] By emphasising the
imagination of the visitor, rather than the ingenuity of
the museologist, 'Blood on the Southern Cross' has
taken an important step away from the notion that
history is a set of facts to be presented and towards
the idea, now current among historians, that it is
something constructed by the reader or viewer.

'Blood on the Southern Cross' makes an instructive
comparison with Ballarat's newest museum, the newly
opened Eureka Interpretation Centre, close to the site
of the rebellion itself. Few museums in Australia have
been born amid such controversy. For months the columns of the *Ballarat Courier* were filled with articles
and letters about the authentic site of the rebellion,
whether the Eureka flag, now in the Ballarat Art

Gallery, should be displayed in the new centre, and especially about how the event itself should be presented. Local Liberal MP Tom Evans, Chancellor of the University of Ballarat Geoffrey Blainey, historian of Ballarat Weston Bate, and historian of Eureka John Molony all became embroiled in the controversy. Central to the row was the expectation of some of the museum's sponsors that the new museum should present an authentic and complete account of the event, not simply a collage of interpretations. 'It must leave the visitor with no questions unanswered,' declared Victorian premier Jeff Kennett at its opening. 'I'd like them to go away with a whole lot of questions,' the historian and manager of the centre Jan Penney responded.[15]

The museum itself skilfully negotiates this dilemma. It reinforces the heroic, even mythic, character of the event with three-times-life-size statues of Peter Lalor and his fellow rebels, blow-ups of Vic O'Connor's and Noel Counihan's stylised black-and-white etchings, and stirring sound and video re-enactments of the most dramatic moments of the episode. But it also provides materials for a more critical reading of the event—a film in which historians debate the causes and consequences of the rebellion and a Hall of Debate, set up like a miniature courtroom, in which visiting school children can deliver their own verdict.

Time travel and tourism

Time travel remains the sustaining fiction of the living history museum. If 'the past is a foreign country' then it must be possible to visit it, and there will be someone only too willing to sell you a ticket. Being able to think of time in this way, as somehow analogous to space, is itself a relatively new phenomenon and some scholars relate it to the abrupt shifts in time–space consciousness that have occurred since the 1970s.[16] The fiction of time travel resonates with that other kind of travel in which most museum visitors are themselves engaged: tourism. We can more easily imagine visiting the past when we are ourselves dressed up in our holiday clothes and ready to go somewhere.

In Australia the idea of time travel connects with other real or metaphorical journeys—the experience of migration, for example, or the journey to the Centre, or perhaps the Great Voyage which, as I argue in Chapter 4, has become the central metaphor of national becoming. Visitors enter Sovereign Hill through 'Voyage to Discovery', a series of dioramas and soundscapes evoking the gold-seekers' passage from the streets of London, their life aboard a crowded immigrant ship, their disembarkation on the Melbourne wharf, and their tramp along the road to the goldfields. At last, they pass through an underground tunnel and emerge amidst the din and frenzied activity of the Red Hill diggings.

The film-set world of Main Street and the diggings is introduced and authenticated by the multiple screen presentations and video displays of 'Voyage to Discovery'. It is as though the past has to be 'seen on TV'—the imaginative gateway to the larger world—before it can be experienced at first hand. In the introductory multi-screen show, 'The Golden Days', sponsored by the mining industry, the theme park becomes the set for a goldfields mini-drama. Two themes—multiculturalism and material advancement—dominate the narrative. A group of young fortune-seekers—English, Scots, Cornish and Irish—brave the physical and financial hazards of the goldrush. Some of their friends and relatives are killed or ruined along the way but by 1861 the young friends, and Ballarat itself, have become rich. The 'Voyage to Discovery' has a happy ending. It is a fable that simultaneously recapitulates the mythology of the 1850s and reinforces the commercial sponsor's message.

Living history promises to transport the visitor into the past. But the illusion is never complete, if only because the illusionists also want the visitors to be impressed with the technical skill by which it is done. At Plimoth Plantation, the recreation of the Pilgrim Fathers' first settlement in New England, visitors enter the village through a display showing how each element of the village has been recreated. At Sovereign Hill visitors watch a video in which the Director Peter Hiscock describes the 'painstaking research' required to produce 'an accurate picture of the past'. The souvenir program for 'Blood on the Southern Cross' looks 'Behind the Scenes' to describe the 17 channels of multiphonic sound, 400 main light sources and 1000 peripheral lights that make it happen. Technique is both the means to creating the show and a sideshow in its own right.

Sometimes technique can so dazzle the visitor that it becomes the main show. Beside the Hume Highway at Glenrowan an eight-metre fibreglass statue of Ned Kelly, in helmet and armour, bails up the tourist buses outside 'Australia's First Computerised Live Theatre'. Inside, beyond the 'authentic replicas' of Kelly armour, and the sales tables of Ned Kelly souvenir tea towels, key rings, T-shirts and ashtrays, the visitors enter an electronic recreation of the famous outlaw's last stand. The show is the brainchild of Bob Hempel, a former Footscray footballer and car salesman, inspired by the commercial success of Queensland's 'Big Pineapple', the movies of Cecil B. De Mille and the technology of Disneyworld. Like other living history museums, 'Ned

Kelly's Last Stand' employs a time-travel device, this time in the form of a life-size animatronic 'magician' who transports visitors back to the year 1880. As they move from room to room, the audience witnesses the Kelly drama unfold—from the carousing in Ann Jones Inn to the shoot-out at Glenrowan and from the simulated burning (by propane gas) of the hotel down to the last dramatic act at Melbourne Gaol. 'Come and see Ned Kelly hang in our newly completed animated computerised Hanging Room' invite the posters outside. In 'Kelly's Last Stand', it is the workings of the life-size computerised marionettes rather than the human story of the outlaw that captures the audience's imagination. The past has become another fantasy land—as far away, as inconsequential and yet as seductive as the world of Nintendo and *Star Wars*.

The past, historians must humbly concede, is only one of the many exotic locations luring the modern tourist, and the success of living history museums is governed more by the vicissitudes of international travel than the historical authenticity of the exhibits. There are ominous signs that the days of the small Australian folk museums may be numbered. Swan Hill Folk Museum, the first of Victoria's small folk museums, once attracted more than 200 000 visitors a year but the busloads of pensioners who once made the trip up from Melbourne to play the pokies on the other side of the Murray now flock to Melbourne's new Crown casino. Other small museums like Coaltown and Old Gippstown open only irregularly with a skeleton staff. Even Sovereign Hill, the most successful of Australian theme parks, experienced a brief downturn after the opening of Melbourne's Crown Casino in the early 1990s. But it took stock, planned some exciting new attractions and made a vigorous marketing push into Asia.

International visitors, mainly Chinese, now comprise over a quarter of Sovereign Hill's patrons. After they leave their buses, they are conducted through the 'Voyage to Discovery' and the Chinese Camp to a 'secret chamber' off the long tunnel mine. There they view a brand new sound-and-light show dramatising—in Mandarin and Cantonese—the adventures of Chin Tem, a Chinese fortune-seeker who travels from Canton to Victoria's 'New Gold Mountain'. The links between Ballarat and Canton were once strong and some of the visitors may even be descendants, or kin, of earlier Chinese immigrants to Australia. But these new travellers come not to seek wealth but to spend it and Ballarat, which once shunned the Chinese, now eagerly solicits their patronage. In the world of global tourism, the futures we anticipate may be the pasts our forebears once sought to escape.

Every day during the holiday season tens of thousands of tourists stop at Glenrowan. But these days it is not the scene of the famous bushranger's last stand that they have stopped to see. The Hume Highway now skirts the old town of Glenrowan and only a trickle of tourists pull off to visit its little tourist strip. Kate Kelly's Tea House looks wanly across the bitumen towards Ned Kelly's Fully Licensed Bistro, while along the street 'Lazy Harry' grinds out yet another electronic rendition of the 'The Wild Colonial Boy'. Bob Hempel, 'Head Dreamer' of Kelly's Last Stand, may be ruing his $1.5 million investment. 'What are you doing in Glenrowan?' a sign on his museum asks the 'visitors and tourist coaches', in a tone that Ned himself might have used.

It is absolutely absurd that after allowing yourself 10 to 20 minutes to take photos, walk up and down the street, buy some souvenirs then leave and tell your friends—'Don't go to Glenrowan, for there is nothing to see'. To be quite honest most visitors to Glenrowan wouldn't know if the country shithouse fell on them. What we are telling you, is to snap out of your preconceived ideas and go and see this magnificent show. If you have a friend who turns out to be a pain in the neck and does not wish to go don't let them spoil your day!

The new Glenrowan, a concrete island of petrol pumps and fast food outlets, is the only stop on the high-speed highway that now stretches all the way from Melbourne to the border. Five minutes and the car is refuelled. The kids are back inside and happily munching their Big Macs and french fries. Soon they will be in the big city, ready for the real holiday. Marooned from that nourishing stream of tourists, Ned Kelly's Last Stand could be Bob Hempel's too.

chapter ten

'A neglected history': Has school history lost the plot?

J UST OVER A century ago a young Australian patriot, failed matriculation candidate and rising poet complained about the teaching of history in Australian schools. Not one in ten of the pupils in the public schools of New South Wales, Henry Lawson alleged, was acquainted with a single historical fact about Australia. Upper-class schoolboys might be able to recite the names of English monarchs but the main events of Australian history—Captain Cook's discovery, the Black Wars, the Eureka Stockade—were entirely unknown to them. One of the few redeeming features of the Centennial Celebrations of 1888 was that, for all the chauvinism and junketing, they had at least set some of the elementary facts of the nation's history before its young people.[1]

A hundred years later patriots are still deploring the lack of historical knowledge among the young. In 1993 a survey conducted by the Civics Expert Group appointed by the Keating government revealed a worrying level of ignorance of the country's constitution and history. 'History is dying in our schools,' a young history lecturer observed a year later. In 1972, Adrian Jones noted, almost three in five final year students in

Victoria took a history subject but by 1995 it was less than one in ten. In New South Wales the situation was almost as bad.

> We are becoming a spiritually impoverished folk. Our students are offered no dreaming. Our prospective citizens are never exposed to any systematic tellings of the history of Australia and Australians.[2]

For more than a century history—often more forgotten than remembered—had been the educational foundation of Australian nationalism. But now those foundations had been disturbed. Aborigines could look back proudly on an ancient past but white children, it seemed, had no dreaming and newcomers would learn none.

Neglect of the nation's history has been a perennial complaint of history teachers, and in the 1990s their concern reached a crescendo. But the historians who identified the problem were more adept at finding culprits than coherent explanations for history's decline. Some blamed the schoolteachers who had misguidedly applied the methods of tertiary history, where students concentrate on theoretical questions of how the past can be known, to the secondary schoolroom where students have to acquire a working map of the past before they can seriously investigate it. Others blamed the university historians who purveyed these unsettling theories of knowledge, and the forms of political disenchantment that sometimes went with them. Educational bureaucrats also came in for a lot of the blame, especially for the recent national 'Studies in Society and Environment' (SOES) curriculum which treats history only under the constricting rubric of 'Time, Continuity and Change' and then with only marginal attention to societies other than Australia.

Parents, understandably anxious for their children's futures, employers insistent on the need for vocational skills, and school principals trying to stretch shrinking school budgets have also been blamed for marginalising allegedly 'non-vocational' subjects like history.

A few observers, less fixed on blame, have pondered the influence of more elusive cultural forces. National history had originated as a secularised form of biblical 'salvation history'—but children reared in an entirely secular environment perhaps no longer took for granted the assumption, fundamental to the Judaeo-Christian tradition, that identity was discovered through the telling of stories. Television, the most powerful cultural force in their lives, had slowly undermined the habit of reading, while the computer had introduced forms of organising knowledge, such as the Internet and hypertext, that were radically subversive of the linear narrative.[3]

It is strange, at first sight, that history should have slumped in the schools just when family history, heritage, local history and other kinds of popular history were booming in the rest of the community. Once it had been the other way about: a generation or two ago history was considered something that children ought to learn but which they might safely forget once school was over. Now, it seemed, Mum and Dad were urging their offspring to forsake history for computer studies at the very moment when they were taking up genealogy themselves. Once a compulsory study for the young, history had now seemingly become a recreational activity of the middle-aged and old.

Obviously, the role of history in the school curriculum has changed radically since Henry Lawson's day. Indeed, it has changed a good deal even in the twenty years or so since I took my own first school history lesson, introducing the young Latvian, Polish and Hungarian immigrants of Form 4D at St Alban's High School to the mysteries of the squatting system. The present crisis in school history is not a sudden arrival, even if the steep fall in student enrolments that dramatised it is relatively recent. It is the most recent passage in a long conversation between historians and educators in which the meanings of both history and education have changed strikingly over the years. To understand how history got into its present parlous condition we need to understand the forces that got us there. One vivid index of those changes has been the school history textbook—until recently the main vehicle by which changes in educational and historical thinking were translated into classroom practice. By reviewing history textbooks over the past 100 years we can tune into the changing terms of that debate.

Henry Lawson was a man ahead of his time in insisting on the teaching of Australian history but his conception of history, and of its educational value, reflected the nineteenth century idea of education as a 'putting in' of knowledge rather than a 'drawing out' of understanding. History, as he and his contemporaries saw it, was essentially a storehouse of moral and political examples. By portraying the heroes and heroines of the past, the history teacher established standards of morality and instilled a love of the country in whose defence the heroes and heroines had carried out their deeds of courage, self-sacrifice and honour. Lawson's complaint was that the heroes and heroines were English rather than Australian; he did not dispute the assumption that the history teacher's main role was to teach morality, instil patriotism and reinforce a sense of national progress.

Heroes and heroines, valiant deeds and notable

events continued to dominate many Australian text-books up to the Great War and even beyond. Often the heroes were British and their deeds were remote in time and place from young Australians' experience. *Deeds that Won the Empire* (1898), the bestselling textbook by Rev. W.H. Fitchett, headmaster of the Methodist Ladies College, recounted British feats of arms in the Napoleonic Wars. 'The tales here told,' he explained, 'are written, not to glorify war, but to nourish patriotism.' The history of the Empire was a treasure 'strangely neglected' in the country's schools: heroic daring, loyalty and honour and love of country were 'the elements of a robust patriotism'.[4]

Any child brought up in the Australian school system before the Second World War is likely to remember more about the exploits of Nelson and Wellington, Clive of India and Gordon of Khartoum than of Arthur Phillip or Henry Parkes. Australia's past was largely bereft of the martial deeds that were the conventional focus of patriotic history, but educationalists viewed the history of exploration and discovery, in which brave men battled a hostile environment instead of hostile Frenchmen or Afghan tribesmen, as a potential substitute. The Fink Royal Commission, which reported on the state of Victorian education in 1898, had recommended that more space be devoted to the teaching of Australian history and geography and had recommended the stories of the explorers as a suitable vehicle. The first textbooks dealing with Australian history—such as Ernest Scott's *Short History of Australia* or George Arnold Wood's *The Voyage of the Endeavour*—emphasised the heroic contribution of great men (and occasionally great women—Caroline Chisholm, for example) to the story of national progress.[5] As British children learned to admire the valour of Drake and

Nelson so young Australians were taught to honour the explorers and pioneers. Their teachers joined the movements to inaugurate 'foundation' and 'discovery' days, and to mark the passage of the explorers across the land with cairns and obelisks.[6] These became the shrines and saints' days of a secular state school system.

In the 1960s and 1970s it became common to question the teaching of patriotism: a society divided over the Vietnam War was wary of the dangers of bringing politics into the classroom. It has taken us another generation to perceive the equal danger of rearing children without an informed sense of citizenship and the role models to instil it. The pedagogy of the first generation of Australian nationalists embodied a heroic, progressive view of history which reflected an individualistic and optimistic view of human nature. Ours, by contrast, is a more sceptical and ironic standpoint. The search for heroes may be a preoccupation of the popular press, as I argue in Chapter 2, but it is the endurance of the common man or woman, rather than the triumph of the exceptional ones, that has become the dominant strain of school history. A seldom considered result of the percolation of the 'new' social history from the universities to the schools may have been to inculcate what the sociologist Dennis Wrong once called an 'oversocialized conception of man'. In stressing social influences—the power of gender, race and class—does the history teacher unwittingly reinforce a sense of victimhood rather than a determination to overcome them?

Adolescence, our educational psychology lecturers used to tell us, is a time of life when hero- or heroine-worship is strong. My own first interest in history was kindled by reading about the lives of boyhood heroes— Louis Fischer's life of Gandhi and George Seaver's life of Albert Schweitzer, for example. Inevitably, of course, I discovered that these idols had feet of clay but biography was a gentle corrective to idealism—less likely, it might be argued, to produce the fatalism or cynicism that may too easily spring from a deterministic social history. In her perceptive review of American history textbooks, *America Revised*, Frances FitzGerald observes that many of the new radically inspired social studies courses of the 1970s had effects quite opposite to those intended, reinforcing rather than breaking down the social gulf between rich and poor, black and white. 'We know we're the ones who get the good end of the deal,' confessed one candid white middle-class pupil. 'We talk about things we don't intend to change. Why change a situation which puts us right where we want, and other people so far away we never even need to know that they exist?' Adolescents, of course, do not cease to have heroes and heroines but they chose them from the international worlds of sport and pop music and do not necessarily expect them to be examples of moral or political conduct.[7]

From the early years of the Commonwealth progressive intellectuals had redirected history teaching to new national goals—the inculcation among young Australians of the rights and, especially, the obligations of citizenship. Teacher-educators, influenced by the ideals of the 'New Education' with its emphasis on child-centred, environmental learning and civic duty, sought to ground the child's love of country in a local and visible past. 'History,' as one of the new Victorian textbooks observed in 1903, 'is the one subject by means of which we can give instruction in citizenship.'[8] The objective, according to the 1904 NSW primary syllabus, was to 'give such an account of the past as will enable the pupil to have some insight into the present and furnish him with noble ideals of life and character upon which he may model his own'.[9] Like their counterparts in Europe and the United States, Australian progressives believed that the life of every citizen should be seen within the context of a drive for 'national efficiency'.

The generation of schoolboys raised on Fitchett's *Deeds that Won the Empire* were to undergo a bitter test of their adolescent idealism on Gallipoli and the Western Front. The history textbooks of the immediate postwar period reflect a turning away from the jingoistic ideals of Empire towards more peaceful themes. In 1919 the Victorian ALP Conference had resolved that 'no articles relating to or extolling wars, battles or heroes of past wars be printed in the State school papers or books' and in 1924, when the party won power, its Minister of Education put the policy into effect.[10] Herbert Heaton's WEA textbook *Modern European History with Special Reference to Australia* (1920) adopted a global perspective on Australian history, placing local developments in agriculture, industry and politics in the broad developmental perspective of the agricultural and industrial revolutions, and the rise of socialism and nationalism. G.V. Portus's *Australia since 1606: A History for Young Australians* (1932) also shows a striking departure from the chauvinism and unguarded optimism of its late nineteenth century counterparts. The explorers are still presented as heroes ('brave and hardy folk') but they discover a land that had been 'rather harshly treated by Nature'. 'To admit this,' Portus believed, 'does not mean that we love our motherland any the less. The love of a poor boy for his poor mother is just as beautiful and sustaining as the love of a rich boy for his rich mother.'

The interwar histories, as this passage implies,

reflected a more independent Australian nationalism yet they continued to view Australian developments in a global perspective. Portus's chapters on the Great War, for example, manage to convey in simple, vivid language something of the tragic inevitability, as well as the causal complexity, of the diplomatic crises that led to the outbreak of hostilities. The Australian part in the story is not relegated to a footnote but, unlike some later Australian textbooks, viewed separately as part of a much larger conflict.[11] In Stephen Roberts' *History of Europe*, a text that dominated the teaching of history at the upper secondary level in New South Wales for more than two decades, Britain takes a subordinate place in the wider history of Europe, a story told, however, in triumphalist vein.[12]

There is much for a present-day reader to criticise in the history textbooks of the interwar period—they are sexist (Portus dedicates his book to the succeeding generation of Australian *boys* and habitually resorts to the imagery of the sporting field: for example, trench warfare is likened to a rugger scrum); they are racist (Aborigines are treated, when they appear at all, as 'stone-age people'); they often adopt a condescending, schoolmasterly tone towards their young readers and they offer little material for active analysis or reflection. But they also display virtues, some of which are rare today. They are often simply, vividly and entertainingly written, with a strong sense of history as story. They convey a sense of Australia's place in the great global movements of history. As sound liberals, they view the past as a series of 'problems' which they present to their young readers, always conscientiously pointing out the 'pros' and 'cons'. History, wrote G.V. Portus at the end of his textbook, 'points to problems which we have to face and try to solve. The story part of history gives us pleasure. The problem part of history makes us think'.[13]

The partnership between History and Civics remained strong in Australian education until after the Second World War. The war itself forced a new attention to problems of foreign policy and political turbulence on Australia's doorstep. R.M. Crawford's *Ourselves and the Pacific* (1943) and Norman Harper's *Our Pacific Neighbours* (1953) expressed a new desire 'to establish and maintain friendly relations' with the 'unsettled region' to Australia's near north.[14] The texts themselves continued in the old problem-centred narrative tradition although the more numerous photographs (ox teams in Asian paddy fields juxtaposed with white-coated Columbo Plan students in Australian university laboratories) reflected a new awareness of the value of visual materials for the teaching of history.

As late as 1962 Victorian matriculation students studying the History of Australasia and the Pacific were asked civics-type questions designed to test their knowledge of the Australian Constitution, the White Australia Policy and Australian Trusteeship in New Guinea. In other parts of Australia the Civics tradition hung on even longer. *Australia's Heritage* (1964), a textbook designed for Queensland schools, emphasised the responsibility of the young student to carry on the traditions of technological progress, material prosperity and democratic institutions bequeathed by 'the pioneers'. A knowledge of the problems faced by the nation in the past would enable the young Australian 'to play a worthy part as an intelligent future citizen of the Australian democracy, where, thanks to the efforts of your great-grandfathers, every man can make his voice heard'.[15]

By the 1960s, however, the connection between the

responsibilities of citizenship and the problem-centred approach to history had begun to weaken. As the universities expanded and academics took a more prominent role as setters of final year examinations, history ceased to be a preparation for citizenship and became a preparation for tertiary education. The standards applied to senior school Australian history were a scaled-down version of the standards that academic historians applied to each other. Matriculation students were now required by the examiners to resolve the historical 'problems' posed in the scholarly literature (Bigge vs. Macquarie, Gipps vs. the squatters etc.). Getting good marks meant reading and distilling the latest articles in *Historical Studies*. Sixth form history teaching therefore readily turned itself into a form of cramming in which teachers and students conspired to memorise model answers to stock examination questions. G. Willis and colleagues' *Issues in Australian History* (1982), which organises the material around 'conflicting interpretations' of standard HSC topics, is one fairly benign example of the 'problem' approach. Clive French's *A Senior Student's Guide to Australian History* (1976) adopts a 'training manual' approach to the subject. With its tips on diet, exercise, sleep and study methods it addresses the young history student in much the same way as a tough old sergeant-major urging a platoon of new recruits through the obstacles on an assault course—which is what the final year of school increasingly became.[16]

Rote-learning and the training manual approach produced a natural reaction in the development of the so-called 'inquiry' or 'discovery' approach to history. The 1970s saw perhaps the most decisive shift in the teaching of history in half a century. There were several major pressures forcing this change. One was the desire of secondary teachers to emancipate their subject from the tutelage of the universities and to accommodate the distinctive needs of schoolchildren. In 1976 Ray Willis, a teacher in the Sunshine region, put this perspective starkly:

> It is fairly clear that the history of an historian is not the history of an educator. While most historians are content to delve into the past for its own sake, the history teacher should not and cannot do this.

The secondary history teachers were themselves coming under pressure from graduates in newer and supposedly 'more relevant' disciplines, especially sociology. If it was to survive in the school curriculum (especially in the middle school curriculum), it seemed likely that history would have to treat with these insistent new specialisations and perhaps settle for a segment within a program of 'liberal' or 'integrated' studies.

So far as teachers in Victoria were concerned, the high point of the 'integrated studies' and 'discovery method' approaches to school history was the conference organised around the visit of the American history educationalist, Jack Fraenkel, in 1976. The textbooks of the post-Fraenkel era look very different from their predecessors. Blackmore, Cotter and Elliott's *Australia's Two Centuries* (1977), designed for middle school pupils, is a good example of the new style. Unlike the old history as story approach, the new textbooks are broken into short gobbets of text broken up by pictures, cartoons, maps, diagrams and time-lines. Passages of authorial narrative are interspersed with real or even made-up documents, questions, suggestions for project work or imaginative writing. Unlike the old Europeancentred narrative histories, which traditionally began with the Dutch and Portugese discoveries, Blackmore, Cotter and Elliott begin their volume by asking pupils to consider the implications of an Aborigine stepping out of a jetliner and claiming possession of England. The new school histories are more frankly 'presentist' than the old. So, for example, in *Australia's Two Centuries* the First World War is presented essentially as a curtain-raiser for Vietnam. The global diplomatic issues, even the history of Gallipoli and trench warfare, recede to make way for 'The Great War Conscription Debate'.[17]

The enquiry method, with its short paragraphs and abundant questions, embraces a pedagogy arguably more appropriate to the children of the television age with their insatiable need for visual stimulus and short attention spans. But it makes it harder to ensure that students acquire a sense of the broader contours of history. Even at HSC level, and perhaps even more under the anticipated new dispensation than the old, students tend to jump, like jet-age tourists, from one exotic island of time to the next with scarcely a glance at the great tracts of time in between. In an attempt to make history digestible, the educationalists had robbed it of its single most compelling feature—the narrative.

The primary function of history in the new school curriculum was twofold: teaching the skills of independent, literate enquiry and the clarification of personal and political values. Students were encouraged to think of themselves as historians, examining, comparing sources, analysing arguments, writing up the findings. They were also encouraged to try to examine the actions of people in the past from their own vantage point. So, while in the 1960s matriculation students were required to review the Australian Constitution or the White Australia Policy, the HSC students of the 1970s were invited to imagine themselves squatters in the 1840s or tailoresses in the 1880s and to describe their outlook on the world.

One of the most popular examples of the 'enquiry' and 'values clarification' approaches was Sue Fabian's *The Changing Australians* (1978). 'Why study the past?' Fabian asks her young readers. Her own answer is threefold: to understand ourselves, to understand our heritage and to learn from past experiences. She emphasises the ways in which words reflect social relationships and the importance of critically examining sources. The 'values clarification' approach implies an open-ended, flexible approach to learning, in which textbook and teacher facilitate the students' discovery of where they stand on the great historical issues of peace and war, equality and inequality, freedom and order. But, as Fabian reminds her young readers, 'history books are written by historians, and historians are human beings. Their words are often wise but never completely gospel'.

This axiom is as true of the new enquiry-centred texts as it is of the old dogmatic ones. So when, in seeking to warn against the prejudices hidden in the religious language of the past, Fabian tells her young readers that words like 'pagan' and 'unbeliever' are 'nowadays mainly used as an exaggerated joke to make fun of the old ideas', does she not insinuate that Christianity itself is an outmoded belief? By implying that the language associated with religious, sexual, racial and class discrimination has 'lost its sting' or 'faded from use' Fabian may be reinforcing an idea of secular progress no less strongly than the more overt

views of national progress fostered by earlier generations of textbook writers.

Fabian has her own heroes and heroines—scientists,
female emancipists, trade union activists—and villains—imperialists, capitalists and wowsers. *The
Changing Australians* illustrates how easily the apparently open and flexible enquiry method may nonetheless
guide the young reader towards a limited range of
conclusions. The students could only 'discover' which
of the alternative versions of the past the textbook
writer had posed for them.[18]

By the 1980s 'integrated studies', the 'enquiry
method' and 'values clarification' had become the ruling
orthodoxy of history education, embodied, for example,
in the Victorian Certificate of Education. In its original
version the VCE History study design gave primary
emphasis to the acquisition of intellectual skills, especially in the analysis of 'representations', and only
secondary attention to the prescription of historical
problems and contexts which were to be left, ostensibly,
to the choice of individual teachers. In practice it did
not always work out this way, since choice of content
was effectively limited by the library resources of the
schools and the previous experience of the teachers. The
old wine of HSC Australian History was often simply
poured into new bottles labelled 'representations of
class', 'representations of race' and 'representations
of gender'. Reforms designed to encourage schools to
create their own innovative history programs often
resulted in the mechanistic application of externally
imposed social categories to attenuated and inert subject matter.

These developments have not been without their
critics. Alan Barcan of Newcastle has been one of the
most incisive and persistent, although even he seems to

regard the struggle to maintain the values he associates with a more traditional history curriculum as doomed to failure:

> The traditional objectives of history make but limited appeal to 'the new society'. History as a humanist study finds an unfriendly climate in an age concerned with techniques rather than content, in a society which believes that 'the medium is the message'. History as citizenship training means little in an age when the state is too strong and the individual too dependent. History as a source of standards is undermined in an age of relativism. History as an intellectual subject is weakened in a period when education is concerned with personal development, entertainment of pupils, and physical movement about the classroom or outside the school.[19]

More recently, the guidelines for the national curriculum in Studies in Environment and Society have drawn similar criticisms from historians. Janet McCalman attacks a misconceived quest for 'relevance' and 'democratisation' for much of the damage. History was now defined pedagogically, in terms of skills, rather than content. 'Children have to be taught how to do things rather than filled with knowledge,' she complains. Many of the teachers are themselves ignorant of the content of what they teach; their job is merely to be a 'technician, a facilitator' rather than 'learned, educated people with something of themselves—wisdom and learning—to impart to students'.[20]

It is clear that history, like much else, ain't what it used to be. But then it never has been. The complaint that history is neglected in our schools has been a perennial one and, while the evidence of recent decline is conclusive, the touch of nostalgia for the golden days of school history that surfaces in the writings of its friends may be equally misplaced. There is relatively little, in my own memories of high school history in the late 1950s, that I cherish: perhaps just a few moments of illumination from an inspired teacher amidst countless hours of mindless transcription from textbooks. I remember meeting few 'learned, educated' teachers before I arrived at university and little that I would describe as wisdom fell from their lips.

If history is to find a new place in the schools—as I believe it should—it will not be just to restore something lost, but to introduce something that a new generation sees as needed. The demand for school history in the 1990s, as in the 1890s, is an essentially conservative one—a desire to reinforce a sense of common identity, group loyalty and national purpose. It gains new strength from fears on both sides of politics that the forces of globalisation, multiculturalism and economic turmoil imperil national and community bonds. But both the concept of nationality and the ways in which it will be instilled must be different from those of earlier eras. In its 1994 report, *Whereas the People*, the Civics Expert Group chaired by Professor Stuart Macintyre affirmed its belief 'that a knowledge and understanding of the history of Australians is an essential foundation for citizenship' and a core element of the curriculum for all students up to leaving age. The Experts had written appreciatively of the first experiments in civics education during the early Commonwealth, which were 'far more than a clumsy attempt to manufacture "good citizens" according to neatly prescribed standards'. Their own recommendations were for courses that would be explicitly pluralist and international rather than simply national in focus.

Unlike the fragmented thematic syllabuses of the 1970s and 1980s, the 'history of Australians' should be based in narrative 'so that students will gain a sense of change over time', as well as 'comparative and reflective' so that Australian history was placed in a larger context. Even heroes and heroines would make a quiet comeback to the schoolroom: young Australians should learn about the lives of 'exemplary individuals'.[21]

In history, more than in many other subjects, the relationship between content and pedagogy is more than accidental. The enquiry method, which invited students to 'discover' the past for themselves, was more than just a means of engaging their interest; it also attempted to reinforce the idea of democratic citizenship, of participating in traditions of open debate. That textbook writers and teachers often guided those choices, and that students were sometimes expected to 'discover' more than their resources enabled them to do should not obscure this important link between the *what* and the *how* of history teaching. In some recent government pronouncements, as in some of the Civics Education curriculum, there is a new and welcome emphasis on the inculcation of a minimum knowledge of Australian history and political institutions. But ensuring that every Australian schoolchild knows the name of the first prime minister will do little for their citizenship unless they are also encouraged to practise the skills of free enquiry and free speech on which the modern Australian state was founded.

In attempting to negotiate a path between the educationalists and their critics the Civics Expert Group has laid some of the intellectual groundwork for a new kind of school history. There are some hopeful signs that such a program might command bipartisan support in the Australian parliament. We must hope so: for the restoration of history to the school curriculum may offer the best hope, not only for fostering a sense of Australian pride and identity, but for maintaining democratic values.

chapter eleven

Community: The uses of local history

'THINK GLOBALLY, ACT LOCALLY.' In a world dominated by transnational corporations, where even nation-states seem reduced to impotence, the little communities of family, neighbourhood and locality acquire renewed significance, if not for their power at least for their consoling intimacy. Even those who act globally, as servants of transnational corporations, sometimes also *think* locally, investing some more intimate part of themselves in a place they can somehow call their own. Local history, which links our aspirations for community to a sense of place, our fragile present to a seemingly more stable past, has a strong claim on the contemporary imagination. Perhaps that is why the history of towns, suburbs and neighbourhoods continues to flourish.

There are now more than 250 local historical societies in New South Wales and some 200 societies affiliated with the Royal Victorian Historical Society.[1] Most of these societies have been founded since the Second World War and especially since the early 1970s. In South Australia 36 new historical societies were founded between 1970 and 1980, more than twice as many as existed at the beginning of the decade, and a further 54 were founded in the 1980s.[2] Everywhere, it seems, Australians are busy collecting, restoring, reviving, researching, recollecting or visiting their local past.

How are we to resolve this paradox? The pasts that schoolchildren do not learn about are rather different, I believe, from the pasts that they and their elders enthusiastically visit in folk museums or view in TV miniseries. It is not just that they are perceived through different lenses—'living history' performances or video images rather than school textbooks and teachers' lectures—although that clearly makes a difference. More importantly, these new pasts answer very different social, psychological and political needs. Our past, in one sense, may be dead and buried but our understandings of it are constantly changing. Each generation inherits a view of the past but it then refashions it according to its own fears, hopes and longings.

Local history has always been one of the most popular forms of historical writing in Australia and its evolution mirrors our changing attitudes towards both locality and history. The excellent bibliographies of Victorian and New South Wales local histories by Carole Beaumont, and by Christine Estlick, Joy Hughes and Ian Jack, enable us for the first time to discern some of the main patterns of local historical activity over the past century or so.[3]

One trend they clearly document is the rapid explosion of local history writing and local history associations over the past fifteen or twenty years. Probably more volumes of local history have appeared in the past two decades—a period, so sociologists tell us, when people's ties to their local suburbs or rural communities have been steadily dissolving—than in the whole previous 180 years of Australian history. Since the late nineteenth century, when local communities first began in substantial numbers to record their past, the goals, methods, style and readership of Australian local history have undergone a series of significant shifts. In the course of that period we can detect at least five broad styles of local history writing—what I will call pioneer history, patriarchal history, professional history, preservationist history and community history. The five styles often coexist, even sometimes in the same work; yet over the past one hundred years we may discern a broad trajectory of development from pioneer to professional, and from professional to community history.

Pioneer history

The first Australian local historians were both makers and chroniclers of their community's past. As the first phase of Australian settlement drew to an end, the pioneer generation were prompted to record their memories and achievements for posterity. In Victoria the ageing of the goldrush generation produced a notable flood of reminiscences, commemorative poems, illuminated addresses and other informal kinds of history-making. In 1891 the self-taught poet and painter Alfred Eustace addressed 'our central city', as he called his home, the north-eastern mining town of Chiltern, in a poem recounting its history and progress. Eustace was conscious that Chiltern's founders were rapidly passing from the scene:

> Thy old identities are fled,
> And laid aside among the dead,
> As one of yore hath truly said,
> All flesh is grass . . .[4]

In the preface to his *History of Ballarat* (1870) W.B. Withers, veteran of Eureka and long-time local journalist, set out his credentials as a contemporary historian. The compiler 'of this "little history",' he wrote, 'has seen the growth of the town from a mere collection of canvas tents among the trees and on the grassy slopes and flats of the wild bush to its present condition'.[5] When he published his first edition in 1870 many of Ballarat's founders were still alive and Withers wrote primarily 'for those who know the place, and knowing it, are proud of it'. For a contemporary like Withers there was no clear boundary between research and recollection, between history and memoir. Re-reading the old files of the *Ballarat Times* he sometimes felt as if 'making a Pilgrimage, after a long absence, through an old burial ground . . . Names forgotten— names even of acquaintances and friends—are recorded in these yellowing and fragile sheets, and as they re-appear, one by one, they almost startle sometimes by the rush of many memories which they produce'.[6]

Pioneer history is a triumphant history, of territory gained, settled and subdued. Its endless lists of firsts— the first discovery, the first river crossing, the first station, the first church service—were the genealogy of communities still striving to establish a sense of legitimacy in newly settled land. Having first possessed the land, the pioneer now laid claim to his portion of its past. It was a history grounded in a sense of personal territory, and the recollections of the pioneer commonly assumed a shape suggested by a walk or ride through a vividly remembered past landscape. It built upon traditions of observation, collection and classification that had been strong for centuries among amateur naturalists and collectors in the lands from which they came, and they often reproduced these traditions in their own local chronicles. When 84-year-old Sir James Fairfax contributed his recollections to the Royal Australian Historical Society in 1918 he focused his narrative upon the people and events associated with those buildings and sites that remained from the Sydney of his youth. In pioneer history tangible remnants of the past become triggers for the sharing of memories.[7]

Pioneer history was the history of European conquest but it did not entirely obliterate the Aboriginal past. Many first generation pioneer histories contain extensive lists of Aboriginal place-names, sites and customs—but they are presented, usually, as the relics of an extinct people, trophies won in the pioneers' warfare with the new land.[8]

Later historians often dismissed the pioneer histories as too 'diffuse', 'anecdotal', 'impressionistic', 'antiquarian', 'jumbled' or 'miscellaneous' for serious consideration as history. 'Patchwork' is Carole Beaumont's favourite epithet for the Victorian examples. Yet their informal, fragmentary, episodic character is a clue to their purpose. They were often the work of plain men or women who lacked the literary artifice for a more sophisticated kind of narrative. 'No pretence has been made at literary style or effect,' confessed the writers of *The Land of the Lyrebird*, the remarkable memoir of pioneering days in the South Gippsland forest, published at the end of the Great War.[9] There is an engaging modesty in the titles the pioneer historians chose for their threepenny pamphlets: 'A Peep at the Past', 'Random Jottings' 'In those Days'. Theirs is a history which does not take itself too seriously and which recognises, more frankly than its professional critics, that all history is partial and contingent. If the logic that shapes the pioneer history sometimes escapes the scientific historian it did not escape the fellow pioneers for whom it was primarily written. For them, the startling contrast between past and present, the lists of local 'firsts', the associations between local landmarks and old identities were the framework of their own colonial book of genesis.

Patriarchal history

By the early twentieth century the mantle of the local historian was passing from the pioneers themselves to their sons and daughters. The new historical societies such as the Australian Historical Society, founded in 1901, and the Victorian Historical Society, founded in 1909, were the vehicle by which the younger generation sought to carry out the trust bequeathed by their pioneering forebears. 'Those whom we esteem as "Pioneers" . . . should not be forgotten,' declared the infant Victorian Historical Society in its founding statement of objectives. 'These pioneers in honour are entitled to have some effort made to record their days. This task devolves upon their descendants.'[10] By conserving the recollections and records of the colonies' founders the lessons of their experience might be transmitted to future generations. Peter Board, Director of the New South Wales Education Department, addressed the Royal Australian Historical Society on the role of history in civic education while Charles Long, editor of the Victorian Education Department's *School Paper,* emphasised the value of 'local chronicles' in 'the guidance of future generations'.[11]

Filial piety is the keynote of pioneer history in its latter phase. It is the homage paid by dutiful children to the memory of their forebears. With the psalmist, the new generation of local historians was apt to exclaim: 'Let us now praise famous men and our fathers that begat us.' Pioneer history is a story of origins; patriarchal history becomes a history of generations.

With the change from pioneer history to patriarchal history there was a subtle change of style and vocabulary: from recollection to recording, from celebration to commemoration, from testimony to chronicle.

A striking number of Australian local or regional histories have been written by women. In the 1920s and 1930s the Country Women's Association took the lead in promoting the study of rural history by sponsoring a competition for women historians, and often it is still the daughter of a local farmer or the wife of a prominent citizen who becomes the chronicler of her community. One day perhaps a woman historian will examine the special contribution of women to the study of Australian local history and I hope she will ponder the subtle blend of family pride and intellectual independence that went into the creation of those three finest of Australian pastoral sagas—Margaret Kiddle's *Men of Yesterday,* Judith Wright's *Generations of Men* and Mary Durack's *Kings in Grass Castles.* To a postfeminist generation, their emphatically masculine choice of titles may seem old-fashioned; but if the historians conveyed a certain devotion to the memory of their forefathers, it was not without recognition of their failings.

The pastoral saga maintains the old pioneer theme of the association of people and the land; but now, it sometimes appears, it is the men who are possessed by the land rather than the other way about. Kiddle, for example, ends her magnificent history of Victoria's Western District with the reminder that all men are grass; it is only the land which endures.[12]

During the early twentieth century the prosperity and progress that had sustained the first generation of pioneer historians was being steadily eroded. A survey of 180 Victorian country towns at the end of the 1930s showed that, while about one-third were continuing to grow, two-thirds were declining or staying still. In the nineteenth century the capital cities had grown as immigrants flowed in from overseas; now an increasing number of small town children headed for the 'big smoke' as soon as their schooldays were over. The 'drift to the city' undermined the economic viability and morale of rural communities.[13]

Local history, reshaped to meet the challenge of new times, became a means of shoring up the community's flagging sense of self-esteem. The interwar years were the heyday of 'back-to' celebrations. Departed residents were invited back to the town for a weekend or even an entire week of get-togethers, social cricket matches, old-time dances, commemorative church services and beauty contests. 'Back-to' week was an opportunity for the 'comebacks' to experience again the old-fashioned friendliness and hospitality of small town life; and it enabled the locals to enjoy the illusion of dance halls and churches once again filled with the hubbub of vigorous community life. The centrepiece of 'back-to' celebrations was usually a commemorative program in which gobbets of hastily compiled local chronicle were interspersed with photographs of the district's beauty spots and advertisements for local traders. In the preface the mayor invited the comebacks to join the locals in honouring 'the wonderful pioneers' of the district. By the 1950s, however, the 'back-to' movement was also on the wane and the honour rolls of 'old identities' featured in their programs were more likely to consist of local grocers, bank managers and stock and station agents than horny-handed pioneers.[14]

In the interwar years some municipalities began to publish commissioned histories. In Victoria, the journalist John Butler Cooper staked out the most promising territory, Melbourne's well-to-do south-eastern suburbs, where he completed sound, but unexciting municipal narratives of St Kilda, Prahran and Malvern. The standard municipal history followed a familar formula, a miniature version of the settlement narratives that dominated the writing of national history. A brief account of the first European 'explorers' in the area was followed by a more detailed narrative, usually accompanied by maps, of the processes of land survey, subdivision and sale, of the first bridges, roads, schools and churches, the establishment of local government and mention of the most notable 'early identities'. 'Progress' was the explicit theme of such narratives which were often illustrated with photographs of notable local buildings and portraits of the most notable early residents. Until the 1950s journalists had the business of commissioned local histories largely to themselves: whatever defects their work might have in the eyes of academics, it was usually capably, even sometimes attractively, written by an author whose byline the customers recognised and to a deadline that was invariably too short for anyone but a fast and fluent writer to meet. The role that Cooper played in the interwar years was later played by other journalists such as C. E. Sayers and F. A. Larcombe.

Professional history

It was not really until the 1950s, as the postwar education boom got under way, that professional historians—bright young men and women with university degrees—began to make a mark on the practice of Australian local history. In 1954 a curly-headed youngster named Geoffrey Blainey, who had just undertaken to write a history of Mount Lyell in Tasmania, expressed some of the professional's reservations about the amateur traditions of 'scissors-and-paste' local history. The author of *Back to Boomerang*, Blainey explained, was inclined to transcribe whole passages from his predecessors tacking the pieces together with brief connecting passages of his own:

> He paves his history with slabs which other writers have constructed. He is like a pavement-maker whose sole aim is to cover the distance. He worries little if the contractor who supplies the materials delivers cracked slabs, he doesn't bother to fill awkward gaps with a mosaic of smaller stones; he doesn't care if his path has weak foundations.[15]

The patchy, informal style of traditional local history offended the professional's desire for a critical evaluation of sources and a consistent narrative. Its preoccupation with origins was damned as mere 'antiquarianism', compared with the professional historians' sophisticated concern with the process and causes of social change. The amateurs' sketchy documentation was disparagingly compared with the professionals' lengthy bibliography, footnotes and scholarly apparatus.

By the mid 1960s the prospects of the professional local historian were improving with the rush of municipal centenaries commemorating the foundation of new shires and boroughs under the New South Wales and Victorian Local Government Acts of the 1860s. University professors persuaded aldermen to look beyond the retired journalists, schoolteachers and town clerks who had traditionally got the job and to engage the services of their bright young graduates. In his preface to Susan Priestley's *Echuca* (1965), Professor Max Crawford of the University of Melbourne took the opportunity to congratulate those 'enlightened councils', like Echuca's, which had had 'the wisdom to turn to trained historians to help them in their task'. 'Australians,' Crawford remarked, a little patronisingly,

> owed a great deal to numbers of devoted local enthusiasts who have sought out, preserved and written up the records of their districts and it is therefore the more disappointing that so often the resultant histories have been unilluminating and virtually unreadable. The fact is that the writing of history is a skilled business. Many people do not understand this, and it is quite common to find that untrained historians suppose that the first occurrence of a thing makes it in some way historical. While they look for the first lamp-post, the important determinants of a community's character pass them by.[16]

Academic credentials, however, were no guarantee of an impeccable job and only a few years later Weston Bate, one of Max Crawford's protégés and author of a model suburban local history, sounded a warning against the tendency of some academics to treat local history as a lesser branch of their trade and to imagine that knocking off a local history was the kind of thing any seasoned professional could do in his or her spare time.[17]

The entry of professional historians has certainly raised the intellectual and literary quality of Australian local history since the 1960s and the path blazed by Bate, Priestley and Blainey has since been followed by many other academically trained local historians. Sometimes it is the local boy, like Bill Gammage, who goes home to write the old town's history; but more often, these days, it is the city-based professional who answers an advertisement in the metropolitan press and drives up, armed with a *curriculum vitae* and a sheaf of academic testimonials, to face the local editorial committee. Ideally, the professional makes the town his or her own for the duration of the project, befriending the old-timers, giving talks to local school and community groups, developing a happy relationship with the editorial committee. But the ideal has not always been attained—the historian has a family back in the city, the newspaper files of the Mitchell or La Trobe beckon and there is a strict deadline to be met. So when the history is finally completed and the locals gather at the Civic Centre to launch it, they may be glad that their history has at last been 'done', but unsure that the handsome volume with the municipal crest on the dust jacket is really their own. Bringing in the professional may have ensured that the documentation is accurate and the prose is sound; but it may leave the locals with the uneasy feeling that their history, like almost everything else, now belongs to the educated folk in Sydney or Melbourne.[18]

It seems almost self-evident that a local history is the history of a community. Pioneer local history was the history of community-building, told by the builders themselves, patriarchal local history was devoted to the defence of community ties against the threat of depopulation. But by the 1970s, as the automobile and the television dissolved the boundaries and undermined the distinctiveness of local communities, the more thoughtful of local historians began to ponder the troubling question of whether the locality had ceased to be a significant unit of study.

Modern local historians end, almost inevitably, on an elegaic note. The communities whose loss they

mourn may be subtly different from one history to the
next, but the tone of nostalgia and regret is almost
ubiquitous. In suburbia, where municipal boundaries
no longer correspond with real communities—if ever
they did—the historian is left to salvage what meaning
he or she can from the history of places where most
residents spend only their sleeping hours. One of the
most common new forms of local history to appear in
the 1970s and 1980s was the school history, written
usually to commemorate the centenary of the school's
foundation under the 'free, compulsory and secular
Education Acts', often by one of the school parents.
They write in celebration of a residual sense of community—that of the young mothers and children who
are now the suburbs' main daytime residents.[19]

Some recent local historians confront the problem
of the dissolution of local ties quite explicitly. Sometimes they protest the persistence of 'community'
amidst the anonymity of the metropolis; sometimes they
redefine it in new, more pluralistic ways; sometimes
they mythologise it. In the most recent edition of his
History of Brighton Professor Weston Bate raises 'the
suggestion of some historians that the process of metropolitan growth in the twentieth century . . . so erodes
the identity of individual suburbs that it is not possible
to write their separate histories effectively'. Brighton,
he contends, had inherited 'the social attitudes and
experiences of generations'. Among the younger generation, and newcomers to the 'suburb, a vague sense of
history, the aura of Brighton's past' somehow helped to
inculcate that sense of private amenity which Bate saw
as the distinctive hallmark of the bayside suburb. The
Brightoners' defence of their foreshore against the depredations of day trippers and bicycle paths was one
indication of 'the locality's fierce sense of its own

identity'. In this process, the appearance of the first edition of Bate's *History* had been a significant moment for the local historical society, founded after its publication in 1962, had been in the van of the movement to conserve the suburb's fast diminishing stock of 'grand old houses' and parklands.[20]

In the eyes of its own historian every locality seems to be distinctive, a last bastion of community values that have disappeared elsewhere. John Lack, historian of Melbourne's western suburbs, shows that Footscray's fierce sense of local identity was based upon a distinctive pattern of local employment and residence.[21] In his history of Strathfield, 'the oasis in the west', Michael Jones recounts the story of how 'a small local community . . . prevented its quality of life from being ruined by the intrusion of factories and high density housing'.[22] In neighbouring Ashfield, however, where the preservationist battle was less successfully fought, Robert and Sheena Coupe celebrate a new pluralist sense of community, 'the cultural richness that derived from the presence in the municipality of people from more than 64 nations'.[23]

Struggletown, Janet McCalman's prize-winning oral history of Richmond, an inner suburb of Melbourne, ends with a lament for the disappearance of 'the old Australian working class and its communal culture'. In the 1950s and 1960s, as the respectable working class moved out to the suburbs, something valuable was lost. 'Richmond,' she writes, 'seemed finished, irredeemably blighted and beyond salvation.'[24] Yet later, when a group of young people employed on a Commonwealth Youth Employment Grant published their own oral history of Richmond, a subtly different picture emerged. There was an ugly xenophobic side to the communal consciousness of the old Richmond working class, more apparent to the immigrant newcomers who endured the locals' taunts of 'Go home to your own country, wog' than it was to McCalman. The authors of *Copping it Sweet* end on a more optimistic note than the author of *Struggletown*, observing the emergence of 'a new cohesive community' among the most recent of Richmondites, the Vietnamese.[25]

Preservationist history

In the affluent middle-class suburbs, too, a new sense of community was being born. As the old folk passed on, or moved out, the young professionals moved in. Geoffrey Blainey ends the latest edition of his *History of Camberwell* in the midst of Melbourne's famous—or notorious—belt of dry suburbs with a wry reflection on the perennial appeal of nostalgia. A generation that had looked backward longingly to a Camberwell of 'green paddocks and post and rail fences' would be succeeded by another who 'recalled the 1940s when Camberwell was overwhelmingly residential, and nearly every house had its own garden and trees, and on Mondays washing flapped on the clothes line in every backyard, and on winter nights the streets smelled of the smoke of briquettes and grey box or mallee roots, and on Sunday everything except the church was closed'.[26] Nostalgia, Blainey implies, is a mind-set among the older folk of any generation. In a few years yet another generation of Camberwell oldsters may look back fondly on memories of villa units, freeways and McDonald's hamburgers.

Yet the community sense and the attitude to the local past fostered among the young professionals of the villa suburbs is subtly different from their predecessors'. We live in a faster moving society and the young upwardly mobile professionals seldom have an ancestral link, or prospects of developing a permanent tie, with the locality in which they sojourn. Their sense of the past is not that of the pioneer, the community-builder; nor even of the dutiful sons and daughters who sought, through the tradition of patriarchal history, to keep the ideals of the founding generation alive. They are often adopted children of the locality who seek, mainly through a love affair with its physical fabric—old buildings, old furniture, old styles of decorating—to simulate an aura of permanence and tradition.

Pioneer history sought to conserve old-time values; preservationist history seeks to conserve old things. 'Heritage', a word used by an older generation to describe its legacy of revered beliefs and traditions, has now become the key word in a movement devoted to the preservation, restoration and—increasingly—to the re-creation and re-enactment of the past. Scan the real estate advertisements in the Saturday papers and you will find that it is the old buildings, not the old folks, who are said to possess 'the charm and character of yesteryear'. Is it nostalgia for a vanished rural past, I wonder, which inspires a suburban real estate agent to advertise a Federation villa as 'The Old Farmhouse'? In the heritage business, it seems, it is the illusion, the veneer of age that counts rather than historical significance. How otherwise are we to explain the selling appeal of a 'two year old colonial homestead' or a 'brand new Victorian townhouse'?

As the metropolis advances, there emerges a longing to conserve the relics of local tradition. Many a struggling country town seeks its salvation in satisfying that yearning. By emphasising its character as a 'historic town', it places itself on the menu of tourist destinations and thus markets its past, not only to the locals but to outsiders as well. A new and glossier kind of local history begins to appear in the gift shops along its freshly restored main street. It is a history grounded less in a sense of community pride than in an appreciation of the picturesque. The town reveals itself to the reader, as it does to the tourist, as a series of quaint facades, romantic ruins and nostalgic vistas. C.H. Bertie's *Old Colonial Byways* (1928) was an early example of the genre. Bertie's evocative descriptions of the 'old world atmosphere' of the 'villages' of the Hawkesbury valley nicely complemented Sydney Ure Smith's delicate etchings of old mills and churches.[27] The bestselling Rigby *Sketchbook* series, begun in the 1960s, popularised the formula and, by the 1980s, visitors to many notable towns were able to choose between a range of attractive historical picturebooks.

Out in these historically conscious towns and suburbs, heritage preservation groups now compete vigorously with historical societies for stewardship of the local past. Sometimes, as Tom Griffiths suggests in his perceptive book *Beechworth: A Country Town and its Past*, it is the city folk, 'the blow-ins' as the locals call them, who head the campaign for preservation against the apathy or hostility of the locals.[28] But often, especially in the suburbs, the battle-lines are more confusingly drawn with different groups of locals—residents' groups and business interests—on either side. The battle often comes to a head in the local council where the claims of planners and heritage experts for local conservation studies compete for municipal funds with requests for local histories of a more conventional kind. Only gradually have the historians begun to win back a little of the ground conceded to the architects and planners and to insist that any evaluation of a locality's built heritage should be based, not only on stylistic criteria, but upon a more complete understanding of its social, economic and political history.

Community history

Preservationist history may be no more than a harmless kind of nostalgia, allied, perhaps, to a defence of one's own real estate; but it may also become the basis for a more active kind of community defence. In 1977 the residents of Surrey Hills, in Melbourne's affluent eastern suburbs, learned of the Road Construction Authority's plans to push an arterial road through the middle of their rather somnolent little shopping centre. One of their first moves—a curious one we might think—was to form a local history group. They took over an old shop and invited residents to bring in their old photographs and to stop and chat about their experiences of Surrey Hills' famous Empire Day celebrations in the 1920s.[29] The battle to stop the arterial road was won, but the meetings in the old shop continued. The local council, concerned to placate feelings of neglect in an area on its borders, established a neighbourhood centre where the 'History Nook', as it has become known, remains the focus, not only for regular meetings of the Surrey Hills History Group, but for other neighbourhood-based activities. Many of them, such as the monthly craft fair and the annual Surrey Hills Day parade, have a strong period flavour.

History has been a powerful ally to residents' associations and other forms of small-scale community politics. The surge in the growth of new local historical societies since 1970 corresponds closely to the period in which resident-based community politics, often with a preservationist or environmentalist trajectory, took off in Australian cities and towns. Such politics are of their nature defensive and backward-looking. The locality the residents seek to defend is often a mythological one—a quiet, healthy, socially integrated town or suburb which its residents locate somewhere in the past—threatened by the imposition, typically from without, of such blights as freeways, high-density housing, powerlines or—in 1990s Victoria —council amalgamations.

The new forms of popular local history, like those developed by the Surrey Hills Group, have much in common with the original phase of pioneer local history. There is a growing move away from the more formal, academic style of official local history and a greater readiness to explore more spontaneous, informal, popular methods of publication, display and performance. The video, the tape recorder and the personal computer have given the local community a new range of ways of exploring their past. Oral history—the recollections of the old days, as the pioneer generation may have called it—and walking tours, rather like Sir James Fairfax's mental peregrinations around Old Sydney, have once again become favoured methods of presenting local history.

In 1991 historians at the University of New South Wales, the home of the Local History Coordination Project sponsored since the late 1980s by the NSW government, decided to rename the project the 'Community History Program'. Support for the old LHCP had been declining; by broadening its base to include other forms of 'community history' the historians sought to improve its prospects of survival. But shifting the program's focus from 'locality' to 'community' was to exchange one problematical concept for another. At its inaugural conference several speakers nibbled, rather tentatively, at the issue—long debated by social scientists—of the nature of the 'community'. Patrick O'Farrell acknowledged that it was 'a concept with a high ethical content' and emphasised ideals of mutual dependence and intercommunication. Lucy Taksa took a more critical tack, raising—but not resolving—the challenging question of whether 'a relationship exists between periods of social fragmentation and a spread of the use of the term community, almost as an aspiration for closer social bonds'. 'Community,' it sometimes seemed, was always in the process of disappearing. It was constituted as a subject of history by the nostalgia of those who mourned its passing as much as the evidence of those who witnessed its persistence.

Two local historians, South Australia's Susan Marsden and New South Wales' Carol Liston also touched on the problematical relationship between 'locality' and 'community'. Many local historians treated their towns and suburbs as 'communities' until the Second World War, Marsden observed, but tended to assume that community disappeared with the coming of 'industrialisation, immigration, and the affordable motor car'. But, she contended, community had not disappeared; it had simply become redefined in terms other than locality. Carol Liston took a similar line: community might be about shared time as much as shared space; historians would need to give special attention to the processes of communication through which these non-localised communities were constituted and maintained.[30]

In these sometimes confused discussions of locality and community there was more than a bit of whistling in the wind. Historians had a vested interest in local history as a regular, if modest, source of commissioned employment, and it might be inconvenient if the foundations of that enterprise were too rudely shaken. Reconceptualising 'community' and cutting the links that had once bound it to locality implied a different kind of local history, more pluralistic, less tied to formal geography. It called into question the old formula of the officially sponsored, authoritative, single-authored local history.

In the mid 1980s residents of Fitzroy, Melbourne's oldest and tiniest suburb, became the recipients of an unusual benefaction. Mrs Margaret Cutten, an old resident, gave a local historical society enough money to sponsor the writing of a history. Fitzroy had once been a working-class suburb but by the 1980s its historical society—like most of its better terrace houses—had become trendified and contained an almost uncomfortable number of professional historians among its members.

Fitzroy: Melbourne's First Suburb, the 350-page volume published by the Cutten History Committee, eschews formal chronology and its 37 chapters written by 35 authors are loosely organised around five main themes—founding and funding, building and bulldozing, working and playing, coming and going, and looking back. Some are formal pieces of academic history; others are informal reminiscence, documents or photo-essays. Some attempt coverage of the whole municipality, others recount an episode, describe a neighbourhood, sketch a theme. 'Fitzroy is now the most heterogeneous of Melbourne's suburbs,' the Preface explains. Its historians respond with a history that is consciously heterogeneous, fragmentary, pluralistic. 'There has been no attempt to reconcile differences of opinion within this book,' they warn the reader. By accident, it seems, they have created a postmodern local history.[31]

Australian local history seemed to have returned to its origins, for in their informality, their blurring of the line between personal reminiscence and impersonal narrative, the new local histories looked strikingly like the old pioneer histories. And indeed the professionals who often wrote them saw themselves merely as the midwives through whom the community itself would write its own history—a fiction that often dissolved, however, in the hard business of actually getting words on paper.

Five years later Fitzroy's neighbour, Brunswick, also published a history. There, where the gentry have yet to firmly establish themselves and the migrant presence is stronger, the historians—many of them postgraduate history students, most of them women—have pushed the implications of the Fitzroy model a stage further. *Brunswick: One History Many Voices* developed through several stages, with questionnaires, exhibitions, radio spots and conferences along the way and its 44 chapters stress the multicultural character of the suburb, not just by the inclusion of many migrants' reminiscences but by publishing them in Italian, Greek, Turkish or Arabic as well as English.[32]

These new local histories celebrate difference but they are reluctant to give up the local historian's old belief in community. In the concluding pages of *Fitzroy* Janet McCalman underlines the 'nasty realities of class' which have divided the suburb between middle-class trendies and a remnant working class, but confides a glimmering hope that 'progress'—that other ghost in the lexicon of local history—might be made if only 'community feeling can be nurtured by street democracy'. On the eve of its amalgamation, Brunswick's historians also invoke 'the tradition of strong community involvement that has characterised so much of Brunswick's history' to repulse the threat to local democracy posed by the Kennett government's local government reforms.

To a sceptical social scientist the sense of community inspired, or supported, by local history may seem to be at odds with the realities of an increasingly mobile, anonymous society. Community, it seems, is always in the process of disappearing. It is constituted as a subject of history more by the nostalgia of those who mourn its passing than the testimony of those who attest its persistence. How can we continue to believe in ideas of community, locality or neighbourhood in a society where all the big decisions are made out of town and where more than half the residents are absent more than half the time?

Yet perhaps it is precisely the *mythic* quality of these ideas that explains their purchase on our imagination. In his superb book *Camden*—Alan Atkinson recounts the story of the Macarthurs' ultimately doomed attempt to create a patriarchal village community in early colonial New South Wales. That experiment would fail as early as the 1860s, as the old Camden succumbed to the pressures of Sydney markets and the liberal ideals of Sydney-based politicians. Yet, as Atkinson reminds us in the book's closing pages, the *idea* of that community, that sense of local attachment lived on, and even acquired a new 'myth-like character' in the minds of the descendants of the old Camden.

Atkinson wrote his book in the belief that 'good local history has something vital to say to a nation whose people are now looking more and more to local government, local environment and heritage, and local leaders, even as they make up their minds at election time'.[33] One of the functions of local history is to keep that sustaining myth of community alive in a society where its extinction has implications too hard to bear. The challenge of local historians, as we approach the millennium, is to create a sense of the past truthful enough to acknowledge the limitations, yet imaginative enough to see the possibilities, of that ideal.

chapter twelve

Turbulent times: The historical vision of modern management

I WAS FLYING BACK to Melbourne when an article in the Qantas flight magazine caught my eye. 'BUSINESS HEAD RECOMMENDS HISTORY' was the headline and the article was by the head of Macquarie University's Business School. How pleasing, I thought, that business leaders were at last recognising the value of history! Perhaps it meant that BHP and IBM would soon be clamouring for history graduates. As I read the article, however, my spirits sank. The Macquarie professor, it turned out, had little interest in Australian history, or even in the history of Australian business. On the contrary, it was a disability, in his eyes, to know too much about the immediate past of your own firm or country since it might trap you into routine or traditional ways of thinking. No, the history that the modern manager needed was of a much more traditional kind. It was through reading the timeless wisdom of Plato, Aristotle, Machiavelli and Hobbes that the corporate high-flyers might hone their political skills for the cutthroat board-room battles of the 1990s.

Academic historians worry that their neighbours in cultural theory and poststructuralism are killing history, but far more lethal enemies lie just across the campus in the faculties of business and economics where beliefs like those of Macquarie's business dean have become a largely uncontested orthodoxy. Half a century ago, history was a vital ingredient in the education of the statesman and public administrator. Understanding the history of the nation and its institutions and of how they have changed, retracing and analysing past episodes of change, knowing how to interpret social and political behaviour, developing a capacity to critically evaluate information and formulate judgments in clear prose—these were the capacities that history was expected to instil in its students, and which the history graduate might bring to the world of business, public administration or politics. Underlying this process of education was the belief that the world of the past was continuous with our present, and that the lessons learned from history were applicable to the present and the future.

Among modern managers this belief is now almost universally denied. The world, it is now suggested, has changed so completely that yesterday's experience is no longer applicable to today. The self-image of the modern manager is of a lonely navigator adrift in a turbulent environment where the winds and tides are variable and unpredictable. Here is a passage from the Australian edition of a popular management textbook on the topic of 'managing change and innovation':

> We can use two very different metaphors to describe the change process. One envisions the organisation as a large ship crossing a calm sea. The ship's captain and crew know exactly where they are going because they have made the trip many times before. Change surfaces as the occasional storm, a brief distraction in an otherwise calm and predictable trip. In the other metaphor, the organisation is seen

as a small raft in a raging river with uninterrupted white-water rapids. Aboard the raft are half-a-dozen people who have never worked together before, who are totally unfamiliar with the river, who are unsure of their eventual destination and, if things were not bad enough, who are travelling in the pitch-dark of night . . . A growing number of managers are coming to accept that their job is similar to [this latter analogy]. The stability and predictability of the calm water metaphor do not exist. . . Many of today's managers never get out of the rapids. They face constant change bordering on chaos. These managers are being forced to play a game they never played before and that is governed by rules that are created as the game progresses.[1]

Consider some of the implications of this passage. The image of the modern manager as a lonely navigator across treacherous seas is at once frightening and heroic: it registers the subjective sense of insecurity felt by the manager in the face of chaotic change, but it also affirms his or her protean role in guiding the organisation through troubled seas. (The Sydney–Hobart yacht race, when business tycoons do battle with each other and with the elements, is a real-life enactment of this imagined drama.) The more dangerous the waters through which the organisation sails, the greater will be its dependence on the heroic helmsman. (Even when naval helicopters were winching Sydney–Hobart sailors from the sea, the skippers insisted on their unfettered right of command.) By treating the environment as intrinsically hostile and unpredictable, the metaphor reinforces the idea of the manager as exercising a distinctive skill, superior to the knowledge of those—such as economists, historians, sociologists—who claim to discern greater order. By picturing the manager and his crew as human, and the environment as inanimate, the image also deflects our attention from the possibility that the unpredictable winds and waves are, at least in part, a product of the very doctrine of uncertainty that unleashes round after round of organisational change as successive cohorts of managers come and go.

Finally, the paired images—the manager as cruise-captain, the manager as raft-captain—rest upon an implied contrast between two historical eras: one in which the lessons of the past could be transferred to the future; and a new age in which all the old rules have been suspended, and the experience of yesterday is irrelevant to tomorrow. Where, we might ask, does this conviction come from? What evidence do we have for its truth?

Management theory often pays a kind of lip-service to history. 'Studying history is a way to achieve strategic thinking, see the big picture, and improve conceptual skills,' another recent textbook declares. 'A historical perspective matters to executives, because it is a way of thinking, a way of searching for patterns and determining whether they recur across time periods.'[2] Yet in the rest of this text history, except in the form of corporate case studies, is largely forgotten. A few managers, such as John Paterson, currently head of the Victorian Department of Infrastructure, have commissioned organisational histories as a step in the process of bureaucratic reform, but his example seems to have been followed by few others.[3] If history was regarded seriously by business schools it would be hard to explain why departments of economic history have almost ceased to exist in Australian universities, and why business and government organisations have recently begun to destroy their libraries and archives. As John Ralston Saul observes, the economic doctrines governing the thinking of most modern executives are largely forgetful of history. 'The only part of this domain [economics] which has some reliable utility,' he claims, 'is economic history, and it is being downgraded in most universities, even eliminated because, tied to events, it is an unfortunate reminder of reality.'[4]

In practice, modern managers are careless of history, when they are not actively hostile to it. Their professional stance is based upon the conviction that management is a *general* science or skill, applicable to any institution, from the stock exchange to the Vatican. Good management, so the jargon goes, is 'content-free'. It screens out historical specificity in order to focus on the underlying organisational issues. The new managers themselves are highly mobile, trained to 'hit the ground running', immune from the sense of institutional identity and loyalty that still imbues many of their employees. As agents of radical change they consciously avoid too close a sense of connection with the organisation and its past. Eradicating institutional memory is a conscious method of control. The last thing the managers want to hear is the voice of the old hand saying, 'We tried it that way a few years ago and it didn't work'. Historical amnesia is supposed to be good for the organisation, freeing it from the outworn practices of the past, but it is also clearly good for the managers in rationalising their insensitivity to institutional memory.

The consequences of this doctrine are now evident throughout the Australian public sector as old employees are sacked, libraries and archives closed or sold off, and new layers of management inserted between professionals and their clients. Recently, I heard that one state government department closed its departmental library because, as the responsible official declared, you could now get all the information you needed on the Internet!

'Sloughing off yesterday'

The textbook image of the manager as a lonely helmsman, bravely navigating uncharted seas, derives, like much of the superstructure of modern management theory, from the writings of the 'management guru', Peter Drucker. In his 1980 book *Managing in Turbulent Times* Drucker invoked the image of the organisation as a storm-tossed vessel.

> After long years of relative calm and predictability, every enterprise—business or non-business public service institution—is likely to be loaded down with yesterday's promises . . . A ship that spends long periods of time at sea needs to be cleansed of its barnacles or their drag will deprive it of speed and maneuverability. An enterprise that has sailed in calm waters for a long time similarly needs to cleanse itself of the products, services, ventures that only absorb resources; the products, services, ventures that have become "yesterday".

'Sloughing off yesterday' is the first axiom of organisational change.[5]

Drucker is himself a historical thinker although not exactly a historian. 'Mr Drucker infuses everything he writes with some historical dimension,' the *Economist* acutely observed. 'In a profession dominated by nanosecond memories, he is happy to range across the centuries, drawing his examples from Tang dynasty

China to Weimar Germany and making bold predictions about the 21st century.'⁶ But the Drucker version of history owes little to the insights of academic historians. Residing in his own Drucker Business School at Claremont College, California, his ideas seldom attract the scrutiny of other social scientists. Among managers, administrators and conservative politicians, however, his writings enjoy enormous influence and, in his nineteeth year, Drucker himself commands prodigious speaking fees. At least one former professor of history, ex-House of Representative Speaker Newt Gingrich, regards him as an oracle.⁷

Drucker was born in early twentieth century Vienna, witnessed the end of the Austro-Hungarian empire and the rise of Hitler, and migrated first to Britain in the 1930s. The Vienna of his childhood, he later wrote, was a city in decay. In August 1914, as a five-year-old child, he overheard a conversation between his father, a senior civil servant, and the Czech patriot Tomás Masaryk. 'This is the end, not just of Austria, but of civilisation,' he remembers one of them saying. And so, at least for his parents' generation, it had. 'All they talked about was life before 1914. I was surrounded by extinct volcanoes.'

From the first he was imbued with a deep sense of discontinuity. History is marked by successive crises, each of which rapidly renders obsolete the assumptions of the preceding era. Already by the late 1930s he had repudiated the ideologies of both Nazism and Marxism and, in his first major book *The End of Economics* (1939), he issued the first of several apocalyptic visions of the coming postindustrial age. In successive books, *Managing in Turbulent Times* (1980), *The New Realities* (1989) and *Post-capitalist Society* (1993), he confidently expounded the same themes: technological progress, smaller government, the critical importance of leadership, the emergence of 'knowledge workers' as the new ruling class and of pension funds as the most important source of financial power. By 1993 he could cite recent events—the fall of the Berlin Wall, the computer revolution, the globalisation of economic life—to vindicate the accuracy of his predictions a quarter of a century before.

Drucker is often described as a 'management guru', a title he disavows but which well expresses the blend of sceptical analysis and bold prophecy that infuses his writings. The world as we knew it, he says, is coming to an end. In 1969, a year of ferment when counter-cultural prophets anticipated the coming of an 'Age of Aquarius', Drucker published *The Age of Discontinuity*, forecasting a very different future.

> This book may be looked at as an "early warning system", reporting discontinuities which, while still below the visible horizon, are already changing the structure and meaning of economy, polity and society. These discontinuities, rather than the massive momentum of apparent trends are likely to mould and shape our tomorrow, the closing decades of the twentieth century.[8]

Before the advent of the microchip and the communications satellite Drucker anticipated that new technologies based on quantum physics, biochemistry, psychology and symbolic logic would create new industries. National markets would give way to a global economy of multinational corporations. Governments and politicians would become less influential than the managers of large corporations. And, most importantly, knowledge would become the most crucial resource of the economy. 'I envy the courage of the seers who tell

us what 2000 may look like; but I have no desire to
emulate them,' he wrote. 'I remember too well what
the future looked like in 1933. No forecaster could then
have imagined our reality of 1969.' Clear-eyed observation of the present, unfettered by sentiment or
ideology, was what he offered his readers. Predicting
the future is intrinsically dangerous; but an attentive
student might at least perceive what *cannot* happen.

To an academic historian, preoccupied with the
complexities of social change, Drucker's historical
vision is impressive for the boldness of its outlines and
the confidence of its forecasts. Like the famous Russian
economic historian, Kondratieff, Drucker divides
modern European history into long cycles. The late
thirteenth century, the late fifteenth, the late eighteenth,
the late twentieth century each marked a historic
'divide'. 'Within a few short decades, society rearranges
itself—its world-view; its basic values, its social and
political structure; its arts, its institutions. Fifty years
later there is a new world.'[9] In such 'turbulent times',
the continuity between past and present is broken.
History is not dead, but it is temporarily disabled.

Envisioning Australia's new age

Drucker's vision of the past is possibly more influential
than that of any contemporary historian. His books
have sold between five and six million copies.[10] Even
more influential are the thousands of newspaper articles, management textbooks, business newsletters and
lectures which constantly reproduce and recirculate his
ideas around the world. Australia's best known business
forecaster, Phil Ruthven of IBIS Business Services, is an
energetic populariser and adapter of Drucker's ideas.

An industrial chemist by training, Ruthven stepped sideways into research and development with the Petersville group in 1969, before founding IBIS in 1971. Like Drucker, Ruthven is a prolific writer, speaker and adviser to corporations.

'There is no theory at IBIS, we have the facts,' the firm's handbook claims.[11] Its main business is the provision of online information to companies on economic and social conditions, both in Australia and internationally. But there is more than a bit of theory in the analysis Ruthven offers the subscribers to his regular bulletins and reports. Like Drucker, he blends a seemingly hard-nosed analysis of present trends with a confident and highly formalistic style of historical analysis. Both the American guru and his Australian disciple anticipate a world radically remade by new technologies, the growth of a service economy, internationalisation, privatisation and smaller government. 'The Industrial Age contest between capitalism and socialism is nearly over. The new order is economic rationalism to be opposed in the 21st century by humanism,' IBIS predicts. Deeply suspicious of 'soap-box ideologies and wild-eyed fanatics', it favours (and predicts) the development of government that is 'logical, sensible, moderate'.[12]

'Societies throughout the world run in eras,' Ruthven declares. 'Of necessity they run the same length as economic cycles.' While Drucker, the big wheel of corporate forecasters, discerns 200-year cycles of global change, his Australian counterpart charts shorter cycles of local economic and social development. Since 1788 Australian history has experienced six main cycles of 'entrepreneurialism', 'expansion', 'maturation', 'degradation' and 'restoration'. Corresponding to each phase of the economic cycle there is a 'social generation' with its own characteristic attitudes. The entrepreneurial phase is dominated by the civic ('we will') generation, the expansion phase by the 'rebellious' ('I want') generation, the maturation phase by the idealist ('you must') generation, the degradation phase by the 'conciliatory' ('we all want') generation and the restoration phase by the return of the civic generation.

In recent times Australia has experienced the entrepreneurial phase of the 1960s dominated by the civic leadership of Menzies, the expansion of the 1970s, dominated by the rebellious attitudes and leadership of the Whitlam era, the maturation phase of the 1980s dominated by the idealist leadership of the Hawke government, phasing into the degradation and conciliatory leadership of the Keating and Howard governments.[13]

In one of their bravest exercises in historical analysis the IBIS researchers have linked fluctuations in Australia's Economic Health Index (as measured by key economic indicators such as unemployment, inflation, interest rates etc.) with the tenure and characteristics of national leaders from Governor Phillip (one of the six strongest point scorers) to Bob Hawke (one of the poorest). Australia's best leader, according to this rather novel form of biographical analysis, is Ben Chifley whose 175 points on the Economic Health Index IBIS attributes to his 'vision' and an ability to give substance to the pent-up desire for social betterment after the Second World War. Good leaders, according to IBIS, are 'usually competent, benevolent autocrats who listen better than democrats, command loyalty (and get it), and lead rather than moderate or manage.[14]

Ruthven has long prophesied a new era of prosperity. In 1987 he anticipated the arrival of 'the New Entrepreneurial Age' after the 'watershed of 1986–93'.[15] But its advent was seemingly postponed. In 1993 he looked forward to 'Australia's Next Golden Age' early in the new century. Like other shifts in Australia's economic fortunes, its approach would be heralded by a revolution of values signalled by the advent of 'New Age' ideals of economic rationalism and cultural convergence. Like other prophets, Ruthven swings between prediction and prescription; he is an ardent advocate of the new order he sees on the horizon.

> Unless we aspire to a new golden age and understand what is required of us to get there, we will remain a morbid economy indefinitely. But not forever: if we do nothing, stewardship of this great island nation continent would pass eventually to other neighbours with vision, energy and appreciation of the country's potential. That time is closer than we dare imagine.[16]

His is a historical vision that imparts both urgency and momentum to the political and economic changes its realisation requires.

Forecasting and forgetting

The version of history purveyed by Drucker and Ruthven is useful to the corporate executive in several ways. It simultaneously conveys a sense of climactic change, of the grand sweep of history, while, paradoxically, making the actual study of history—the complex interplay of personality, events and circumstance—largely irrelevant. While explicitly rejecting the claims of those, such as Marx, who sought to read the future from the past, it nevertheless identifies a historical dynamic with which, it suggests, nations and their leaders must cooperate or risk disaster. The corporate leader must focus on this 'big picture' of global change, rather than its complex and disquieting local consequences. Because history is on their side, the managers can slash and burn, confident that new growth will come in its place. Like Marxism, the histories of Drucker and Ruthven endow a new class—the managers and knowledge workers—with the leading role in achieving this transformation.

In fact, management history can be seen as a kind of inverted Marxism. While Marx viewed leaders as the embodiment of class interests and politics as a reflection of shifting social relationships, managerialists are inclined to see social conditions and values as the product of good or bad leadership ('new ages are created by true visionaries, true leaders'). While politics is unchanging ('the Ten Commandments of *good politics* [emphasis added] . . . seem not to have changed since Machiavelli wrote *The Prince*, which has remained the bible ever since')[17] good government or leadership requires 'vision' and 'clear focus', a concentration on preordained goals rather than the democratic skills of consultation, mediation and compromise.

This is a vision congenial in many ways to the mood of our times—our pragmatism, our preoccupation with material survival, our fatalism, our disillusionment with formal politics. It has a particular appeal to managers, endowing them with a sense of historical mission, reinforcing their personal authority and expertise, and marginalising all local, traditional or political sources of resistance.

But it rests on assumptions that other historians might wish to contest. Is it yet clear that the rapid changes of the 1980s and 1990s constitute such a sharp break in national and international history that they render all previous experience irrelevant? The managerialists, like other prophets of discontinuity (such as postmodernists) draw strength from the pervasive pessimism and apocalyptic mood of the approaching millennium. As in the 1890s, when *fin-de-siècle* pessimism was also rife, such moods may be more indicative of the sensation of rapid social change than of the inherent disconnectedness of the present from the past. The lonely helmsman may *feel* that he is alone amidst the storm, but his vessel is propelled by forces that are intrinsically as calculable as those that produce calmer weather.

Drucker and Ruthven are themselves selective in their view of what changes and what survives from the past: the wisdom of Machiavelli is timeless but the ideas of Rousseau and Marx are superseded.

Their histories also rest upon an unexamined theory of cyclical change. Such theories probably have an inherent appeal to business people and economic liberals. The ups and downs of the stock market and business cycle create an expectation that social and political life should follow a similar cyclical pattern. Geoffrey Blainey's *The Great See-Saw*, which charts cycles of optimism and pessimism in western society since 1750, and Trevor Sykes' several studies of Australian corporate failures, are two popular local examples of this outlook.[18] As plausible as they may seem, however, such cycles should be recognised as theoretical constructs rather than as facts of nature. The 200-year cycles that Drucker detects in western history, and the fifty-year cycles that Ruthven discerns in Australian history may be more in the eye of the historian than in the rhythm of events.

If history really follows cycles then the manager or politician may hope to apply the lessons of the last cycle to the challenges of the next. In practice, managerialists are ambivalent about this possibility. Sometimes they confidently extrapolate from the past to the present; sometimes they insist that the past has been superseded. What governs this selective application of history is an implied hierarchy of values. Global forces prevail over local ones, technology over culture, economics over politics, reason over emotion. It is a history in which the past is shaped in the service of a future ideal. So long as the managers agree about it, however, it has at least an outside chance of being realised.

In one sense there is nothing unusual about this: we all, even professional historians, tend to write history with an eye on the present and the future as well as the past. But the historical vision of modern management is distinctive in its confidence, its formalism, its contempt for institutional memory, its hermetic isolation from other historical discourses. It is seemingly impervious to the processes of critical debate that govern other forms of historical knowledge.

Confident of their own wisdom, modern managers often fail to recognise the costs of ignoring history. A few years ago, just as it was about to be corporatised, a metropolitan water and sewerage authority decided to commission two academics to write its history. Even while the historians were at work the process of 'downsizing' and 'contracting out' was under way. Each day as they entered the building fresh notices appeared by the lifts announcing farewells for the old-timers 'taking the package'. The new managers had initiated a ruthless rationalisation of resources. Even the organisation's long-established library and map collection were marked for disposal and sale.

No sooner had the last of the old-time employees left than the managers faced a crisis. Suddenly there were reports from several suburbs that raw sewage was escaping into the streets. Quite apart from the unpleasant odour, there were fears for the health of people in the neighbourhood. The underground system of tunnels that conveyed the sewage to market gardens on the city fringe was almost a century old—still serviceable, but only when it was run by engineers who knew, by long experience, its idiosyncrasies and weak spots. Once the system began to break down, the new managers had no choice but to rehire the old hands as consultants, at a substantial advance on their old salaries. It was a cheap way of appropriating the knowledge accumulated over decades of 'permanent' employment, but when the old-timers finally pass on who will be there to take their place?

This is not an unusual story. In Auckland a newly privatised power company sacked the old operatives and got a massive power breakdown. In Sydney a sudden increase in the level of bacteria in the water followed the corporatisation of the water supply authority. Who knows how many smaller disasters have attended the structural transformation of other public bodies? They are illustrative of the dangers that accompany the attempt to divorce management from content, decision-making from institutional memory.

More enlightened managers might look to history to help conserve, rather than systematically destroy, institutional memory. History might heighten the manager's sense of the complexity of social and institutional change. It reminds us of the contingent and the unforeseen. It brings the corrective of experience to the confidence of dogma. Too much complexity, some managers may argue, is as disabling to the person of action as it is fascinating to the scholar; but managers will surely be wiser for knowing the limits as well as the reach of their actions.

History redresses the managers' confidence in the

universal principles of management theory with an awareness of the cultural specificity and enduring power of institutions, localities and folkways. While they may live in a borderless world of transnational corporations, those who work for them belong to families, neighbourhoods, religious and ethnic groups with competing identities and loyalties. History matters to them, even if it doesn't matter to the boss. Their sense of identity, loyalty and memory is a force with which the manager might seek to cooperate rather than compete. Knowing 'where people are coming from', as the phrase goes, means sharing a sense of their collective past, knowing their personal and institutional histories.

History might even alert managers to the historical contingency of their own management doctrines. Knowing where management theory came from—its authorship, its ideological and scientific antecedents, its social and political implications—may arm managers with a healthy dose of scepticism towards the gurus, forecasters and think-tanks who offer to make their history for them. 'Everyman,' the American historian Carl Becker remarked in 1931, 'makes his own history.' So should every manager, relying on as wide and critical an understanding of the past as, in a busy life, he or she can afford.

chapter thirteen

'A vote, a rifle and a farm': Unnatural rights and invented histories

MODERN POLITICS IS saturated with the language of rights.[1] Americans were endowed by their Constitution with the right to 'life, liberty and the pursuit of happiness'. The French uphold the right to 'liberty, equality and fraternity'. Australia's Constitution contains no such elevating charter of rights, although according to recent decisions of the High Court some rights, such as freedom of speech, are 'implied' in it.

The rights invoked each day by modern Australians, however, go far beyond those guaranteed by any constitution. Advocates of euthanasia invoke a person's right to die as well as their right to live. Pro-abortionists invoke a woman's right to control her own body while anti-abortionists plead for an unborn baby's right to life. Some homosexuals want the right to marry, or to share superannuation entitlements with their partners. Some social benefits—health care, pensions, education, unemployment benefits—are also often described as rights. And now, in the strangest twist of all, some Australians are asserting their 'right'—as white people already here—to curtail the 'rights' of some Asian people who want to come here, or to send back some of those already here.

Where do these rights come from? The Enlightenment philosophers who inspired the French and
American constitutions believed that political rights
were natural, inherent in our character as human beings
living in society. Having been enshrined in constitutions
written by the founders of the modern nation-states,
and revered by succeeding generations of democrats,
they also became, in a sense, historic rights. In recent
years postmodernists and others have challenged the
'enlightenment project' and the concepts of liberal
democracy that allegedly flowed from it; yet, in spite
of the widespread cynicism towards politicians and
formal politics in general (or perhaps because of it),
people go on finding new rights every day.

Such a proliferation of rights, John Hirst has
argued, may eventually so weaken our institutions that
they will no longer be able to function effectively. With
the assertion of each new right the fabric of obligations
is weakened. The Left, he says, has been especially
active in inventing new rights, extending within institutions such as schools and public housing estates the
liberties properly exercised only in relation to society
at large.[2] But the invention of new rights is not a
monopoly of the Left, or even of the economic rationalist wing of the New Right, which Hirst sees as an
unconscious ally in the attack on our institutions.
Rights have also more recently become a thread in the
rhetoric of the populist Right, led by Pauline Hanson.

Pauline Hanson is a novice in political philosophy
but she thinks she knows her rights. Among them is
the Australian's alleged right to bear arms, or more
precisely, to own a high-powered semi-automatic rifle.
Since her emergence Mrs Hanson and her One Nation
Party have danced a dangerous *pas de deux* with the
political leaders of the gun lobby. Much of her program

of populist nationalism challenges liberal values, especially in the economic sphere: she is against free trade, free immigration, unregulated competition. But she is *for* the Australian's right to bear arms. Her policy on firearms, released in May 1998, declares that 'Australians have a right to defend themselves and their families in their own homes'. Reform of gun laws was first in the list of political demands by her newly elected followers in the Queensland election.

In the notorious and now suppressed apologia, *Pauline Hanson—The Truth*, one of Mrs Hanson's ghost-writers claimed that the right to bear arms was a 'traditional right' of Englishmen, guaranteed by the Bill of Rights of 1688, and that, since that Bill remains part of Australian common law, the right to bear arms should likewise persist in Australia. 'Many gun owners believe that they have a Constitutional right to bear arms,' but this, the writers acknowledge, is a moot point since the Australian Constitution, unlike the American Constitution, contains no analogous definition of rights. Moreover, even if such a traditional right subsisted in Australian common law, it is unlikely to be upheld by the Courts because 'the Australian legal system, even more than the universities, is in the vice-like grip of the new class elites' "new morality" '.[3]

The idea that owning and carrying guns is a British, and hence an Australian, right has a curious history. One of its curiosities is that Australians of earlier generations would almost certainly have been surprised to know of its existence. Gun-owning may have been a long-established *custom* in colonial society, but there is scant evidence that our Australian forefathers exalted it into a *right,* as did the founding fathers of the American Constitution who famously enshrined a 'right to bear arms' in the Second Amendment. The current

Australian government, through its Attorney-General, has specifically repudiated the idea of such a constitutional right. 'Gun ownership is not a right,' declared Daryl Williams in May 1996. 'Rather it should be seen as a conditional privilege reserved for those with a genuine reason and subject to appropriate controls.'[4] In a formal sense he is right; for most of the past 200 years, colonial and national governments have assumed, and most citizens have accorded them, wide powers to control the access of Australians to firearms. As British subjects, Australians perhaps saw the possession of arms as a privilege granted by the Crown rather than a right inherent in their status as citizens.

In fact, the 'Australian right to bear arms' is perhaps better described as a recently imported, rather than an invented, right, for it derives, most immediately, from the ideological dependence of the Australian gun lobby on its American parent. Only after the American gun lobby had discovered the British origins of their own (republican) right to bear arms did their Australian counterparts—monarchists for the most part—uncover a similar pedigree. Yet while the history that Australian gun lobbyists now claim may be a recently invented myth, it draws strength from beliefs and practices more deeply rooted in the history of rural Australia. For guns, as we shall see, have long occcupied an important place in rural life and the proposal to fetter their use, at a time when much else in the farmer's way of life is under threat, excites emotions that run deep in the life of those who live beyond the capital cities.

The idea of an Australian right to bear arms is, I suggest, an abuse of history. Under the influence of postmodernists and deconstructionists the line between fact and fiction, history and myth, has become increasingly blurred. All narratives, we are told, are fictions, tales told from a particular viewpoint which select from the evidence in accordance with the writer's purpose. If so, what is there to distinguish the Hansonites' populist version of history, with its lineage of a suppressed or forgotten right to bear arms, from other attempts to recover 'hidden histories' of the poor and disadvantaged? Can we choose between, say, Hanson's history of gun laws and Henry Reynolds' history of Aboriginal land rights on any basis other than our concurrence, or otherwise, with the political positions of their authors?

One answer is that the abuse of history involves an abrogation of the rules of proper historical method: a failure to observe chronological sequence, the wilful ignoring of contradictory evidence, an inattention to contemporary context. Demonstrating its abusive character, however, requires something more. We need to investigate the origins and moral tendency of that history, the ways in which the invention of a historic right to bear arms is linked, psychologically as well as logically, to the social origins of the Hansonite phenomenon. In this essay I investigate three interconnected issues: the origins of the American right to bear arms and its importation to Australia; the history of gun-use and firearms legislation in Australian society; and the modern politics of rural decline. Together, they illustrate how the past may be perverted to reinforce old prejudices and how easily folk belief, insulated from criticism, may parade itself as history.

The American right to bear arms

Few words in American political discourse have been so intensely scrutinised, and so often misconstrued, as

those of the Second Amendment: 'A well-regulated militia being necessary to the security of a free State, the
right of the people to bear arms shall not be infringed.'
More than 200 years after they were proposed to the
Congress by James Madison, historians continue to
debate their intent. Did the Congress invest citizens
with an unfettered right to own and carry arms, of
whatever kind they chose? Or was that right circum-
scribed by the context established by the first clause of
the amendment—the responsibility of citizens to render
service to the state as part of a 'well-regulated militia'?
Individual rights or communal responsibility—which
was paramount in the minds of the nation's founding
fathers?

A school of conservative historians and lawyers—
upholders of the so-called 'Standard Model' of interpretation—trace a continuous lineage of ideas grounded in
the concept of the citizen and householder defending his
home and family, and joining with other like-minded
individuals to defend the community. Such ideas, they
argue, emerged first within the English common law
tradition, were inscribed in the English Bill of Rights of
1688, codified in Blackstone's *Commentaries on the
English Law*, exercised by the revolutionists and
enshrined in the Second Amendment. The exercise
of arms, whether in hunting game or defending the community, contributed to that 'boldness, enterprise and
independence' which Jefferson had seen as the hallmark
of the virtuous citizen. According to their interpretation, the right to bear arms was, in the first instance, a
right vested in the individual rather than the political
community. How otherwise, they ask, could citizens over-
throw a tyrannical government?[5] Whether that traditional
right should remain unfettered in the changed circumstances of the late twentieth century might be open to

debate; but there can be no question, say the Standard
Modellers, that the men of the eighteenth century understood them so.

In a derivative version, this is the argument that
sections of the gun lobby have recently sought to extend
to Australia. In 1992 Owen Dare, President of the
Firearms Association of Australia, declared that the
licensing and registration of firearms was 'in breach of
the rights guaranteed us by the Bill of Rights 1688 and
Magna Carta, which clearly provide for the possession
and use of arms for our defence'. Ian McNiven of the
same association later defended his possession of a gun
as a 'fundamental right in law . . . guaranteed under
the 1688 English Bill of Rights'.[6] Such arguments have
circulated among Australian gun lobbyists since the
early 1980s. In 1984 Carl Vandal of the Australian
Firearm Law Institute argued that, since the American
constitutional right to bear arms was grounded in
English common law precedents, the same right was
vested in the pre-Federation Australian colonies.
Because the Australian Constitution is silent on the
matter, he continued, that right must be intact under
Australian law.[7]

The Standard Model has some able defenders but
it also has some penetrating critics.[8] Only by attending
to the precise contexts in which the Bill of Rights and
the Second Amendment were drafted, they argue, can
we correctly interpret their spirit and scope. The Bill
of Rights was written at the time of the Protestant
Restoration; in granting the right to bear arms to
Protestant freeholders it sought to bar the way to a
Catholic restoration. If the rights enshrined in the Bill
still stand, then only propertied Protestant males are
entitled to bear arms![9] When America's founding fathers
inscribed a right to 'bear arms' they were speaking not

of the right of an individual to resort to arms in defence of himself or his family, but of the right of the political community, organised as a 'well-ordered militia', to defend itself against tyrants and foreign enemies. The arms they used, moreover, were not the automatic and semi-automatic rifles that the modern gun lobby asserts its right to bear, but barrel-loaded muskets. The founding fathers of the Republic—groups of farmers organised as small communities—could hardly have anticipated the immensely greater destructive potential of modern weaponry or the anomic isolation of alienated individuals who now raise arms against the rest of the community.

When we think of popular American attitudes to the use of firearms, images of the backwoodsman with his rifle, the cowboy with his six-shooter, even perhaps the gangster with his tommy-gun come to mind. America, it seems, was a society in which firearms had been part of the fabric of everyday life for two centuries or more. We Australians are inclined to congratulate ourselves on being a less violent society, less prone to resort to arms. Yet it is far from clear that this was always the case. According to a recent and persuasive study by Michael Bellesiles, firearms were rare possessions in American households in post-revolutionary America. In antebellum America only about one household in five possessed a firearm and militia commanders constantly complained of the difficulty of finding enough firearms to drill. Guns were responsible for only about 20 per cent of homicides, a similar proportion to that in early colonial Australia.[10] Only after the Civil War, when the whole society became militarised and the local small arms industry boomed, did America begin to earn its reputation as a trigger-happy society.

Australians and guns

The idea of an Australian right to bear arms is a legal invention. There is no sign in statute or common law that Australians, either in colonial times or since, ever considered that the provisions of the English Bill of Rights applied in Australia, or that they limited the capacity of Australian legislatures to regulate the ownership and use of firearms. On the contrary, since convict times the use of force, and with it the use of lethal weapons, has usually been seen as a monopoly of the Crown to be delegated with care to the individual citizen.

Yet this, unfortunately, is not the end of the matter. For while Australian judges may not recognise a right to bear arms, many of their countrymen, especially in the bush, are heirs to traditions of gun use which have acquired, in their eyes, some of the characteristics of rights. Custom, not law, governs the attitudes of many Australians to the use of guns. But the custom is deeply engrained, and in the eyes of its upholders the threat to end it feels like a loss of rights. 'I think that it's more or less a right,' a 27-year-old Gippsland maintenance worker declares, explaining why he joined other shooters in a protest march in June 1996. 'I have had my automatic shotgun since I was 16. It was the first thing I ever bought.'[11]

In Australia, as in the United States, guns were an essential instrument of colonisation. 'Frontier society bristled with guns,' notes Henry Reynolds. Guns were both a defensive and offensive weapon in the conflict with Aborigines. 'Your gun is always ready to your hand, and your hand ready to act instinctively,' one British visitor noted in the 1840s.[12] The muskets, pistols and rifles used by Australian colonists in the 1830s and

1840s were far less lethal than the modern automatic rifle, and an Aborigine with a spear was often at an advantage over a settler with a cumbersome and unreliable rifle. But by the late nineteenth century repeating rifles and revolvers shifted the balance of force sharply towards the colonists. Well into the twentieth century, unarmed Aborigines were being shot by white men with guns. How far, one may wonder, does this long folk memory of frontier violence contribute to the assertion by sections of the gun lobby, especially in Queensland and Western Australia, of a right to bear arms? Is it possible to disentangle the politics of firearms from the politics of race?

Many shooters would say yes. Guns were also for hunting game, for culling stock, for eradicating pests, or simply for sport. One of the new democratic freedoms of Australia was the opportunity to shoot. 'In England,' Tony Dingle observes, 'hunting was the preserve of the rich and game laws of great severity protected their quarry from the depredations of common folk. When the common folk reached these shores they revelled in the new found freedom to shoot what they liked. The resulting slaughter was one of the less attractive features of an egalitarian society.'[13] In 1884 a journalist, 'the Vagabond', toured the Victorian countryside. Everywhere, it seemed, he came across bands of men with rifles, engaged in shooting rabbits, kangaroos, ducks, wonga pigeons, platypus—virtually anything that moved. On the Murray he encountered a fellow Englishman. 'The Britisher and myself go ashore, he armed, full of his countrymen's idea that the height of enjoyment is in shooting and killing something.'[14]

In the minds of many country people the right to shoot was an expression of their independence. It might seem only a short step to assert a more general right to bear arms in defence of their personal and political liberty. Yet only rarely—and then usually only under the direct influence of Americans—have Australians flirted with this doctrine. Australian gun lobbyists sometimes call to their support the example of the Eureka rebels. By taking up arms in defence of their rights and liberties, and swearing oaths to a republican flag, the Eureka rebels were invoking the precedents of both the American and the more recent European revolutions. Yet most of the men in the stockade were armed only with pikes; the important exception was a band of Americans, the Independent Californian Rifle (or Revolver) Brigade.

Firearms and political rights were themes closely interwoven in the history of the Californian goldrush, where vigilantes were often the only source of public order. Americans carrying revolvers and bowie knives were also conspicuous on the Australian fields. An American merchant, George Train, was responsible for the importation of more than £15 000 worth of firearms during the rush. In 1852 the Englishman William Howitt noted the miners' fondness for firearms. 'The diggers seem to have two especial propensities, those of firing guns and felling trees,' he noted. 'All are armed, and all fire off their guns at night in rapid succession. [They] seem like children, who are immensely delighted with the sound of gunpowder.'[15]

But though many diggers seem to have possessed firearms—usually handguns—and although American immigrants occasionally appealed to arms in defence of their liberties, most Australian colonists were wary of linking political rights with the exercise of physical force. Daniel and Annette Potts, who have made the most thorough study of the American presence on the goldfields, note the contemporary fear of American traditions of frontier justice but emphasise the determination of both Americans and other colonists to observe what were seen as British traditions of moderation and constitutionalism.[16]

Appeals to republican ideals of armed citizenship, often directly inspired by American example, were an occasional and controversial feature of Australian democracy after the goldrush. In 1860, when Victorian radicals were campaigning for the right to free selection of small farms, one of their spokesmen, the lawyer and radical parliamentarian Wilson Gray, speaking to a torchlight demonstration outside the Victorian parliament, invoked the popular right to 'A Vote, a Rifle and a Farm'. Gray, who had come to Victoria by way of the United States, was consciously drawing upon American ideals of frontier democracy.

> He wished to see every man in the position of an armed citizen . . . And whether in the case of invasion by a foreign enemy or even against domestic foes, he [Mr Gray] would say it was desirable that everyone in the country should have a sense of independence, both moral and physical. If there were a thorough sympathy between the House and the people, there was no harm in saying here, as in America, that they should have a vote, a rifle and a farm.

His, however, was a lone voice. Conservatives attacked him for attempting to intimidate the Legislative Assembly by threatening armed revolution. Most of his fellow radicals conspicuously refused to support him: those of British birth were mindful, perhaps, of the demise of 'physical force' Chartism only a decade before, and reluctant to sanction the use of arms, especially against 'domestic foes'.[17]

Appeals to arms remained a rare feature of Australian domestic politics. When a Melbourne anarchist called upon unemployed workmen in the 1890s to support the doctrine of 'one man, one rifle', his cry was greeted with laughter. A Sydney firebrand who espoused the same doctrine complained that he had been expelled from the Australian Socialist League.[18] The use of arms against 'foreign enemies', on the other hand, was increasingly accepted and even encouraged. As imperial rivalries intensified in the closing decade of the nineteenth century, the ideal of an armed colonial citizenry was reinforced, first, through the official encouragement of rifle clubs and volunteer regiments and, from 1909, through a Commonwealth government scheme for the compulsory military training of young Australian men. The war historian Charles Bean would later celebrate the frontier skills of riding, camping and shooting which made Australians such good soldiers. But experienced military officers were dismayed by the total unfamiliarity of most young Australian men with firearms. 'Not three percent of Australians can handle a rifle with safety either to themselves or to those in their immediate vicintity,' a senior officer observed in 1907. 'There are rifle clubs dotted about the Commonwealth, but they represent infrequent drops in an ocean of desolation, and their membership roll is in most cases pathetically small . . . [I]n the two qualities which stood so well to the Transvaal Boers in the late war—namely the ability to ride and shoot—our young men are lamentably deficient.' Rifle drill was a prescribed part of the training scheme, but the available rifles were antiquated and in short supply. Trainees were not permitted, as their Swiss counterparts were, to keep their service rifles at home and obtained at most one or two opportunities to fire them on the range.[19]

An armed citizenry was less a foundation of the Anzac tradition than a product of it. During the Great War thousands of Australian men were trained to use rifles, revolvers, machine guns and other lethal weapons. When hostilities ceased, many of them were permitted to keep their service rifles and thousands of other arms, including revolvers, were sold through army disposals. Police and coroners reported an increase in the number of violent deaths from gunshot, including a number of returned soldiers killing themselves with service revolvers. 'It is, perhaps, one of the results of war that people are more handy with deadly weapons than they were previously and are tempted to use them on occasions when they should not,' a Victorian MP and ex-serviceman observed mildly in 1921. American cowboy films, which had begun to appear in the early 1920s, were seen as another sinister influence.[20] Statistically, the increase in shootings was only slight but it was enough for the Commonwealth to prompt the states to pass legislation controlling the sale, purchase, possession and carriage of handguns.[21]

Australian legislation generally followed the pattern set by the 1920 British Firearms Act but, while exercising tight control over the ownership and use of handguns, it left long guns largely uncontrolled.[22] Debates on the legislation revealed a clear distinction in the minds of politicians between a concern, on the one hand, to prevent the use of concealed weapons in urban areas, especially by criminals, and a high degree of latitude in the use of long guns by people, even including children, in the countryside. 'I am against doing anything that would cause youngsters to be prevented from receiving toy guns as presents,' a senior

NSW policeman declared. '[If] Australia is to remain white, many more of us will probable [sic] have to handle guns in the future.' The Sydney City Coroner, John Jamison, who had witnessed the bloody results of several shootings with handguns and wished to outlaw the carriage of concealed weapons in public places, was less certain about prohibiting the private possession of guns. 'I feel so strongly about a man having the means to protect his family and goods that I would not care to offer an opinion.'[23]

Moves to limit the use of firearms by legislation have been influenced more by political responses to individual gun outrages than by any clear evidence of increased hazard. Renewed concerns about the possession of ex-military weapons, including machine guns, at the end of the Second World War produced a further round of legislation in the early 1950s, although the number of deaths by firearms, whether homicides, suicides or accidents, was actually fewer than in the 1930s. From 1915 to 1994 the proportion of homicides through firearms has remained roughly constant, while suicides and accidents from firearms have fallen steadily in relative, and in the case of accidents, in absolute terms. But shocking incidents such as the Father's Day massacre at Milperra in September 1984, the Hoddle Street massacre of August 1987, the Queen Street killings of December 1987, the Strathfield Plaza massacre of 1991 and the Port Arthur massacre of April 1996 have created a perception of increasing danger, each provoking demands for increased gun controls.

Any killing, by gun or otherwise, is a tragedy and a civilised society will surely do its best to prevent it. Yet the fear that Australian society may be heading down the same path as the United States, with rising levels of gun use and abuse, is simply not borne out

by the evidence. For both gun lobbyists and gun con-
trollers, arms are an emotive and symbolic issue. For
the largely urban and female leadership of the gun-
control movement, guns may symbolise forces of male
aggression and chauvinism, while the attempt to curb
their use draws upon that longer tradition of moral
control which founded the modern temperance, feminist, animal rights and peace movements. Guns are a
touchstone for distinguishing between members of what
the psychologist Hans Eysenck once dubbed the 'tough-
minded' and 'tender-minded' approaches to politics.

The symbolism of the gun

The gun is more than a weapon. To its owners it is a
symbol of independence; to its opponents a symbol of
violence. When the people of rural Queensland rise in
defence of their right to bear arms, they are drawing
from a well of popular sentiment largely incomprehen-
sible to the urban sophisticates of Sydney and
Melbourne, most of whom have never handled or fired
a gun. In the bush, guns were for hunting, for killing
wounded stock, for sport, for warning off interlopers,
for self-defence and, perhaps—if their country called—
for war. They embodied a language of self-sufficiency,
self-reliance, self-defence, self-respect. They were a
reminder that the veneer of civilisation was thinner in
the bush, that bush people stood closer to the rawness
of nature and the struggle for existence. There was more
than enough folk memory—recollections of families kept
alive by the rabbits shot from the front porch, of
suffering bullocks put out of their misery, of trespassers
scared off by a mounted farmer with a shotgun—to
reinforce a determination among bush people not to give

up their guns. An attack on the right to have a gun was an attack, not only on a useful weapon, but on the bushman's sense of personal autonomy.

What makes the Hansonites' defence of their guns so distinctive, and so troubling, is its domestic orientation. It is expressed, not just in terms of the sportsman's right to shoot duck or wild pigs, or of the farmer's right to kill pests, but of the householder's right to defend his own home. The image of the defiant householder barring the threshold with a loaded gun is a male fantasy. It springs, deep down, from that primitive belief in the male as the hunter, the head of the house, provider for his wife and children, defender of their safety and reputation. Once it expressed itself in the Labor ideal of the basic wage—an amount sufficient to keep a man, his wife and two children in 'frugal comfort'. It was embodied in the free selection movement and in the soldier settlement schemes after both wars. When drought, depression and lack of capital defeated them, the victims often saw the disaster as a failure of manly responsibility.[24] This was the ideal that often underlay the great Australian dream of home ownership. 'One of the best instincts in us,' declared Robert Menzies in his famous 'Forgotten People' speech of 1942, 'is that which induces us to have one little piece of earth which is ours, to which we can withdraw, in which we can be among our friends, *into which no stranger can come against our will*'.[25] [emphasis added]

Menzies spoke in the aftermath of the Great Depression and, in summoning up the spectre of the stranger at the door, he called to mind those unwelcome visitors, the landlords and bailiffs who had ejected defaulting tenants from their houses. The 1930s was the last great visitation of right-wing populism in Australia. There is a discomforting resemblance between the 'anti-political politics' of the early 1930s and those of the 1990s.[26] The distrust of professional politicians and international financiers, the appeal to the folk wisdom and folk prejudice of those shut out from conventional politics, strains of nativism and xenophobia and gestures of armed resistance against unpatriotic or foreign elements—these were as characteristic of the populist movements of earlier eras as they are of our own. Both feed upon the same undercurrents of disappointment and distrust; the same fear that, as the fabric of communities dissolves, families have no one to rely upon but themselves.

In the good times that followed during the long boom from the 1950s to the 1970s, that threatening stranger was kept at a distance, but in the 1990s he has reappeared in new guise. He is the bailiff come to foreclose on the family farm, the Family Court officer come to reinforce the wife's right to custody, the Aborigine come to claim the pastoral lease, the foreign company come to buy up the farm or close down the local factory. This is the recurrent fantasy in the writings of the populist right. 'The battler, the hardworking, honourable man, comes home from work to find that his wife has been raped, his children have been murdered and his property has been burnt to the ground, he is dispossessed and is now a slave.' So begins an article, 'Revolution in Australia', by the Queensland gun merchant and right-wing activist Ron Owen in *Lock, Stock and Barrel.*[27] The stranger on the threshold is the personification of that more generalised sense of threat and embattlement that Hugh Mackay and other social researchers have detected among growing numbers of Australians. This is a society in which people increasingly turn off the evening news and tune into garden and home maintenance shows, in which politics and politicians are scorned and civic virtue is derided. Now and again desperate men actually take to arms, barricade the doors of the family home and hold the world at defiance in a 'gun siege'. The world looks on via live television, scorning the desperado, pushing down the fears in their own hearts. Only a few ideologues may join secret armies to prepare for a threatened invasion of the country or to resist the corrupt 'New Order' government in Canberra. But while few Australians would actually join them, a disturbing number evidently share the conviction that, in a society where the market rules, the last line of defence is a man's front door and his only weapon a gun.

The politics of distrust and the abuse of history

How should historians confront such abuses of history as the invention of 'the Australian right to bear arms'? Exploding the myth—demonstrating its legal and historical falsity—is a necessary but strictly limited response. For the history in which it is grounded is not, ultimately, that of the 1688 settlement, or the American Second Amendment, or some long-suppressed Australian constitutional right. Demonstrating its factual inaccuracy may not extinguish its power since its followers are simply not tuned into the language of argument and refutation. It is also important to criticise its uses, to show its moral and political tendency. In the last resort the Australian right to bear arms is a myth—a feral version of the Australian Legend, which turns independence to defiance, egalitarianism to resentment, mateship to distrust. It presents a narrative of loss and resentment, a white riposte to the story of

Aboriginal dispossession. 'We are losers too,' it says. It grows in the space vacated by more hopeful versions of the Australian past. It is symptomatic of the inability of our leaders to provide a new and inclusive national story. 'Among many other things, leaders must be story-tellers, and Mr Howard isn't,' observes Hugh Mackay.[28]

A poor story-teller, Howard is nevertheless a master of political compromise. In mid 1999 he agreed with new Senator Aden Ridgway on the details of a proposed Preamble to the Australian Constitution to be put to the people in November. Howard had surrendered his desire to include a reference to the bush creed of mateship (it was too blokey for the feminists) and agreed to the insertion of a passage 'regretting' past injustices to Australia's indigenous people. The Preamble is a less than inspiring document, more revealing of our difficulties in agreeing on the nation's founding ideals than of those ideals themselves. The fault lies, however, not in the story-telling abilities of the Prime Minister, but in the lack of a single national story to tell. The assertion of a constitutional right to bear arms is the attempt of one group of disenchanted Australians to fill that void. Their attempt will not succeed, but it illustrates how deep a gulf has now opened up between the new Australia and the old.

chapter fourteen

Conclusion: Is history useful?

W HY DOES HISTORY matter? Not the *past*, mind you. The past, as the preceding chapters show, is always with us, lending itself to myriad causes: frivolous, venal, hopeful, hateful, desperate, sometimes doomed. But history—the critical, methodical, consecutive study of the past for its own sake. Why does *it* matter? What is it useful for?

In January 1999, with the centenary of Federation on the horizon, the Australian government launched an advertising campaign designed to remedy the shameful public ignorance of the nation's past. Every American, it was said, knew the name of Washington and could recite the Bill of Rights, but not one in ten Australians knew the name of our first prime minister, let alone the contents of our Constitution. Newspaper editorials were sympathetic to the government's objective, although some questioned whether a brief advertising campaign could remedy years of educational neglect.

But there were a few sceptics who doubted the value of history. 'Is history really relevant in the real world?' asked R. R. Wise, a correspondent to the Melbourne *Age*. 'There are millions of Australians living perfectly happy and successful lives who know little or nothing about their nation's history . . . They may find themselves saying: "Australian history is fine for those who are interested in that sort of thing, but back in the real world I'm not sure how knowing what happened at Tenterfield in 1889 will help me get a job, build a better relationship with my kids, or tell me Saturday night's lottery numbers".'[1]

This is a sad but probably accurate characterisation of the conscious attitude of many Australians. History, for them, is a satisfactory hobby for a few, but irrelevant to the main concerns of their lives. Their attitude reflects both a narrow idea of history—a collection of arcane dates and facts—and a decent but limited idea of the good life—a job, a functional family and a small chance of getting rich. 'Happy is the country without a history,' declared the famous Italian jurist Beccaria. Forgetting the past was a habit for many Australians, part of that illusion of happiness ('The Lucky Country') which long sustained our sense of national identity. History was other nations' afflictions—wars, religious and ethnic conflicts, deep-buried grievances, inherited dreams of a better life—all the things that Australians hoped to leave behind. But in the 1990s the world, and with it the claims of history, have come home to Australia. Even the happily employed suburban family, gathered around the TV to watch the Lotto draw, is not immune from the claims of the past.

The happy family, careless of history, is a caricature, shorn of the real-life characteristics that make history important to people. It could not be a family of Serbian or Macedonian or Irish or Vietnamese immigrants, for history has followed them here and even as Australians they cannot forget it. It could not be an Aboriginal family for history, both the pre-European past and the history of colonisation and settlement, continues to shape its members' everyday lives. The family could not be Catholic or Protestant, Jewish or Greek Orthodox, or they would regularly participate in beliefs and rituals grounded in history. It could not include sons and daughters of ex-servicemen from any of Australia's wars, for the pride and sorrow of past battles and imprisonment are still felt in their lives. And it could not be politically active, at any level; otherwise it would participate in debates about rights and obligations that can only be understood historically.

Changing history is often first among the political objectives of those who seek to change the future. Even before the Chinese government had resumed its rule in Hong Kong, it had begun to change the school history textbooks. As they drove Albanian Kosovars across the border and destroyed their homes and villages, Serbian militia were already burning papers in the archives, extinguishing all evidence of the Albanian presence in land records, birth and marriage registers, creating a history as well as a geography that had been 'ethnically cleansed'.

All societies have a consciousness of the past, which influences them willy-nilly. Serbians and Kosovars, Republicans and Monarchists, Catholics and Masons each have views of the past—the real question is whether our views of the past are to be critical or superstitious, educated or uninformed, open or dogmatic. The past may be past but our beliefs about it are powerful, for good or ill. Living without some sense of the past is not an option. Studying it critically and rationally, in an arena of open debate, is a kind of insurance against the prevalence of prejudice and hate.

The uses of history—then and now

To some traditionalists it is surprising, even offensive, that anyone should question the value of history. Yet a historian of history would have to admit that it is not useful in quite the way it used to be. History emerged as an academic discipline only about a century ago when its distinctive procedures were first codified by professors at Oxford and Cambridge, Berlin and Paris, and later adopted at Sydney and Melbourne. Then it was conceived primarily as a genealogy of the nation-state, designed for those who would devote their lives to serving it. History, wrote Sir John Seeley in 1895, was past politics, and politics was present history.[2] By studying past heroes, the young politician or public servant was inspired with patriotism and instructed in the arts of statesmanship. By following the narrative of national history, he (it was usually a man) gained a sense of progress, a capacity to read the lessons of the past for the future. While patriotism provided the impetus to historical study, those who made it a subject of university study were also deeply imbued with scientific ideals. The critical use of sources, the organisation of archives, the establishment of scholarly historical journals with systems of peer review, the public discussion of historical interpretation among professionals who had undergone a rigorous training in historical method were all designed to eradicate, or at least minimise, the worst abuses of the past.

A century later, several of the intellectual pillars on which academic history was first erected are shaking or have actually collapsed.[3] Hero-worship, as we saw in Chapter 2, may retain a lingering appeal to many people as a reason for studying history, but most historians are more adept at debunking than boosting the reputation of the mighty dead and people find their heroes without much help from historians. Cultural critics and historians themselves have undermined the pretensions of academic history to scientific objectivity.

Historians may claim to offer more artful, imaginative, better researched versions of the past; but they are not necessarily more objective.

The twentieth century has also dashed the hopes of those who sought to apply the lessons of history to foretell or shape the future. The fall of the Berlin Wall destroyed the dream of a Marxist utopia and delivered what seemed like a final blow to perhaps the most influential modern version of the idea of a purposeful past. The expectation that history has lessons to teach us nevertheless remains strong. A critic of the sceptical R.R. Wise cited several 'lessons from history . . . relevant to our present circumstances'. The failure of the free market, the value of trade unions and the dangers of racism would all be apparent to the careful student of the past, he claimed. History, according to this view, has a mainly prophylactic value: it inoculates the politician or public servant against the confident predictions of doctrinaire reformers, such as the managerialists discussed in Chapter 12, even if it does not itself provide us with a road map of the future.

Recently it has become common to defend history mainly as a set of intellectual skills rather than as a body of useful knowledge. 'The study of history encourages clear articulation of thought and the development of investigative skills,' wrote another correspondent in the *Age*. This was the rationale that underlay much history teaching not only in universities but, as we saw in Chapter 10, in secondary and primary schools in the 1960s and 1970s. These skills were seen as useful both for employment and for life. There is something in these arguments, and many employers do indeed value the intellectual skills acquired by history graduates, but history is not the only subject that can legitimately claim to teach us to think and write clearly.

The study of history is surely something more than an intellectual gymnasium. It is the *what* as well as the *how* of history that matters. We need a serviceable map of the past as well as the skills to read it. Only as they have seen their subject merged into generalised 'Studies of Society and Environment' have historians and teachers awakened to the loss that occurs when historical content is divorced from its chronological framework and from historical methods of interpretation. Something more is involved in studying events in sequence and in their historical context than treating those events as isolated specimens of 'revolution', or 'race relations' or 'gender politics'.

So how, at the end of the twentieth century can history show its usefulness? Each historian will give his or her own defence of the discipline. Some would object even to the idea that history should have to be useful. History, they say, is like art or religion—an activity that any civilised society should sponsor for its own sake, not because it serves some other purpose. To defend history on utilitarian grounds is to accept the ground rules of history's enemies. I respect this view, but I believe that in a utilitarian age it may be equally dangerous to concede the uselessness of something that, in other hands, is also potentially harmful. When history is under threat historians will offer a range of arguments in its defence, not all of them equally valid. The most convincing ones, it seems to me, centre round four key ideas: identity, cultural sensitivity, social change and citizenship. History, I suggest, tells who we are, gives us imaginative and sympathetic insight into the lives of others, encourages a critical attitude to questions of social and political change, and equips us to participate in a political community.

History and identity

History became professionalised as the story of the nation-state, but in our time it has also become the story of the class, the ethnic group, the neighbourhood and the gender group. What is common to all these forms of history is their focus on questions of identity. Reclaiming a sense of one's collective past has been an essential step in the liberationist projects of nationalists, trade unions, ethnic groups, women, gays and other oppressed or emergent groups.

How do such histories serve the interests of their constituents? By recognising a sense of continuity in the past, they reinforce bonds of solidarity in the present. By reciting a narrative of past wrongs and injustices they strengthen claims for justice and restitution in the present. By discovering patterns of forward movement in the past they strengthen the momentum for change in the present.

As communications grow speedier and cheaper, and trade and cultural barriers come down, so people seek to shore up their fading sense of personal and communal identity. Jewish grandfathers, who have fought to break down racial antagonisms and fostered the ideal of a secular Jewish state, watch with bemusement as their children embrace religious orthodoxy. Aborigines, reared in Christian missions where they were encouraged to assimilate, devote their mature lives to rediscovering their Aboriginal heritage. Material prosperity and social progress were the watchwords of history in the 1950s and 1960s; community and identity are its watchwords in the 1980s and 1990s. As we saw in Chapter 5 family history—the search for personal identity—has become a paradigm for other forms of identity history—the history of the community, the ethnic group and the nation-state.

Identity history is one of the most powerful forms of history in the contemporary world. But it is also one of the most dangerous. While it serves the interests of women's liberation and Aboriginal emancipation, it also serves the interests of ethnic cleansing in Bosnia and Kosovo and Protestant and Catholic separatism in Northern Ireland. In appealing to sentiments of group pride and solidarity it can also reinforce racial, ethnic, religious and national divisions. Once, in both the West and the East, these pressures were contained by over-arching attachments to the nation or internationalist loyalties to the Papacy or the Kremlin. But since 1989 and the breakdown of the Communist bloc, identity politics has broken free of these fetters.

Narrowing the focus of history to issues of identity raises some troubling ideas. The narratives constructed by oppressed or emergent groups can perform a powerful role in their emancipation. Historians sympathetic to their cause may sometimes treat such narratives less sceptically than they would the sustaining stories of others. Alex Haley's *Roots*, in which the Black-American author traced his family history back to Africa, won widespread approval among historians eager to support an emergent black consciousness movement in the 1970s; only years later did they acknowledge the obvious flaws in Haley's historical method. In Australia, supporters of Aboriginal land rights, such as Henry Reynolds, have consciously sought to provide a historical lineage both for the concept of native title and for the 'First Land Rights Movement' which upheld it. Reynolds' work has done much to advance the Aboriginal cause but, as Peter Cochrane has recently suggested, he often gives the appearance of being 'more a hunter in the past than a cultured traveller', more an avid seeker after supportive evidence than a curious explorer of a foreign country.[4]

Australia has largely escaped the most virulent forms of identity politics and identity history. But we still need to ask, with the distinguished European historian Eric Hobsbawm, whether identity history is enough. Rather than stressing common humanity, identity history celebrates cultural difference. An Australian republic, say its defenders, will be founded on a tolerance and respect for gender, racial and cultural difference. This is an admirable but fragile enterprise. By regarding all humans as children of God, Christianity laid the basis for the Enlightenment idea of equal natural rights. But the acknowledgement of difference does not, of itself, confer such an equality of respect; on the contrary, recognition of difference has more often been combined with an explicit or implicit sense of discrimination. It is perhaps only because Enlightenment ideas of liberty and equality are so deeply engrained in western societies, and still so influential, that claims for the recognition of minority cultures can be made without bringing a cultural and political backlash.

The greatest abuse of history, Hobsbawm argues, is not the temptation to lie, to knowingly suppress the truth, but to 'isolate the history of one part of humanity—the historians' own, by birth or choice—from its wider context'. The pressures to do so, he concedes, are often great, especially if the historian's own group is threatened or persecuted, as Jews for example often were. Yet the professional historian, he argues, owes a duty to humanity as a whole which overrides his or her group loyalties. 'A history which is designed *only* for Jews (or African-Americans, or Greeks, or women, or proletarians, or homosexuals) cannot be good history, though it may be comforting history to those who practise it.'⁵

Writing on behalf of humanity, not just one's own group, may seem a loftier goal than most historians can attain. Half the historian's training is devoted to systematically revealing the hidden, often unconscious, ways in which other historians construe the past in their own image. Many students quickly succumb to the belief that objectivity and critical detachment are merely shibboleths of a discredited professional orthodoxy. The distinction between history and propaganda, some suggest, 'serves mainly to delegitimize histories which challenge dominant ideology'. It is more important to have the confidence of one's convictions than confidence in one's facts.⁶

But even if we can never completely escape our own prejudices, something is gained in the conscientious attempt to overcome them. Historians have generally proved resistant to the more extreme forms of cultural relativism, precisely because they know that in practice the scope for interpretation is always bounded. They are constrained both by the 'evidence'—those traces of the past that survive into the present—and by the standards of interpretation shared with their fellow professional historians.⁷ Indeed, the truthfulness of history lies as much in being true to one's readers as in being true to one's convictions. Partisanship has a role to play in the conversation about the past we call history, and we often edge closer to truth through the dialogue of opposing viewpoints. We should honour those whose originality enables us to see the past in fresh ways. But a historian who writes in isolation from others, and heedless of their criticisms, conducts a conversation of the deaf.

Understanding others

History not only endows us with a sense of who we are; ideally, it stretches our imaginative capacity to understand others. The forces of globalisation, which threaten the survival of ethnic, national and local particularity, also increase the need for intercultural and international understanding. The skills required to cross the border between present and past may also enable us to transcend other kinds of cultural difference.

Yet visiting the past, as we saw in Chapter 9, is not exactly like visiting another country. While Sovereign Hill may promise to transport you back to the heady days of the goldrush, it is in the last resort only a facsimile of the past that we experience. Whereas a foreign visitor or anthropologist can always be corrected by the natives, the inhabitants of the past are dead and unable to answer our questions except indirectly. That, perhaps, is why history often seems a step closer to fiction than to anthropology.

Every historian recognises the thrill and the challenge of stepping into a past world where suddenly all our preconceptions about right and wrong, up and down, are overturned. History is written in the elusive space between what we can find—in documents, pictures, buildings—and what we can imagine. Discerning patterns from incomplete data, reconstructing motives and ideas from hints and gestures, looking for the unstated assumptions behind the words—these are the skills of the historian; but they are also the skills of the diplomat, the business negotiator, the journalist.

Would we have better international business people, diplomats, aid experts, tourist consultants if they learned more history? What is the real benefit to a graduate or an employer of a major in, say, Asian

history compared with a major in marketing or ac-
countancy? Hands-on vocational skills have a natural
advantage in the educational marketplace over generic
cultural studies like history. They deliver what seem like
measurable, immediately applicable skills while history
or anthropology has a more subtle, but more profound
influence on attitudes, frames of reference, styles of
cultural interaction. Technical skills can be regularly
upgraded through life, but the ability to read and
understand other cultures is a personal disposition, an
imaginative quality, which education can foster and
develop although never guarantee to produce.

History and change

History promises us insight into the reasons why the
world has changed in the past and wisdom about how
we might act to change it in the future. For the reasons
already discussed, history cannot claim to be a predictive science. Our knowledge of the present is too scanty
and our insight into the dynamics of change too
primitive to be able to foretell the future. But history
can sometimes suggest what is unlikely to happen. It
educates our guesses, refines our calculation of prob-
abilities. It can sensitise us to the way in which the
forces promoting and inhibiting change interact in time.
When a crisis occurs in a foreign country and we watch
anxiously to see what will happen next, we look to the
historian to tell us, not only what led up to the event
but how the actors have reacted to such situations in
the past. This may not tell us what will happen next,
but it helps to frame the possibilities. An American
exponent of 'applied history' calls these skills 'the discipline of historical context'. They may seem like

modest insights compared with the bold predictions of
'futurologists', but they may be more securely based.

Historians are so conscious of the abuses of what
the philosopher Karl Popper called 'historicism'—the
attempt by Marxists and Fascists to read the future
from the past—that they may now succumb to the
opposite failing, a cynical or fatalistic belief that
the past is totally disconnected from the present and
future.[8] Even Nietszche, the prophet of historical relativism, deplored the tendency of critical history to
induce 'a dangerous condition of irony with regard to
itself, and a still more dangerous state of cynicism'.
Since history never repeats itself exactly, it is hazardous
to read 'lessons' from one historical episode to another.
Yet it is surely just as dangerous to ignore the experience of the past. One of the challenges for historians
approaching the millennium is to reaffirm the value of
the past to the present, not in the misleading form of
a predictive science, but as a study that illuminates the
subtle interaction between environmental, social, political and personal forces in the process of historical
change. In universities, where the world is divided
between specialised disciplines, history remains one of
the few studies that attempts to see it whole.

History deepens our conversation about the causes
and direction of social change. Recent debates about
'economic rationalism' have taken place largely without
reference to the eighteenth and nineteenth century economists whose doctrines free market apologists invoke.
Few of those Australians who uphold these doctrines
are aware of where they originated or of the qualifica-
tions and refutations made by contemporaries. It is as
though a whole layer of historical experience and
memory has been obliterated. How many economic
rationalists who invoke the name of Adam Smith

understand the moral doctrines that sustained his life and writing?

History may give insight, not only into why things change but why they stay the same. Economists sometimes speak of 'path determinacy'—the inertia that prevents institutions departing from their historical path of development. Why are so many Australians concentrated in our capital cities? Why do they continue to sprawl along a long suburban frontier? Each of these trends has deep foundations in the colonial past and has been reinforced by successive decisions. Planners and politicians who set out to reverse these trends, by promoting 'urban consolidation', for example, should at least know the strength of the forces they are up against.[9]

'Those who cannot remember the past are condemned to repeat it,' was George Santayana's famous aphorism. If we recalled past mistakes, he supposed, we would be more likely to avoid repeating them. Yet learning from the past is a tricky business. In seeking *not* to repeat the errors of the past we may unwittingly increase the likelihood of committing new errors. For a generation after the Second World War, politicians on both sides of the Iron Curtain were so determined to avoid the error of 'Appeasement' that they probably reinforced the mutual suspicions of the Cold War.

One of the boldest attempts to apply historical insight to contemporary problems is the course in applied history at the Kennedy School of Government at Harvard, described by its originator, Ernest May, in his book *'The Lessons of the Past'* (1973).[10] Students in the course were invited to review past episodes in diplomatic or military history and draw lessons for future action. Generals, it is often said, are always refighting their last war. Politicians, too, are often influenced, sometimes half-consciously, by historical precedents. In declaring Australia's support for the Gulf War, Prime Minister Hawke cited the Munich crisis as evidence of the perils of not confronting dictators. Such reasoning, Ernest May argues, should be disciplined by a critical understanding of the past. If they are tempted to draw lessons from the past, politicians should at least ensure that the analogies they draw between one episode and another are soundly based.

It is hard to gainsay the logic of May's argument, yet it must be conceded that the acknowledged successes of such exercises in applied history are few. This may be in the nature of the undertaking: for just as it is difficult to identify the causes of a historical calamity, so is it difficult to be sure that, in avoiding a calamity or securing success, the politician has successfully applied the lessons of history or just got lucky. A more modest, but sounder, claim is that history informs the context in which the politician or general acts. It does not prescribe answers but it helps to define the question.

History and citizenship

History is useful, finally, as an education for citizenship. That happy family of consumers, identified by the correspondent in the *Age*, might seem to have little use for history. Citizenship—the rights and obligations of participating in a political community—is something that they do not have to exercise. Yet the world has a way of crowding in, even on the happy suburban family. Knowing one's rights—whether it is to deal with unruly neighbours, negligent tradesmen, extortionate retailers, unwelcome calls for jury duty—draws us into a fabric of laws, customs and institutions that can only be understood historically.

Knowing the national past is necessary both for a sense of national pride and for an understanding of how our institutions evolved and work. It is the lack of such an understanding, as demonstrated for example by surveys conducted by the Keating government's Civics Education enquiry, that inspires the Australian government's current advertising campaign. History, according to this view, is a stock of agreed knowledge that every citizen (or civilised person) should know. As such, it gives a national inflection to a broader educational argument: that history inculcates what some recent American commentators call 'cultural literacy'.

While this is a popular view, it is perhaps not the strongest argument for the usefulness of history. While politicians and historians may deplore the ignorance of their fellow citizens about the national past, the connection between historical knowledge and responsible citizenship is far from clear, especially if history is defined in narrowly factual terms. Does it really matter if younger Australians are more likely to recognise Michael Jordan or Shane Warne than Edmund Barton or Alfred Deakin? An imaginative advertising campaign, preferably backed by financial inducements such as free lottery tickets or tickets to a sporting event, might ensure that every Australian child can recognise the names of the Founding Fathers of the Commonwealth, or recite all the verses of the National Anthem. This might relieve some of the shame felt by Australian politicians in the face of their apparently more patriotic American cousins, but it would do little to promote patriotism let alone the arts of citizenship.

There *is* a connection between history and the cultivation of citizenship, but it depends more upon habits of free enquiry and debate, a critical reconstruction and analysis of the national past, than it does upon rote knowledge of the facts of Australian history. Considered in its wider bearings, historical enquiry calls for the exercise of independent judgment, clear speech and argument, a weighing of alternative courses of action, a sense of responsibility to the community.

Like the call for new heroes discussed in Chapter 2, the advertising campaign to teach young Australians about our founding fathers reflects an anxiety among the political elite about the apparent disenchantment of the nation's youth. Citizenship education is the binding force that will transform Generation X into a proud united nation. It will inculcate that sense of 'social responsibility' that shapes other parts of the political agenda of the late 1990s, such as Work for the Dole.

The teaching of history, many historians will say, should have wider goals than the promotion of citizenship; but civic education remains the best chance in this generation for reclaiming a small share of the school curriculum for history. Once it is back there, enlightened teachers may shape the curriculum along more generous lines to promote a history that exercises the imagination as well as the memory, embraces the world as well as the nation, and inculcates hope for the future as well as reverence for the past.

Conclusion

History in the 1990s is on the defence. It is threatened, not primarily by the cuts to university history departments and school curricula, harmful though they are, but by a limited idea of its usefulness and, in some quarters, a calculated assault on historical memory.

Modern governments still call upon historians to instil patriotism or reinforce a sense of civic duty but their support for history is strictly conditional. Political conservatives, who once sought to learn from the past, have now redefined themselves around radical programs of deregulation, privatisation and outsourcing that are hostile to the preservation of institutional memory. Modern managers prefer information to be packaged, standardised and controlled, not—as history inevitably is—unbounded, unstable and controversial.

But history has always been on the defence, outnumbered by forces that seek to use the past for other purposes. Historians sometimes join them, making alliances—political, sentimental, pragmatic—with heritage, genealogy, museology, tourism, civics education, perhaps even with managerialism. But as professionals they retain an overriding obligation to understand the past, as far as possible, in its own terms. In standing against the self-interested uses of the past by others, historians may demonstrate their greatest usefulness.

That is what citizens should require of them. By taking the lid off the history business and showing how the interpretation of the past is implicated in our public and private lives, this book is a small attempt to open up the conversation between historians and citizens. We are all, consciously or otherwise, users of history. And we all stand to gain or lose, as it is used or abused.

Notes

Chapter 1   Introduction

1. The following paragraphs are based on Paul Keating, *Major Speeches of the First Year*, Australian Labor Party, Barton n.d. and Mark Ryan (ed.), *Advancing Australia. The Speeches of Paul Keating, Prime Minister*, Big Picture Publications, Sydney, 1995. Most of these speeches were the work of the historian Don Watson. Keating, who left school at 17 with little formal study of history, must have acquired a good working knowledge of Australian historiography simply by reading Dr Watson's well-researched speeches.
2. Ryan (ed.), *Advancing Australia*, p. 279.
3. John Howard, Sir Thomas Playford Memorial Lecture, 5 July 1996.
4. For example, David Mandelson, 'Guilt, Shame and Reconciliation', *Quadrant*, July–August 1997, pp. 96–99.
5. See, for example, the debate over the Smithsonian Museum's proposed exhibit on the *Enola Gay*, the aircraft that led the raid on Hiroshima, discussed in Edward T. Linenthal and Tom Engelhart (eds), *History Wars. The Enola Gay and other Battles for the American Past*, Metropolitan Books, New York, 1997.
6. Charles Maier, *The Unmasterable Past History, Holocaust, and German National Identity*, Harvard University Press, Cambridge, Mass. 1987, p. 14.
7. Friedrich Nietzsche, *The Use and Abuse of History*, translated by Adrian Collis, Bobbs-Merrill, Indianapolis, 1957, pp. 12–13.
8. ibid., p. 18.
9. *The Past is a Foreign Country*, CUP, Cambridge, 1985, p. 384.
10. *A New Britannia*, Penguin Books, Ringwood, 1970, p. 12.

11. Nietzsche, *The Use and Abuse*, p. 42.
12. A key text is Michel Foucault, 'Nietzsche, Genealogy, History', in Paul Rabinow (ed.), *The Foucault Reader. An Introduction to Foucault's Thought*, Penguin, London, 1984, pp. 76–100. See discussion in Joyce Appleby, Lynn Hunt and Margaret Jacob, *Telling the Truth about History*, W.W. Norton, New York, 1994, ch. 6; and compare Keith Windshuttle, *The Killing of History; How a Discipline is being Murdered by Literary Critics and Social Theorists*, Macleay Press, Sydney, 1994.
13. Geoffrey Blainey, 'They View Australia's History as a Saga of Shame', Annual Community Lecture sponsored by Mt Eliza Uniting Church 1985, in *Eye on Australia. Speeches and Essays of Geoffrey Blainey*, Schwartz Books, Melbourne, 1991, pp. 46–51.
14. Geoffrey Blainey, 'Drawing Up a Balance Sheet of our History' (Latham Lecture), *Quadrant,* July–August 1993, pp. 10–15.

Chapter 2   The last hero?

1. *Age*, 12, 13 July 1993.
2. See K. S. Inglis, *Sacred Places. War Memorials in the Australian Landcape*, Melbourne, 1998, ch. 9.
3. Thomas Carlyle, *On Heroes, Hero-worship and the Heroic in History* (1841), Collis, London, n.d., p. 21.
4. Watkin Tench, *A Narrative of the Expedition to Botany Bay and An Account of the Settlement at Port Jackson* [1789 and 1793], Empire Book Association, Brentwood Essex, 1986, p. 19.
5. *When Australia was a Woman: Images of a Nation*, Western Australian Museum 1998, p. 60.
6. *Official History of Australia in the War of 1914–18*, vol. 1, The Story of Anzac, Angus & Robertson, Sydney, 1933, p. 48.
7. *The Australian Commonwealth. A Picture of the Community 1901–1955*, MUP, Melbourne, 1961, p. 209.
8. *Life, Collector's Edition, Celebrating our Heroes*, May 1997, p. 43.
9. N.T Feather, 'Attitudes toward high achievers and reactions to their fall: theory and research concerning tall poppies', *Advances in Experimental Social Psychology*, vol. 26, 1994, esp. pp. 46–48, 56–58. A less formal poll among students in Sydney and Melbourne secondary schools found that American

sports stars, such as Michael Jordan, ranked ahead of most local heroes and, although Fred Hollows and Nelson Mandela had their admirers, the survey suggested 'that the idea that a hero is one who overcomes fear or serious personal risk for the greater good is no longer widespread currency'. *Australian* 10–11 June 1995.

10. *Whereas the People. Civics and Citizenship Education: Report of the Civics Expert Group*, AGPS, Canberra, 1994, p. 52.

11. G. M. Trevelyan, *Clio, a Muse and other Essays Literary and Pedestrian*, London, 1914, as quoted in Stephen Vaughn (ed.), *The Vital Past. Writings on the Uses of History*, Georgia University Press, Athens Ga., 1985, p. 195.

12. Peter Cochrane, *Simpson and the Donkey. The Making of a Legend*, MUP, Melbourne, 1992, p. 4; and compare his 'The new heroes—inventing a heritage' in David Headon, Joy Hooton and Donald Horne (eds), *The Abundant Culture: Meaning and Significance in everyday Australia*, Allen & Unwin, Sydney, 1994, pp. 16–25.

13. *Age,* 23 July 1994.

14. *Australian Book Review*, May 1994, pp. 24–25.

15. *Sunday Age,* 15 May 1994.

16. *Sunday Age*, 22, 29 May 1994.

17. Thomas Carlyle, *On Heroes, Hero-worship and the Heroic in History* (1840), Collins edition, London n.d., p. 21.

18. Manning Clark, 'Heroes' in Stephen B. Graubard, *Australia: The Daedalus Symposium*, Angus & Robertson, North Ryde, 1985, pp. 81–82.

19. A trait that, as Hank Nelson notes, was as evident in 1945 as it was fifty years later; see Sir Edward Dunlop, 'Reflections, 1946 and 1991' in Gavan McCormack and Hank Nelson (eds), *The Burma-Thailand Railway*, Allen & Unwin, Sydney, 1993, pp. 144–50.

20. 'My Australia' (1988), reprinted in *Age*, 5 July 1993.

21. K.S. Inglis, *This is the ABC. Australian Broadcasting Commission 1932–1983*, MUP, Melbourne, 1983, pp. 35, 90–93.

22. *Herald-Sun*, 3 July 1993. Dunlop himself had actually seen the conduct of his fellow POWs as a conclusive refutation of the practicability of socialism: 'I would dearly have loved to see a few people with socialist convictions watching the conduct of this camp and knowing the inner story. If socialism

doesn't work amongst a few men under these conditions, it surely is impractical on a national basis.' E.E. Dunlop, *The War Diaries of Weary Dunlop: Java and the Burma-Thailand Railway*, Penguin, Melbourne, 1986, p. 124.

23. Ebury, *Weary*, p. 598; and compare Bob Millington, 'Dunlop was not a saint' but 'a good man made great by circumstances', *Age,* 29 December 1994.

24. *Age*, 5 July 1993 (reprint of 1988 article).

25. Statue: *Canberra Times*, 15 July 1993, *Mufti,* 31 August 1994; House Museum: *Sunday Age,* 17 July 1994; street, *Age,* 30 April 1994; international fellowships: *Age*, 6, 20 July 1993, *Canberra Times,* 29 July 1993; medical fellowships: *Age,* 13 April, 21 September 1994; coin: *Age,* 16 February 1995.

26. For example, David Selbourne, *The Principle of Duty: An Essay on the Foundations of the Civic Order,* Sinclair & Stevenson, London, 1994.

27. *Whereas the People,* p. 15.

28. Trevelyan, p. 195.

Chapter 3   Monumental history

1. David Cannadine, 'The Context, Performance and Meaning of Ritual: The British Monarchy and the "Invention of Tradition", c.1820–1977' in Eric Hobsbawm and Terence Ranger (eds), *The Invention of Tradition*, CUP, Cambridge, 1983; Benedict Anderson, *Imagined Communities*, Verso, London, 1991.

2. B. Field, *First Fruits of Australian Poetry* (1819), Edwards & Shaw, Sydney, 1941, p. 15.

3. A. Atkinson and M. Aveling (eds), *Australians 1838*, Fairfax Syme & Weldon, Sydney, 1987, pp. 4–5; K.S. Inglis, *The Australian Colonists: An Exploration of Social History 1788– 1870*, Melbourne University Press, Melbourne, 1974, p. 239.

4. *Australian*, 12 April 1842.

5. David Goodman, 'Fear of Circuses: Founding the National Museum of Victoria', *Continuum*, vol. 3, no. 1, 1990, pp. 18–34; idem., *Goldseeking: Victoria and California in the 1850*s, Sydney, 1994, ch. 3; Helen Proudfoot, 'Sydney changes Scale: The impact of James Barnet's Australian Museum Building on the town of Sydney' in Lenore Coltheart (ed.),

   Significant Sites: History and Public Works in New South Wales, Sydney 1989, pp. 52–66.

6. *Unveiling of Captain Cook Statue 25 February 1879*, Sydney, 1879, p. 6. An instructive later discussion of the public uses of statuary is H. G. Turner, 'Why Flinders should have a memorial in Melbourne', *Victorian Geographical Journal*, vol. 30, 1913, pp. 22–25.

7. 'Memorials of the Great War', *Australian Cultural History*, no. 6, 1987, pp. 5–17; *The Australian Colonists*, ch. 15; *Sacred Places: War Memorials in the Australian Landscape*, Miegunyah Press, Melbourne, 1998.

8. For example, J.A Reid, *The Australian Reader: Selections from Leading Journals on Memorable Historic Events*, Whitelaw & Son, Carlton, 1882.

9. The following observations are based mainly on Council of the City of Sydney, *List of Fountains, Obelisks, Statues and Memorials*, Sydney, n.d.; Melbourne City Council, *Melbourne's Parks and Gardens: History, Features and Statistics*, Melbourne, 1974; City of Adelaide, *Reference Book,* Adelaide, 1983, pp. 111–25; Queensland Society of Sculptors, *Brisbane Sculpture Guide*, Brisbane, 1988; Ronald Ridley, *Melbourne's Monuments*, MUP, Melbourne, 1996.

10. *Argus*, 24 August 1887.

11. *Argus*, 11 January 1856, 28 October 1857.

12. P. O'Farrell, 'A Note on the Statues of Cardinal Moran and Archbishop Kelly' in *St Mary's Cathedral Sydney 1821–1971*, The Cathedral, Sydney, 1987, pp. 52, 310.

13. C.R. Long, *The Aim and Method in History and Civics*, Macmillan, Melbourne and London, 1909, p. 19; *British Worthies and Other Men of Might*, Robertson & Mullens, Melbourne, 1933; 'Monuments, Local Histories and Commemoration Days' in J. Barrett (ed.), *Save Australia: A Plea for the Right Use of our Flora and Fauna*, Macmillan, Melbourne, 1925.

14. C. Daley and J. Barrett (eds), *Victorian Historical Memorials to Explorers and Discoverers* [Victorian Historical Society], Melbourne, 1944. Parallel developments are described in K.R. Cramp, 'Some Historical Monuments and Buildings', *Journal of the Royal Australian Historical Society,* vol. 19. 1933, pp. 3ff.

15. For example, E. Scott, *A Short History of Australia*, OUP,

Melbourne, 1916, *Australian Discovery*, OUP, Melbourne, 1929; G. A. Wood, *The Discovery of Australia*, Macmillan, London, 1922; and compare Stuart Macintyre, *A History for a Nation: Ernest Scott and the Making of Australian History*, MUP, Melbourne, 1994, esp. ch. 9.

16. J. Reynolds, 'Some Recollections of the Tasman Memorial Controversy', *Tasmanian Historical Research Association Papers and Proceedings*, vol. 13, 1966, pp. 39–49.

17. B. McMahon, 'Sydney's Monuments', *PFA Magazine*, March 1921, pp. 21–22.

18. See remarks at dedicatory speeches for statues of C.C. Kingston and Charles Sturt, *Advertiser*, 27 May, 22 December 1916.

19. OUP, Oxford, 1925, p. 141.

20. Inglis, 'Memorials of the Great War', pp. 5–17; and compare Peter Cochrane, *Simpson and the Donkey*, MUP, Melbourne, 1992.

21. On the theme of mourning see Inglis, *Sacred Places*, pp. 97–106; Jay Winter, *Sites of Memory, Sites of Mourning: The Great War in European Cultural History*, CUP, Cambridge, 1995, ch. 4.

22. *Sydney Morning Herald*, 20 July 1932.

23. *The Book of the Anzac Memorial*, Sydney, 1934, pp, 46, 49.

24. *King George V Memorial Fund: Suggestions for the Consideration of the Committee* [Sydney], 1936, mimeograph.

25. *Sydney Morning Herald*, 6 February 1954.

26. *Advertiser*, 12 December 1927.

27. *Advertiser*, 21 April 1941.

28. *Canberra and the New Parliament House*, Lansdowne, Sydney, 1983; K.S. Inglis, 'Ceremonies in a Capital City Landscape: Scenes in the making of Canberra, *Daedalus*, vol. 114, 1985, pp. 85–126; Canberra National Memorials Committee, 'Report in respect to the Naming of Canberra's Streets and Suburbs', 27 March 1928, *Commonwealth Parliamentary Papers*, 1926–28, vol. 2, pp. 1311–17.

29. National Capital Development Commission, *Works of Art in Canberra*, 2 vols, Canberra, 1980, 1986.

30. Alexis de Tocqueville, *Democracy in America*, translated by Henry Reeve, revised edition, New York 1836–40, vol. 2, p. 56.

31. *The Culture of Cities*, as cited in C.M. Howett, 'The Vietnam

Veterans Memorial: Public Art and Politics', *Landscape*, vol. 28, no. 2, 1985, p. 1; and see also J. Hargrove, 'A Social History of the Public Monument in Ohio' in M. Doezema and J. Hargrove (eds), *The Public Monument and its Audience*, Cleveland Museum of Art, Cleveland, 1977, pp. 23–63.

32. Mitchell, Giurgola and Thorpe, Stage Two Completion Report, as quoted in *Canberra and the New Parliament House*, p. 80.

33. T. Duggan, 'House of Art and Enlightenment', *Age*, 18 December 1987; compare M. Davie's similar response in 'Monument to Democracy in the Style of a Hill Fort', *Age*, 30 January 1988.

34. Funeral Service of the Unknown Australian Soldier, 11 November 1993, *Journal of the Australian War Memorial*, 24 April 1994, pp. 4–5.

Chapter 4   The Great Voyage

1. Graeme Davison, 'Welcoming the World: The 1956 Olympics and the Re-presentation of Melbourne' in Judith Smart and John Murphy (eds), *The Forgotten Fifties*, MUP, *Australian Historical Studies* Special Issue, November 1997, pp. 64–77.

2. For a discussion of Melbourne's foundation myth see Graeme Davison, *The Rise and Fall of Marvellous Melbourne*, MUP, Melbourne, 1978, pp. 240–46.

3. Henry Reynolds, *Fate of a Free People: A Radical Re-examination of the Tasmanian Aborigines*, Penguin, Melbourne 1995, ch. 5.

4. The foremost study is Michael Kammen, *A Season of Youth: The American Revolution and the Historical Imagination*, Knopf, New York, 1978.

5. John Jennings, *Boston Cradle of Liberty 1630–1776*, Doubleday, New York, 1947, offers a clear narrative but more illuminating are several essays by social historians: Alfred F. Young, 'English Plebeian Culture and Eighteenth Century American Radicalism' in Margaret Jacob and James Jacob (eds), *The Origins of Anglo-American Radicalism*, Allen & Unwin, Boston and London 1984, pp. 155–213; Dirk Hoerder, 'Boston Leaders and Boston Crowds, 1765–1776' in Alfred F. Young (ed.), *The American Revolution: Explorations in the History of American Radicalism*, North Illinois University Press, de Kalb, 1976, pp. 233–71; Alfred F. Young, 'George

Robert Hewes (1742–1840): A Boston Shoemaker and the Memory of the American Revolution', *William and Mary Quarterly*, vol. XXXVII, 1981, pp. 559–623.

6. Michael Cowan, *The City of the West: Emerson, America and the Urban Metaphor*, Yale UP, New Haven, 1967; Robert A. Gross, 'Transcendentalism and Urbanism: Concord, Boston and the Wider World', *Journal of American Studies*, vol. 18, 1984, pp. 36–81.

7. ibid.

8. *Boston Evening Transcript,* 18 June 1875.

9. ibid., 19 April 1875.

10. ibid.

11. *Boston Evening Transcript*, 18 June 1875.

12. *Boston Globe*, 4 July 1976.

13. American Revolution Bicentennial Administration, *The Bicentennial of the United States of America: A Final Report to the People*, vol. 1, Washington DC, 1977.

14. *Congressional Record*, vol. 116, Part 23, p. 31334 (11 September 1970)

15. *Boston Globe*, 17 December 1973; *The Bicentennial of the United States of America*, vol. 1, p. 106. On the People's Bicentennial Commision and earlier 'revolutionary' responses to the anniversary, see Philip S. Foner (ed.), *We, The Other People*, University of Illinois Press, Urbana, 1976.

16. *Boston Globe*, 20 April 1975.

17. ibid., 12 July 1976.

18. *New South Wales Parliamentary Debates*, vol. 19, 1886, p. 1656. A fuller account of the centenary celebrations is contained in Graeme Davison, 'Centennial Celebrations' in Graeme Davison, J.W. McCarty and Ailsa McLeary (eds), *Australians 1888*, Fairfax, Syme & Weldon, Sydney, 1987, pp. 1–29. On American comparisons, see Noel McLachlan, 'The Future America; some bicentennial reflections', *Historical Studies*, vol. 17 no. 68, 1977, pp. 361–83.

19. ibid., vol. 23, 1886, p. 5064.

20. Davison, 'Centennial Celebrations', p. 15.

21. *NSWPD*, vol. 23, 1886, p. 5062.

22. 'The Day We Ought to Celebrate', *Bulletin*, 21 January 1888.

23. Nicholas Hawken, *NSWPD*, vol. 30, 1887–88, p. 2683.

24. Henry Parkes, ibid., vol. 27, 1887, pp. 2325 ff.

25. *Sydney Morning Herald*, 1 July 1887 (editorial).

26. Gavin Souter, 'Stormy Passage of a Celebration', *Age*, 12 September 1987; Peter Spearritt, 'Celebration of a Nation: The Triumph of Spectacle' in Susan Janson and Stuart Macintyre (eds), *Making the Bicentenary, Australian Historical Studies*, vol. 21, no. 91, November 1988, pp. 3–20; Tony Bennett et al. (eds), *Celebrating the Nation: A Critical Study of Australia's Bicentenary*, Allen & Unwin, Sydney, 1992.

27. Jonathan King's view of the affair is in his *The Battle for the Bicentenary*, Hutchinson, Sydney, 1989. The conservative response to the ABA program is illustrated in Ken Baker, 'The Bicentenary: Celebration or Apology?', *IPA Review*, vol. 38, 1985, pp. 175–82 and Peter Coleman, 'The Great Australian Death Wish', *Quadrant*, May 1985, pp. 7–8.

28. Jack Horner and Marcia Langton, 'The Day of Mourning' in Bill Gammage and Peter Spearritt (eds), *Australians 1938*, Sydney, 1987, pp. 29–35; Andrew Markus, *Blood from a Stone: William Cooper and the Australian Aborigines' League*, Allen & Unwin, Sydney, 1988.

29. Souter, 'Stormy Passage'.

30. *The Bicentennial of the United States of America*, vol. 1, pp. 44, 92–93. Among other features of the Australian Bicentenary apparently borrowed from the American program were a travelling exhibition, heritage grants and a national historic records search. Compare Australian Bicentennial Authority, *Annual Reports*, 1988, 1989.

31. Phillip to Lord Sydney, 15 May 1788, as quoted in Alan Frost, *Arthur Phillip 1738–1814: His Voyaging*, MUP, Melbourne, 1987, p. 166.

32. *Age*, 15 January 1988.

33. Ann Bickford, 'Romantic Ruins' in Graeme Davison and Chris McConville (eds), *A Heritage Handbook*, Allen & Unwin, Sydney, 1991, pp. 78–82; John Mulvaney, *A Good Foundation: Reflections on the Heritage of the First Government House*, AGPS, Canberra, 1985.

34. *Age, Sydney Morning Herald*, 27 January 1988.

35. *The Bicentennial of the United States of America*, vol. 1, pp. 130, 193; and compare *Age*, 15 October 1987, Eve Fesl, 'What is there to celebrate in 1988?, *Age*, 12 May 1987, *Age*, 26 August 1987.

36. *Age*, 1, 22 January 1988.
37. New Zealand Government advertisement, *New Zealand Herald*, 5 February 1990. Claudia Orange, *The Treaty of Waitangi*, Allen & Unwin and Port Nicholson Press, Wellington, 1987, pp. 40–41 brings out the ambiguities created by the use of the English word 'sovereignty' and the Maori 'kawanatanga' (governorship) in the two versions of the Treaty. (I am grateful to Bain Attwood for discussion of this point.)
38. *New Zealand Times*, 22 January 1890; and see description of the day in Keith Sinclair, *A Destiny Apart: New Zealand's Search for National Identity*, Allen & Unwin and Port Nicholson Press, Wellington, 1986, ch. 12.
39. ibid., 23 January 1890.
40. *Dominion*, 23 January 1940 and see Sinclair, pp. 239–40.
41. *New Zealand Herald*, 23 January 1940.
42. ibid., 7 February 1940.
43. *New Zealand Herald*, 25 January 1990.
44. *New Zealand Herald*, 7 February 1990.
45. See Bernard Smith, *The Spectre of Trugannini*, ABC, Sydney 1980 and compare Graeme Davison, *Australia—The First Postmodern Republic?* Robert Menzies Centre, London, 1995.
46. *New Zealand Herald*, 7 February 1990.
47. ibid., 5 February 1990.
48. ibid., 7 February 1990.

Chapter 5   Ancestors

1. Nick Vine Hall, 'Establishing an Identity', *Society of Australian Genealogists 1932–1982: Golden Jubilee History*, Sydney, 1982, pp. 82–93; and compare his 'Genealogy and the Writing of History' in Geoffrey Burkhardt and Peter Procter, *Bridging the Generations: Fourth Australasian Congress on Genealogy and Heraldry*, Canberra, 1986, pp. 391–99; for recent statistics showing a levelling-off of growth, see *Descent: Official Organ of the Society of Australian Genealogists*, vol. 22, no. 3, September 1992, p. 101.
2. Winsome A.N. van den Bossche, Amateur Historical Inquiry in the Tracing of Ancestry: Establishing a Profile of a Genealogist, A Victorian Survey, M.Ed. Thesis, University of Melbourne, 1988. The questionnaire was circulated through the two main

Victorian genealogical societies and the genealogical research centre at the State Library of Victoria and is possibly biased towards the more stable element in a floating population of enthusiasts; also compare Noeline Kyle, 'Our Women Ancestors: Illuminating Women on the Family Tree' in Burkhardt and Procter, *Bridging the Generations*, pp. 217–25.

3. Herbert Rumsey, 'The Collection of Family History', *Australian Genealogist*, vol. 1, Part 1, January 1933, p. 2.

4. June Elliott, *They Came from Somerset: The Story of Stephen and Emma Harris and their Descendents*, privately printed, Adelaide n.d., pp. 4–10.

5. R.M. Taylor, 'Summoning the Wandering Tribes: Genealogy and Family Reunions in American History', *Journal of Social History*, vol. 16, no. 2, 1982, pp. 21–38.

6. 'Kaleidoscope', *Genealogist*, vol. 2, no. 6, June 1978, p. 156.

7. A. Ollier, 'Personal Experiences in Genealogical Research', *Victorian Genealogist*, December 1963, p. 66.

8. M. Fleay Beasy, *'Belonging': A Research into the Fleay Family through Six Centuries by a Descendant of the Family*, privately printed, Burleigh Heads, 1979, p. ix.

9. In his article 'Organizing a Family Reunion', *Genealogist*, vol. 3, March 1981, pp. 143–54, F.J. Robinson gives instructions on how to organise a thanksgiving service 'general' enough to accommodate 'widely varying branches of the Christian faith'.

10. Editorials in *Descent*, vol. 1, Part 1, 1960 and *Victorian Genealogist*, September 1961, p. 21.

11. W.H. Bossence, 'Genealogy at Kyabram', *Victorian Genealogist*, April 1965, pp. 97–98.

12. *Genealogist*, vol. 2, no. 3, September 1977, p. 92; and compare Phil Brotchie, 'Genealogy and Genetics', ibid., vol. 3, March 1981, pp. 156–58.

13. *Victorian Genealogist*, April 1967, p. 147.

14. *Genealogist*, vol.2, no.3, September 1977.

15. June Elliott, *They came from Somerset: The Story of Stephen and Emma Harris and their Descendants*, privately printed, Adelaide n.d., p 4.

16. John Hirst, 'The Pioneer Tradition' in John Carroll (ed.), *Intruders in the Bush*, OUP, Melbourne, 1982, pp. 14–37; and also see his 'Egalitarianism' in S. Goldberg and F.B. Smith (eds), *Australian Cultural History*, CUP, Melbourne, 1988, pp. 58–77.

17. Paul de Serville, *Pounds and Pedigrees: The Upper Class in Victoria 1850–80*, OUP, Melbourne, 1991, pp. 191–92.

18. Douglas Cole, 'The Crimson Thread of Kinship', *Historical Studies*, vol. 14, no. 56, April 1971, pp. 511–25.

19. Gavin Souter, *Lion and Kangaroo: Australia: 1901–1919 The Rise of a Nation*, Fontana Edition, Sydney, 1978, p. 48.

20. 'Compiling a Family History',*Victorian Genealogist*, vol. 2, Part 3, 1965, p. 85.

21. Women's Pioneer Society of Australia, *Annual Reports*, 1958–60; V.M.E. Goodlin, 'The Hon. T. D. Mutch and his Work', *Descent,* vol. 1, no. 1, 1960, pp. 5–11; K.S. Inglis, '1788 to 1988', *Overland*, no. 106, March 1987, pp. 11–13.

22. *Pioneer Families of Australia*, Sydney, 1948, 4th edition, n.p.

23. Alexander Henderson, *Henderson's Australian Families*, vol. 1, A. Henderson, Melbourne, 1941.

24. Henderson, p. 121 (entry on Yuille family).

25. Tom Griffiths, *Hunters and Collectors*, ch. 5.

26. *Kings in Grass Castles*, Constable, London, 1959, p. xiii–xiv.

27. *The Generations of Men*, OUP, Melbourne, 1959, p. 222.

28. ibid., pp. 14, 32.

29. *The Cry for the Dead*, OUP, Melbourne, 1981, pp. 279–80; and compare her *Born of the Conquerors*, Aboriginal Studies Press, Canberra, 1991.

30. See, for example, her *Sons in the Saddle*, Constable, London, 1983, *To Be Heirs Forever*, Constable, London, 1976 and the preface to Ingrid Drysdale and Mary Durack, *The End of the Dreaming*, Rigby, Adelaide, 1974.

31. Jill Ker Conway, *The Road from Coorain: An Australian Memoir*, Mandarin, London, 1989, p. 238.

32. Mary Durack, *To Be Heirs Forever*, Constable, London, 1976, p. 19.

33. Robert Murray as quoted in Peter Read (ed.), *Down There on the Cowra Mission: An Oral History of Erambie Aboriginal Reserve, Cowra, New South Wales*, Pergamon, Sydney, 1984, p. 15; and compare Read, *The Stolen Generations: The Removal of Aboriginal Children in New South Wales, 1883–1969*, New South Wales Ministry of Aboriginal Affairs Occasional Paper No. 1, n.d.

34. See, for example, the description of the part played by Family History and Genealogy Workshops in community development

projects in South Australia in Jane Jacobs, 'Women Talking Up Big: Aboriginal Women as Cultural Custodians, A South Australian Example' in Peggy Brock (ed.), *Women, Rites and Sites: Aboriginal Women's Cultural Knowledge*, Allen & Unwin, Sydney, 1989, pp. 91–93. In 1992 one of the most famous Aborigines, Evonne Goolagong-Cawley, returned to Australia after 17 years' residence in the United States and has since been continuously occupied in researching her family's past. See Greg Roberts, 'Evonne's Greatest Return', *Good Weekend*, 16 January 1993, pp. 8–11.

35. Diane Smith and Boronia Halstead, *Lookin for Your Mob: A Guide to Tracing Aboriginal Family Trees*, Aboriginal Studies Press, Canberra, 1990, p. ix.

36. *My Place*, Fremantle Arts Press, Fremantle, 1987, p. 152.

37. Compare with the perceptive discussion in Bain Attwood, 'Portrait of the Aboriginal as an Artist: Sally Morgan and the Construction of Aboriginality, *Australian Historical Studies*, vol. 25, no. 99, October 1992, pp. 302–18.

38. Germaine Greer, *Daddy, We Hardly Knew You*, Penguin, London, 1989; Drusilla Modjeska, *Poppy*, Penguin, Ringwood, Victoria, 1990; Arnold Zable, *Jewels and Ashes*, Scribe, Newnham, Victoria, 1991.

39. Greer, p. 271.

40. Modjeska, pp. 77, 90.

41. See Greer, p. 9 and Modjeska, especially chs 4 and 5.

42. Greer, p. 303.

43. Modjeska, p. 260.

44. Zable, p. 63.

45. Modjeska, p. 5.

46. Greer, p. 6.

47. Greer, pp. 6, 311.

48. Zable, pp. 7, 163.

49. See the exchange between Robert Manne, Stuart Macintyre, Janet McCalman and Graeme Davison in 'The Inaugural Melbourne Debate: That Australia's Historians Should Wear Black Armbands', *Melbourne Historical Journal*, vol. 26, 1998, pp. 1–16.

Chapter 6   Heritage

1. For reflections on the relationship of heritage to nationalism, see David Lowenthal, 'Identity, Heritage, and History' in John

R. Gillis (ed.), *Commemorations: The Politics of National Identity*, Princeton University Press, Princeton, 1988, pp. 41–57; and compare his *The Heritage Crusade and the Spoils of History*, Viking, London, 1996.

2. Tim Bonyhady, 'The Stuff of Heritage' in Bonyhady and Tom Griffiths (eds), *Prehistory to Politics: John Mulvaney, the Humanities and the Public Intellectual*, MUP, Melbourne, 1996, pp. 144–62.

3. Elizabeth Mulloy, *History of the National Trust for Historic Preservation 1963–73*, Washington, Preservation Press, 1976, p. 14.

4. *Report of the Enquiry on the National Estate* (the Hope Report), AGPS, Canberra, 1974.

5. *The Heritage of Australia: The Illustrated Register of the National Estate*, Macmillan, Melbourne, 1981, pp. 9–11.

6. *The Heritage Industry*, London, 1987, p. 32.

7. David Lowenthal, *The Past is a Foreign Country*, CUP, Cambridge, 1985, p. 399.

8. Fred Davis, *Yearning for Yesterday: The Sociology of Nostalgia*, Free Press, New York, 1979.

9. Patrick Wright, *On Living in an Old Country*, Verso, London, 1985, ch. 1.

10. *National Estate*, pp. 21, 23.

11. Tony Bennett, *The Birth of the Museum: History, Theory, Politics*, Routledge, London, 1995, ch. 5—'Out of which Past?' This chapter was previously published as a limited circulation monograph by Griffith University in 1988.

12. Tony Bennett, *The Birth of the Museum*, p. 141.

13. *Possessed by the Past: The Heritage Crusade and the Spoils of History*, Free Press, New York, 1996, p. 121.

14. Chris McConville, '"In Trust": Heritage and History', *Melbourne Historical Journal*, vol. 16, 1984, pp. 60–74.

15. Jenny Walker, *South Australia's Heritage*, State Heritage Board, Adelaide, 1986, p. ix.

16. *On Living in an Old Country*, p. 47.

17. McConville, '"In Trust"', p. 69.

18. Compare Raphael Samuel, *Theatres of Memory: Volume 1 The Past and Present in Contemporary Culture*, Verso, London, 1994, pp. 158–64.

19. Dennis Jeans and Peter Spearritt, *The Open Air Museum*, Allen & Unwin, Sydney, 1980, pp. 82–98.

20. *The Heritage of Australia*, pp. 9–11.

21. Walker, *South Australia's Heritage,* p. ix.

22. Joan Domicelj, Helen Halliday and Peter James, 'Australia's Cultural Estate Framework for the assessment of Australia's cultural properties against the World Heritage criteria', vol. 3, 1996; *World Heritage Listing: What Does It Really Mean?*, Department of Environment, Sport and Territories, 1996.

23. For criticism of one version of the thematic approach see Davison, 'History and Heritage' in Terry Kass (ed.), *The Role of History in Conservation Work*, Professional Historians Association, Sydney, 1990, pp. 13–15; also Norman Etherington, Peggy Brock, John Dallwitz, Tom Stannage and Jenny Gregory, Principal Australian Historic Themes Project, vol. 1 Presentation and Discussion of a Thematic Framework, Australian Heritage Commission, May 1995.

24. *The Birth of the Museum*, p. 151.

25. This issue is the main focus of Isabel McBryde (ed.), *Who Owns the Past?*, OUP, Melbourne, 1985.

26. Tom Griffiths, *Beechworth: An Australian Country Town and its Past*, Greenhouse, Melbourne, 1987, pp. 96–104.

27. Peter Read, *Returning to Nothing: The Meaning of Lost Places*, CUP, Melbourne, 1996, p. 200.

28. *What is Social Value? A Discussion Paper*, Australian Heritage Commission Technical Publication Series, no. 3, 1992; *People's Places: Identifying and Assessing Social Value for Communities*, Technical Workshop Series, no. 6, Australian Heritage Commission, September 1994.

Chapter 7   Antiques, shrines and documents

1. Anthony Trollope, *Australia and New Zealand,* Melbourne 1873, abridged edition Alan Sutton, Gloucester, 1987, p. 239.

2. J. W. Beattie, *Port Arthur, Van Diemen's Land*, Hobart n.d. [1920?]; later developments are sketched in E. R. Pretyman, *Some Notes on the Penal Settlement at Port Arthur, Tasmania*, Tasmanian Museum and Art Gallery Hobart, 1966.

3. Helen Proudfoot's unpublished paper 'The Concept of Historical Significance in Relation to Heritage', Australian Heritage Commission 1988, reviews some of the central issues; see also the contributions of Miles Lewis, Chris McConville and Alison

Blake to Bill Logan (ed.), *Planning the Past,* Proceedings of ANZAAS Seminar, Monash University, Melbourne, 1985.

4. John Ruskin's reflections on the contribution of age and famous events to our sense of historic significance are found in his *Seven Lamps of Architecture,* G. Allen, Orphington, 1886, pp. 186–87.

5. 'Twentieth Century Buildings: Preserving the Commonplace', *Heritage Australia,* vol. 1, no. 1, March 1982, pp. 28–31.

6. Ruskin, *Seven Lamps,* pp. 186–87.

7. Hermon Gill, *Captain Cook's Cottage,* Lothian, Melbourne, 1934, pp. 13–14.

8. Graeme Davison, 'Centennial Celebrations' in Davison, J.W. McCarty and Ailsa McLeary (eds), *Australians 1888,* Fairfax, Syme & Weldon, Sydney, 1987, pp. 4–5.

9. John Summerson, 'Town Buildings' in James Lees-Milne (ed.), *The National Trust: A Record of Fifty Years' Achievement,* B. T. Batsford, London, 1945, pp. 98–99.

10. Ruskin's arguments against the preservation of commonplace buildings are in his *The Poetry of Architecture,* Routledge, London, 1907, p. 117.

11. Robin E. Datel, 'Preservation and a Sense of Orientation for American Cities', *Geographical Review,* vol. 75, no. 2, 1985, pp. 125–41.

Chapter 8   Sacred sites

1. Chris Johnson, *What is Social Value? A Discussion Paper,* Australian Heritage Commission, Canberra, 1992, p. 12.

2. The Healesville episode is reconstructed from articles in *Mountain News* and the *Lilydale and Yarra Valley Express* from October to December 1986.

3. *Peninsula and Westernport Post,* 15 January 1986; *Diamond Valley News,* 8 July 1986; *Portland Observer,* 2 December 1985.

4. *Returning to Nothing: The Meaning of Lost Places,* CUP, Melbourne, 1996, p. 22.

5. Compare the discussion of postcolonial ideas of 'sacredness' in Ken Gelder and Jane M. Jacobs, *Uncanny Australia: Sacredness and Identity in a Postcolonial Nation,* Melbourne, 1998.

6. Statement by Rev. C. Cohen to Historic Buildings Council, 15 October 1986.

7. As quoted in Leslie F. Church, *The Early Methodist People*, Epworth, London, 1948, p. 54; R. Dolbey, *The Architectural Expression of Methodism*, Epworth, London, 1964, p. 182.
8. *The Past is a Foreign Country*, CUP, Cambridge, 1985, p. 384.
9. Raphael Samuel observes 'the recognisable religious element in heritage': *Theatres of Memory, vol. 1 Past and Present in Contemporary Culture*, Verso, London, 1994, pp. 229–31.
10. *Islands and Beaches: Discourses on a Silent Land*, MUP, Melbourne, 1980, p. 199.
11. Peter Carey, *Oscar and Lucinda*, QUP, St Lucia, 1989, p. 429.
12. Penelope Lively, *Judgement Day*, Penguin, London, 1982.
13. Keith Castle, 'From Significance to Respect: The Philosophy of Conservation and its Implications for Church Buildings', Master of Environment and Planning Report, Macquarie University, 1992, Appendix 4.
14. Address at the Twelfth Annual Meeting of the Society for the Protection of Ancient Buildings, 3 July 1889, in May Morris (ed.), *William Morris: Artist, Writer, Socialist*, vol. 1, Blackwell, Oxford, p. 151.
15. Marcus Binney and Peter Burman, *Chapels and Churches: Who Cares?* British Tourist Authority, London, 1977, p. 116.
16. Kevin Greenhatch, Statement to Historic Buildings Council Hearing, 12 May 1987.
17. *Ballarat News*, 5 June 1986.
18. *Boston Globe*, 30 October 1988.
19. Helen Smith, 'Paving paradise: How we use our empty churches', *Canadian Heritage*, October 1987, pp. 22–29.

Chapter 9   Living history

1. Roger Trudgeon, *Museums in Victoria: A Report on the Victorian Museums Survey 1982/3*, Museums Advisory Board, Melbourne, 1984, pp. 98–100.
2. See, for example, Tom Griffiths, *Beechworth: An Australian Country Town and its Past*, Greenhouse Publications, Melbourne, 1987, pp. 86–90; and compare Chris Healy, *From the Ruins of Colonialism: History as Social Memory*, MUP, Melbourne, 1997, ch. 3.
3. David Lowenthal, *The Past is a Foreign Country*, CUP, Cambridge, 1985. p. 4.
4. Adelaide, 1975, p. 1.

5. *Life was Simple Then: A Pictorial Celebration of Australia's Past*, Dreamweaver Press, Sydney 1983, p. 9.
6. *Museums in Australia 1975: Report of a Committee of Inquiry on Museums and National Collections*, AGPS, Canberra, 1975, pp. 25–27.
7. *Your Introduction to Sovereign Hill: Guide to the Goldmining Township*, Sovereign Hill Historical Park, Ballarat, 1987, p. 7.
8. See, for example, Mike Wallace, 'Visiting the Past: History Museums in the United States', *Radical History Review*, vol. 25, 1981, pp. 63–96; idem., *Mickey Mouse History and Other Essays on American Memory*, Temple University Press, Philadelphia, 1996.
9. N. Valentine, *First Act: Sovereign Hill—and How It All Began*, Sovereign Hill Historic Park, Ballarat, 1980, p. 7.
10. Weston Bate, *Lucky City: The First Generation at Ballarat*, MUP, Melbourne, 1978, ch. 6.
11. Michael Evans, 'Historical Interpretation at Sovereign Hill' in John Rickard and Peter Spearritt (eds), *Packaging the Past: Public Histories*, Special issue of *Australian Historical Studies*, vol. 24, no. 96, April 1991, pp. 142–52.
12. Tony Bennett, Chilla Bulbeck and Mark Finnane, *Accessing the Past*, Institute for Cultural Policy Studies, Griffith University, Brisbane, n.d., p. 60.
13. Umberto Eco, *Travels in Hyper Reality*, Harland, Brace Jovanovich, New York, 1986, ch. 1.
14. *Blood on the Southern Cross: The Story of Eureka*, Ballarat n.d., p. [3].
15. *Ballarat Courier*, Eureka Stockade Centre Supplement, 27 March 1998.
16. Kevin Walsh, *The Representation of the Past: Museums and Heritage in the Postmodern World*, Routledge, London, 1992, esp. pp. 65–7, 94–115; and compare Graeme Davison, *The Unforgiving Minute: How Australia learned to tell the Time*, OUP, Melbourne, 1993, pp. 145 ff.

Chapter 10   'A neglected history'

1. 'A Neglected History' (1888) in Henry Lawson, *Autobiographical and other Writings*, edited by Colin Roderick, Angus & Robertson, Sydney, 1972, pp. 5–7.

2. Adrian Jones, *Australian History Teacher*, vol. 22, 1995, pp. 43–4; see also *Australian*, 21 August 1996.

3. See Sven Birkerts, *The Gutenberg Elegies: The Fate of Reading in an Electronic Age*, Fawcett Columbine, New York, 1994, p. 129; Graeme Davison, 'History and Hypertext', *Electronic Journal of Australian and New Zealand History*, 23 August 1997, http//www.jcu.edu.au/aff/history/elehist/davison/htm

4. *Deeds that Won the Empire: Historic Battle Scenes*, George Bell and Son, London, 1898, pp. v–vi.

5. Compare Stuart Macintyre, *A History for a Nation: Ernest Scott and the Making of Australian History*, MUP, Carlton, 1994, esp. pp. 182–85; Brian Fletcher, *Australian History in New South Wales, 1888–1938*, University of New South Wales Press, Sydney, 1993, p. 77.

6. Tom Griffiths, *Hunters and Collectors: The Antiquarian Imagination in Australia*, CUP, Melbourne, 1996, ch. 7; Chris Healy, *From the Ruins of Colonialism: History as Social Memory*, MUP, Melbourne, 1997, ch. 4.

7. *America Revised: History Schoolbooks in the Twentieth Century*, Little Brown, Boston, 1979, pp. 201–2.

8. As quoted in P. W. Musgrave, *To be an Australian? Victorian School Textbooks and National Identity 1895–1965*, Paradigm Papers no. 1 [Melbourne] 1996, p. 30.

9. Peter Board, 'Australian Citizenship', *Journal of the Royal Australian Historical Society*, vol. 5, Part 4, 1919, pp. 196–200; see also 'History and Australian History', ibid., vol. 3, Part 6, 1916, pp. 290–93.

10. As quoted in Musgrave, *To be an Australian?* p. 25.

11. OUP, Melbourne, 1932, pp. 204–5.

12. Deryck Schreuder, 'An Unconventional Founder: Stephen Roberts and the Professionalisation of the Historical Discipline' in Stuart Macintyre and Julian Thomas (eds), *The Discovery of Australian History 1890–1939*, MUP, Carlton, Melbourne, 1995, p. 132.

13. Portus, *Australia since 1606*, p. 234.

14. Crawford, *Ourselves and the Pacific*, MUP, Melbourne, 1943; Harper, *Our Pacific Neighbours*, Cheshire, 1960.

15. W.P. Logue et al., *Australia's Heritage*, Lansdowne, Brisbane, 1964, pp. 11–12.

16. Cassell Australia, Stanmore, NSW, 1978.

17. W.H. Blackmore, R.E. Cotter and M. J. Elliott, *Australia's Two Centuries: A Survey of Australian History,* Eureka, Warranwood, Victoria, 1977.

18. *The Changing Australians: A Social History*, Rigby, Adelaide, 1978, esp. p. 5.

19. *Social Science, History and the New Curriculum*, Sidney Hicks Limited for WEA, Sydney, 1971, p. 63.

20. 'Students losing out as history goes unheeded', *Age*, 10 December 1996.

21. *Whereas the People: Civics and Citizenship Education, Report of the Civics Expert Group*, AGPS, Canberra, 1994, pp. 30, 52; compare Stuart Macintyre, *Rethinking Australian Citizenship*, Cunningham Lecture, Academy of the Social Sciences in Australia, Canberra, 1992.

Chapter 11   Community

1. Gail Griffith, 'The Historical View from the Royal Australian Historical Society' in *Locating Australia's Past*, UNSW Press, Kensington, 1988, p. 12; Victorian statistics from RHSV.

2. Brian Crozier, *Owning the Past: Historical Societies in South Australia*, Community History Unit, History Trust of South Australia, Adelaide, 1990.

3. Carole Beaumont, *Local History in Victoria*, La Trobe University Library, Melbourne, 1980; Christine Estlick, Joy Hughes and Ian Jack, *New South Wales Local History*, Sydney, 1987.

4. *A.W. Eustace of Chiltern 1820–1907, Selected Verse*, Chiltern Atheneum Trust, 1992, p. 8.

5. Ballarat, 1887, Preface to the First Edition 1870, p. 1. For the background to Withers' *History*, see Weston Bate, *Lucky City: The First Generation at Ballarat 1851–1907*, MUP, Melbourne, 1978, p. 191 and compare John Hirst, 'The Pioneer Legend', *Historical Studies*, no. 71, October 1978, pp. 317–18.

6. Withers, *History*, p. 322.

7. 'Some Recollections of Old Sydney', *Journal of the Royal Australian Historical Society*, vol. 5, Part 1, 1919, pp. 1–37.

8. This paragraph draws on Tom Griffiths, *Hunters and Collectors: The Antiquarian Imagination in Australia*, CUP, Melbourne, 1996, esp. ch. 3.

9. Korumburra, 1920, p. xvii.

10. 'Objects of the Victorian Historical Society' quoted in Ellie V. Pullin, 'What has the Society done in Seventy Years?' *Victorian Historical Journal*, vol. 50, no. 20, May 1979; for the origins of the Society see Tom Griffiths, *Hunters and Collectors*, pp. 206–11.

11. Peter Board, 'Australian Citizenship', *JRAHS*, vol. 5, Part 4, 1919, pp. 196–97; Charles Long, 'Local Chronicles', *Victorian Historical Magazine*, vol. 1, no. 2, April 1911, pp. 33–35.

12. *Men of Yesterday*, MUP, Melbourne, 1961, pp. 511–14.

13. A.J. and J.J. McIntyre, *Country Towns of Victoria*, MUP, Melbourne, 1944, p. 59.

14. These observations are based upon a count of titles in the Beaumont and Estlick bibliographies and a selection of Victorian examples: *Back to Heathcote* (1925), *Back to Donald* (1952) and *Back to Benalla* (1960).

15. 'Scissors and Paste in Local History', *Historical Studies*, vol. 21, November 1954, p. 340.

16. Susan Priestley, *Echuca*, Heinemann, Melbourne, 1965, p. v.

17. Weston Bate, 'The Good Old Cause in Local History', *Historical Studies*, vol. 11 no. 41, October 1963, pp. 120–24.

18. See, especially, the criticism of Chris Healy, 'Community-based History' in *The Politics of History*, special issue of *Melbourne Historical Journal*, vol. 16. 1984, pp. 6–14.

19. Elaine Warne, *Errol Street: The First Hundred Years, 1857–1957*, Errol Street Centenary Committee [Melbourne], 1974; Faye Schutt, *Rathdowne Street 1884–1984: A Centenary History*, Carlton Primary School [Melbourne] 1984.

20. *A History of Brighton*, second edition, MUP, Melbourne, 1983, pp. 403, 420–37.

21. 'Residence, Workplace, Community: Local History in Metropolitan Melbourne', *Historical Studies*, no. 74, April 1980, pp. 16–40.

22. *Oasis in the West: Strathfield's First Hundred Years*, Allen & Unwin, Sydney, 1985, pp. 144–45.

23. *Speed the Plough: Ashfield 1788–1988*, Ashfield Council, Sydney, 1989, p. 246.

24. *Struggletown: Public and Private Life in Richmond 1900–1965*, MUP, Melbourne, 1984, pp. 296–97.

25. *Copping it Sweet: Shared Memories of Richmond*, Richmond City Council, Melbourne, 1988; see esp. 'Culture Shock', pp. 195–214, 250.

26. *A History of Camberwell*, revised edition, Jacaranda, Melbourne, 1980, pp. 117–18.

27. *Old Colonial Byways*, Ure Smith, Sydney, 1928.

28. *Beechworth*, Greenhouse, Melbourne, 1987, pp. 95–104.

29. *Surrey Hills: In Celebration of the Centennial 1883–1983*, Surrey Hills Association, 1983.

30. Patrick O'Farrell and Louella McCarthy (eds), *Community in Australia*, UNSW Community History Project, Sydney, 1994, pp. 16–18, 22–25. Compare Richard Broome, 'Reflections on the Flesh and Bones of Local History', *Victorian Historical Journal*, vol. 61, no. 1, March 1990, pp. 33–51; and for a parallel discussion among Melbourne historians see Graeme Davison, Tony Dingle and Seamus O'Hanlon (eds), *The Cream Brick Frontier: Histories of Australian Suburbia*, Monash History Monographs, Melbourne, 1995, ch. 12.

31. Cutten History Committee of the Fitzroy History Society, *Fitzroy: Melbourne's First Suburb*, Hyland House, Melbourne, 1989.

32. Helen Penrose (ed.), *Brunswick: One History Many Voices*, MUP, Melbourne, 1994, esp. p. 294.

33. Atkinson, *Camden Farm and Village Life in Early New South Wales*, OUP, Melbourne, 1988, p. xv.

Chapter 12   Turbulent times

1. Stephen P. Robbins, Rolf Bergman and Ian Stagg, *Management*, Prentice Hall, Sydney, 1997, pp. 437–38.

2. Richard L. Daft, *Management*, Dryden Press, Fort Worth, 1997, pp. 40–41.

3. See, for example, Patrick Troy and Clem Lloyd, *For the Public Health The Hunter District Water Board, 1892–1992*, Longman Cheshire, Melbourne, 1992, commissioned by Paterson when he was in charge of the Hunter District Water Board, and J.W. Powell, *Watering the Garden State*, Allen & Unwin, Sydney, 1989, commissioned when Paterson headed the Water Commission.

4. John Ralston Saul, *The Unconscious Civilization*, Penguin, Ringwood, 1997, p. 4. Paterson has also been the most outspoken defender of managerialism in the public sector—see 'A Managerialist Strikes Back' in Mark Considine and Martin Painter (eds), *Managerialism, The Great Debate*, Melbourne University Press, Carlton, 1997, pp. 72–87.

5. Peter F. Drucker, *Managing in Turbulent Times*, Harper & Row, New York, 1980, pp. 43–45.

6. 'Peter Drucker, Salvationist', *Economist*, 1 October 1994, p. 81.

7. *Inc*, vol. 20, March 1998.

8. Peter F. Drucker, *The Age of Discontinuity*, Heinemann, London, 1969, pp. vii, 1–9.

9. Peter F. Drucker, *Post-capitalist Society*, Butterworths, London, 1993, p. 1.

10. Jack Beatty, *The World according to Drucker: The Life and Work of the World's Greatest Management Thinker*, Orion Business Books, New York, 1998, p. 19.

11. James Sarros, *The Executives*, Lothian, Melbourne, 1991, p. 226.

12. *The New Age: What it is, and the Implications for Business*, IBIS Business Papers, December 1994, pp. 43–45.

13. *Leadership in Australia: Past, Present and Future*, IBIS Business Papers, February 1993, pp. vi, 2, 4.

14. *Outlook Australia*, April 1994, p. 40.

15. P. K. Ruthven, 'The Economic, Financial, Political and Social Outlook', Luncheon Address, Old Scotch Collegians Association, 3 April 1987.

16. *Australia's Next Golden Age*, IBIS Business Papers, January 1993, p. ii.

17. *Outlook Australia*, April 1994, p. 41. Compare with Auren Uris, *101 of the Greatest Ideas in Management*, John Wiley & Sons, New York, 1986, p. 211: 'Machiavelli's rules for the nobles of Renaissance Italy are still relevant to the twentieth century managers, just as Newton's laws of gravity will always retain their validity.'

18. Geoffrey Blainey, *The Great See-Saw: A New View of the Western World*, Macmillan, Basingstoke, 1988; Trevor Sykes, *The Bold Riders: Behind Australia's Corporate Collapses*, Allen & Unwin, Sydney, 1994.

Chapter 13   'A vote, a rifle and a farm'

1. For assistance in locating material for this essay I wish to thank Ian Mylchreest and John Iremonger.

2. John Hirst, 'The Left and New Rights', *Overland*, no. 125, Summmer 1991, pp. 23–28.

3. *Pauline Hanson—The Truth*, Parkholme SA, 1997, ch. 8, 'The Gun Control Debate'.

4. *Sydney Morning Herald,* 11 May 1996, as quoted in Marie Swain, *Gun Control: Historical Perspective and Contemporary Overview,* NSW Parliamentary Research Service, Briefing Paper No. 11/99, p. 29.

5. For scholarly defence of this interpretation see Robert A. Shalhope, 'The Ideological Origins of the Second Amendment', *Journal of American History,* vol. 69, no. 3, 1982, pp. 599–614; Joyce Lee Malcolm, *To Keep and Bear Arms: The Origins of an Anglo-American Right,* Harvard University Press, Cambridge Mass., 1994.

6. Gareth Griffith, *A Right to Bear Arms in New South Wales?* NSW Parliamentary Library Research Service Briefing Paper No. 10/96, p. 3.

7. Carl Vandal, *Firearms Control,* Melbourne 1984, pp. 16 ff.

8. Lawrence Delbert Cress, 'An Armed Community: The Origins and Meaning of the Right to Bear Arms', *Journal of American History,* vol. 71, no. 1, June 1984, pp. 22–42; Garry Wills, 'To Keep and Bear Arms', *New York Review of Books,* 21 September 1995, pp. 62–72.

9. Griffith, *A Right to Bear Arms in New South Wales?* p. 12.

10. Michael Bellesiles, 'The Origins of Gun Culture in the United States, 1760–1865', *Journal of American History,* vol. 83, no. 2, September 1996, pp. 425–544; compare Michael Sturma, *Vice in a Vicious Society: Crime and Convicts in Mid-Nineteenth Century New South Wales,* UQP, St Lucia 1983, p. 95.

11. *Age,* 2 June 1996.

12. Henry Reynolds, *Frontier Aborigines, Settlers and the Land,* Allen & Unwin, Sydney, 1987, pp. 13–16.

13. Tony Dingle, *Settling,* Fairfax, Syme & Weldon, Sydney, 1984, p. 140.

14. *Vagabond Country: Australian Bush and Town Life in the Victorian Age,* Hyland House, Melbourne, 1981, p. 49.

15. William Howitt, *Land, Labour and Gold,* London 1855, SUP, Sydney, 1972, p. 176; and compare data on gun imports during the goldrush in Christopher Halls, *Guns in Australia,* Hamlyn, Sydney, 1974, pp. 92–93.

16. E. Daniel Potts and Annette Potts, *Young America and Australian Gold: Americans and the Goldrush of the 1850s,* UQP, St Lucia, 1974, pp. 164–68.

17. *Argus,* 29 August 1860; and compare Geoffrey Serle, *The Golden Age,* MUP, Melbourne, 1963, pp. 298–99.

18. Graeme Davison, *The Rise and Fall of Marvellous Melbourne*, MUP, Melbourne, 1978, p. 218; Verity Burgmann, '*In Our Time*' *Socialism and the Rise of Labor 1885–1905*, Allen & Unwin, Sydney 1985, p. 59.

19. John Barrett, *Falling In: Australians and 'Boy Conscription'*, *1911–1915*, Hale & Iremonger, Sydney, 1979, p. 33.

20. *Victorian Parliamentary Debates*, vol. 158, p. 227.

21. Satyanshu Mukherjee and Carlos Carcach, *Violent Deaths and Firearms in Australia: Data and Trends*, Australian Institute of Criminology, Canberra, 1996, pp. 5–10.

22. John Crook, *Under the Gun: High Noon for Australian Gun Laws*, Chelsea, Vic., 1994, pp. 5–6.

23. Final Report of the Committee on the Possession of Firearms, *New South Wales Parliamentary Papers*, vol. 4, 1920, pp. iv, 105, 146–47.

24. Marilyn Lake, *The Limits of Hope: Soldier Settlement in Victoria 1915–38*, OUP, Melbourne, 1987, chs 6–8; Stephen Garton, *The Cost of War: Australians Return*, OUP, Melbourne 1996, ch. 4.

25. As quoted in Judith Brett, *Robert Menzies' Forgotten People*, Macmillan, Melbourne 1992, pp. 7–8.

26. Peter Loveday, 'Anti-Political Political Thought' in Robert Cooksey (ed.), *The Great Depression in Australia, Labour History No. 17*, 1970, pp. 121–35.

27. *Lock, Stock and Barrel*, edition 24, p. 55.

28. *Age*, 23 July 1998.

Chapter 14   Conclusion

1. *Age*, 10, 13 February 1999.

2. Sir John Seeley as quoted in Richard Evans, *In Defence of History*, Granta, London, 1997, p. 161.

3. For a fuller account see, for example, Joyce Appleby, Lynn Hunt and Margaret Jacob, *Telling the Truth about History*, Norton, New York, ch. 7.

4. Peter Cochrane, 'Hunting not Travelling', *Eureka Street*, vol. 8, no. 8, October 1998, pp. 32–40.

5. Eric Hobsbawm, *On History*, pp. 276–77.

6. As summarised in Evans, *In Defence of History*, p. 205.

7. Here I support the general position of Appleby et al., *Telling the Truth*, ch. 7.

8. Karl Popper, *The Poverty of Historicism*, Routledge, London, 1957.

9. See Lionel Frost and Tony Dingle, 'Sustaining Suburbia: An Historical Perspective on Australia's Urban Growth' in Patrick Troy (ed), *Australian Cities: Issues, Strategies and Policies for Urban Australia in the 1990s*, Cambridge University Press, Melbourne, 1993, pp. 20–21.

10. Ernest May, *'The Lessons of the Past': The Use and Misuse of History in American Foreign Policy*, New York, 1973; and compare the more recent Ernest May and Richard Neustadt, *Thinking in Time: The Uses of History for Decisionmakers*, New York, 1986. For a more extended discussion of applied history, see my 'Paradigms of Public History' in John Rickard and Peter Spearritt (eds), *Packaging the Past: Public Histories*, special issue of *Australian Historical Studies*, 1991, pp. 4–15.

Index